Judicial Review
and the Law
of the Constitution

SYLVIA SNOWISS

Judicial Review
and the Law
of the Constitution

Yale University Press

New Haven and London

Designed by April Leidig-Higgins.
Set in Sabon type by Keystone Typesetting, Inc., Orwigsburg, Pennsylvania.
Printed in the United States of America by BookCrafters, Inc., Chelsea, Michigan.

Library of Congress Cataloging-in-Publication Data
Snowiss, Sylvia, 1939–
     Judicial review and the law of the constitution / Sylvia Snowiss.
          p.   cm.
     ISBN 0-300-04665-0 (alk. paper)
          1. Judicial review—United States. I. Title.
KF4575.S66   1990
347.73'12—dc20
[347.30712]   89-21543
                                                                    CIP

The paper in this book meets the guidelines for permanence and durability of the Committee on Production Guidelines for Book Longevity of the Council on Library Resources.

10   9   8   7   6   5   4   3   2   1

CONTENTS

Preface vii

CHAPTER ONE
Fundamental Law and Ordinary Law 1

CHAPTER TWO
Period 1: From Independence to *Federalist 78* 13

CHAPTER THREE
Period 2: From *Federalist 78* to *Marbury* 45

CHAPTER FOUR
Enforcing and Expounding the Constitution 90

CHAPTER FIVE
Period 3: The Marshall Court 109

CHAPTER SIX
The Province and Duty of the Judicial Department 176

CHAPTER SEVEN
The Rediscovery of Fundamental Law 195

Index 223

FOR A LONG time the question of whether the framers of the U.S. Constitution intended to establish judicial review of legislation was the subject of extensive and repeated investigation. There has been no definitive resolution of the issue, the consequence, it is widely agreed, of ambiguities and internal contradictions in the early record. More recently interest in intent on the establishment of judicial review has declined, along with fundamental opposition to the practice.

In the aftermath of the Court crisis of the 1930s constitutional law was dominated by the controversy between judicial self-restraint and judicial activism, as led by Justices Felix Frankfurter and Hugo Black, respectively. Frankfurter's doctrine of self-restraint insisted on a systematic judicial deference to legislative interpretation of the Constitution, whereas Black was committed, albeit under specified constraints, to its authoritative judicial exposition and enforcement. By the 1970s Frankfurter's position had been largely abandoned as advocates of self-restraint adopted significant parts of Black's constitutional law. This shift brought with it renewed interest in intent, but discussion no longer focused on whether the framers had intended judicial review itself. In the inconclusiveness of historical investigation of the issue and with widespread acceptance of the practice, that inquiry rests with the assumption that the framers contemplated some kind of judicial review. Intent is discussed today as part of a debate over the proper relationship between the framers' substantive intentions for the meaning of the Constitution and the character and substance of contemporary constitutional law.

I will, here, reopen the question of intent on the establishment of judicial review itself and present still another interpretation of its origin—one that removes the inconclusiveness and ambiguities of existing interpretations and resolves the purported inconsistencies of the pre-Marshall record. The reinterpretation presented here uses no new material but consists in a rereading of existing sources. I will argue that although there was substantial support for a judicial check on legislation before John Marshall assumed the chief justiceship of the U.S. Supreme Court, the check then contemplated was fundamentally different from that which Marshall built. I will argue, further, that Marshall's role was far more innovative and decisive than has ever been recognized. Marshall did not, as is widely assumed, simply reinforce or extend ideas partially or wholly accepted. He built instead an essentially new practice, and did so by effecting a radical transformation in existing conceptions of the Constitution and of the judicial relationship to it. Marshall achieved this transformation, moreover, with no public discussion or acknowledgment of his purposes or methods. He disguised his actions in the clear understanding that the changes he was introducing could not be supported by existing legal or political norms. His superb skill in manipulating and exploiting existing agreement, the seeming superficiality of the changes he introduced, and the public receptivity to these innovations allowed them to escape recognition by his own and succeeding generations. Among the consequences have been a misreading of pre-Marshall sources, and the inability to establish original intent conclusively and to understand fully the terms of the contemporary practice.

I do not offer this reinterpretation as a way of attacking or defending the institution of judicial review. I share the prevailing view that judicial authority over legislation has by now generated sufficient support to be unaffected by assessments of original intent. I have been motivated by the inadequacy of existing explanations and by the growing conviction, as I worked with material connected with the founding of the nation, that the purported ambiguities and inconsistencies of the pre-Marshall record masked an unrecognized, underlying coherence.

This book is primarily an attempt to answer unanswered historical questions. At the same time, the reinterpretation of intent offered here is not only of historical interest but can contribute to the contemporary debate over the proper practice of judicial review. For one thing, it challenges assumptions about intent made implicitly and explicitly by contending sides in present day controversies. More important, it reopens and recasts what I take to be the most basic issue of American constitutional law—the relationship between its legal and political components. The last chapter probes some of the implications for current practice that grow out of this account of the origin of judicial review.

A briefer statement of the argument made here appeared in 1987 under the title "From Fundamental Law to the Supreme Law of the Land" in *Studies in American Political Development*, volume 2. The next year G. Edward White's *The Marshall Court and Cultural Change, 1815–35*, volumes 3 and 4 of *The Oliver Wendell Holmes Devise History of the Supreme Court of the United States*, was published. My discussion in chapter 5 has benefited much from Professor White's work and is the only part of this book that differs significantly from comparable parts of the shorter version.

I am greatly indebted to Mary Cornelia Porter for her support and encouragement on this project for close to ten years. I would also like to thank Karen Orren and Stephen Skowronek, editors of *Studies in American Political Development*, for their substantial contributions to the presentation of the argument. Martin Shapiro and Rogers D. Smith read various versions of the manuscript and made helpful comments and suggestions for which I am grateful. I have also profited from my many conversations with Lonnie S. Turner and from suggestions made by Leslie Friedman Goldstein. Last, I acknowledge with thanks the financial support provided by the National Endowment for the Humanities, the Earhart Foundation, Ann Arbor, Michigan, and the California State University Foundation, Northridge.

Judicial Review
and the Law
of the Constitution

CHAPTER ONE

Fundamental Law
and Ordinary Law

JUDICIAL AUTHORITY to enforce the Constitution against unconstitutional acts is conventionally traced to Chief Justice John Marshall's opinion in *Marbury* v. *Madison* and its claim that the written Constitution is included within that law for which it is "the province and duty of the judicial department to say what the law is."[1] The extent to which Marshall's assertion reflected a shared agreement has yet to be conclusively determined, while powerful criticism of the *Marbury* reasoning made over succeeding centuries stands unanswered.[2] Nevertheless, the *Marbury* claim remains the basis for judicial authority to invalidate legislation and overrule executive action.[3]

I shall argue here that this proposition was no part of the understanding of those who before *Marbury* supported a judicial check on legislation, and that the conventional reading of *Marbury* did not develop until some time in the middle of the nineteenth century. Judicial review as we know it developed over three distinct periods: from Independence to *Federalist 78; Federalist 78* to *Marbury;* and from *Marbury* to the end of Marshall's tenure on the Court. During the first period judicial authority over unconstitutional acts was often claimed, but its legitimacy was just as often denied. In this unresolved controversy, judicial invalidation of legislation remained an essentially controversial practice. Moreover, the judicial power then claimed, although resembling modern judicial review, was nevertheless decisively

1. *Marbury* v. *Madison,* 5 U.S. (1 Cr.) 137, 177 (1803).

2. The classic critique of *Marbury* is Alexander M. Bickel, *The Least Dangerous Branch* (Indianapolis: Bobbs-Merrill, 1962), 1–14.

3. See, e.g., *Cooper* v. *Aaron,* 358 U.S. 1, 18 (1958), and *United States* v. *Nixon,* 418 U.S. 683, 703 (1974).

different from it. In its most important difference, it understood the
Constitution, or fundamental law, to be a political instrument different in kind from ordinary law. As a restraint on sovereign power
rather than individual behavior fundamental law was no part of that
law subject to authoritative judicial application and interpretation.
The judicial authority to enforce the Constitution asserted in period 1
was, accordingly, understood to be an extraordinary political act, a
judicial substitute for revolution. Although it was to be exercised by
the judiciary in the course of its enforcement of ordinary law, constitutional enforcement was not part of conventional legal responsibility.
During period 1, however, there existed no coherent or uniform
defense of this power. In refusing to execute particular laws, period 1
judges leaned on a variety of justifications, all of which were closer to
outdated English precedent than subsequent American doctrine.

Period 2 provided the coherent defense of judicial authority over
unconstitutional legislation that had been absent in period 1. It was
presented first by James Iredell in a North Carolina newspaper in
1786[4] and reformulated and popularized by Alexander Hamilton in
Federalist 78 and James Wilson in *Lectures on the Law*. It quickly
gained widespread support, putting opposition to judicial authority
over unconstitutional legislation on the defensive—as it had not been
before but has remained ever since—and articulating for the first time
a single standard defense.

This period 2 argument was the forerunner of the *Marbury* doctrine, but it did not then carry the meaning since attributed to *Marbury*. Period 2 judicial review, first, was not derived from the written
constitution per se, as *Marbury* suggests, but from the existence in the
American states of real, explicit social contracts or fundamental law,
which came into being in the aftermath of the revolutionary break
from England. The distinctive characteristics of American as opposed
to European fundamental law, which made the former enforceable in
court, were the reality of American social contracts, in contrast to the
fictional or imaginary status of European ones, and the explicitness of

---

4. "To the Public," in *Life and Correspondence of James Iredell*, ed. Grif-
fith J. McRee (New York: Peter Smith, 1949), 2:145–49.

its content, in contrast to the traditional and customary content of European fundamental law. That American fundamental law was written was, before Marshall, only of incidental importance, serving merely as the vehicle for its explicitness. The most telling evidence of the relative unimportance of the American state and national Constitutions' commitment to writing is the absence of any mention of, or reliance on it in the three major period 2 defenses of judicial review: Iredell's "To the Public," Hamilton's *Federalist 78*, and Wilson's *Lectures on the Law*.

Next, period 2 judicial review maintained the period 1 understanding that judicial enforcement of the Constitution was an extraordinary political act, a judicial substitute for revolution. Its great achievement was the demonstration that this act was one which judges were nevertheless allowed and even required to perform. Period 2 judicial review, furthermore, derived its authority over legislation from an equality of the governmental branches under explicit fundamental law, not, as does the *Marbury* doctrine, from a uniquely judicial responsibility to a written constitution. Last, its exercise was accompanied by political restraints appropriate for judicial defense of fundamental law.

Period 3 began with Marshall's assumption of the chief justiceship and consisted of his reworking of the period 2 position. Marshall's key innovations did not come in *Marbury*, which was only a peculiarly worded restatement of the ground already won in period 2, but in the way he treated the Constitution in his opinions of the 1810s and 1820s. First, Marshall ended seriatim opinion writing and, with it, public airing of alternate approaches to fundamental law. Next, under this near monopoly of opinion writing, he introduced an unprecedented application to the Constitution of the rules for statutory interpretation, an application not to be found in period 2 cases or in the Court, concurring, or dissenting opinions of his Supreme Court colleagues. Last, he effected a seemingly slight but portentous shift in the significance to be attributed to the written constitution. In Marshall's hands the written constitution lost its period 2 meaning as vehicle of explicit fundamental law and became instead testimony to the Constitution's status as supreme ordinary law. Through this use of the written constitution, coupled with its subjection to the rules for statutory interpretation, Marshall transformed explicit fundamental law, different in kind from ordinary law, into supreme written law, different only in degree. In the process judicial enforcement of the Constitution lost its character as revolutionary defense of explicit fundamental law and became judicial application and interpretation of supreme written law. At the same time the restraints that had been part of period 2 judicial review lost their applicability. This changed the character and enlarged the scope of judicial control over legislation while introducing the judicial supremacy that had been absent from period 2 judicial review but that remains the controversial core of the modern practice.

Legalization of the Constitution took about half a century to complete. Although there was some recognition that Marshall's actions exceeded the terms of the period 2 agreement, there was no general awareness of the magnitude or import of his innovations. Marshall was able to achieve this silent unrecognized legalization and judicial enforcement of the Constitution through maintenance of period 2 language and form, by virtue of the seeming superficiality of the difference between explicit fundamental law and supreme written law, and by confining his results to those which could be accommodated under period 2 terms. At the same time, the rapid elimination of the circumstances that had given rise to the original practice, and Marshall's skillful manipulation and exploitation of the agreement underlying that practice, have blinded succeeding generations to the original understanding and to Marshall's transformation of it.

From the beginning the legalized form of judicial review was accorded deep public acceptance. There has also been a certain scholarly awareness that in the course of its development American constitutional law was, in some way, "legalized."[5] But to the extent the issue is addressed, it is assumed that legalization was the product of an evolving consensus achieved before *Marbury*. There has been no recognition that it was the product of Marshall's deliberate actions

5. See Martin Shapiro and Douglas S. Hobbs, eds., *The Politics of Constitutional Law* (Cambridge: Winthrop, 1974), 12–13.

and, more important, that it came to be accepted with no public awareness of its implications and commitments. This has resulted in a confessed inconclusiveness in our understanding of the pre-Marshall sources and, in place of understanding, attribution to them of internal contradiction and ambiguity.[6] It has also thwarted our capacity to come to terms with the complex legal-political institution that is modern judicial review. This failure is reflected in the perpetual controversy and periodic crisis that accompanies constitutional law.

On Reading Period 1 and 2 Sources

The misreading of period 1 and 2 sources pervades all modern discussion and will take several chapters to delineate and document. Underlying all these misreadings is our loss of access to the depth of the differences that originally separated fundamental law from ordinary law. Fundamental law used much of the terminology of ordinary law: it was called law, it was spoken of as binding, and violations were termed "illegal" or "void." But fundamental law was the attempt to bind sovereign power whereas ordinary law bound individual action. It was on this ground understood to be a political instrument that could bind only politically and morally, not legally.

During periods 1 and 2 it was universally recognized, as it is now only incompletely perceived, that it is impossible to enforce restraints on sovereign power in the routine way ordinary law is enforced. As sovereign power is by definition the strongest force in the community, it cannot be made to accede to limits it will not voluntarily accept. Fundamental law, consequently, was to be enforced by electoral or other political action. If these were insufficient, revolution or the threat of revolution was the only recourse. If the judiciary attempted

---

6. See, e.g., Jesse H. Choper, *Judicial Review and the National Political Process* (Chicago: University of Chicago Press, 1980), 62–63 and accompanying notes; Walter F. Murphy and C. Herman Pritchett, eds., *Courts, Judges, and Politics*, 3rd ed. (New York: Random House, 1979), 12; and Gordon S. Wood, *The Creation of the American Republic, 1776–1787* (Chapel Hill: University of North Carolina Press, 1969; repr. New York: W. W. Norton, 1972), chap. 7, particularly pp. 291–305.

to enforce fundamental law, as period 2 judicial review successfully argued it could, the judiciary functioned necessarily as a substitute for revolution.

Second, just as it was understood that fundamental law could not be routinely enforced against determined violation, it was also recognized that short of such violation, fundamental law was not in need of authoritative exposition in particular cases. Fundamental law contemplated unresolved controversy over contending legitimate interpretations and unlike ordinary law did not need authoritative resolution of this controversy in order to maintain its efficacy. In the absence of authoritative determination of fundamental law's meaning, challenged governmental action stood, debate continued, and constitutional principles retained all their vitality. Controversy among contending legitimate interpretations of constitutional principle was, moreover, self-evidently one of policy rightly reserved for political and popular, not judicial, resolution. In the inability routinely to enforce fundamental law against genuine violation, in the absence of any need for its authoritative exposition short of the genuine violation, and in the inappropriateness of judicial resolution of political controversy, it was never contemplated until far into the nineteenth century that fundamental law was included in that law for which it is the province and duty of the judicial department to say what the law is.

As a consequence of these differences enlistment of the judiciary in the period 2 defense of fundamental law was understood to be an entirely separate undertaking from the judicial enforcement of ordinary law. As such it had its own standards and limits. It was the judicial authority to enforce, but not to expound, fundamental law and was limited to the concededly unconstitutional act. These distinctions are incoherent when applied to modern judicial review, but in the context of period 2 ideas and circumstances they were the basis of an internally consistent position of significant practical application.[7]

---

7. James Bradley Thayer, in "The Origin and Scope of the American Doctrine of Constitutional Law" (*Harvard Law Review* 7 [October 1893]: 129–56), recognized that period 2 judicial review was limited to the concededly unconstitutional act and urged his contemporaries to return to this

Period 2 judicial enforcement of fundamental law was one response to the political instability and untested republicanism of the revolutionary era. It was motivated by the fear that democratic legislatures would not respect previously established principles limiting the exercise of political power. Period 2 judicial review saw itself as rallying and reasserting these principles, not as applying and expounding law. Moreover, during the course of the 1790s, as fear of legislative irresponsibility abated with the passing of the revolutionary era and the success of the Constitution of 1787, this newly won judicial power over legislation began to atrophy.

All period 1 and 2 sources recognized the differences in kind between fundamental law and ordinary law, but none discussed or articulated them. These differences went unarticulated not because they were unimportant but because they were then universally shared and thus manifestly self-evident. They remained unarticulated because it served Marshall's purposes to keep them so, while he presented period 3 judicial review as though it were a continuation of the period 2 understanding. Over the course of his long tenure on the Court the original distinctions eventually became inaccessible. Subsequent generations have, as a result, read back into period 1 and 2 discussions assumptions that did not develop until at least half a century later. We have assumed that judicial enforcement of the Constitution was always an extension of ordinary law enforcement and, as such, that it carried with it authority to expound it, to say what the law of the Constitution is. At the same time, we have failed to recognize and to appreciate the internal coherence of the distinctions that accompanied and limited period 2 practice. Taken together these misperceptions are the source of the contention that pre-Marshall judicial review was characterized by ambiguity and inconsistency.

Gordon Wood, in his study of American political thought at the time of independence, noted that Americans initially shared much of

standard. I am not trying here to revive Thayer's position but rather to show that it was only partially correct. Thayer did not understand that this standard was part of an essentially different practice from that which developed during the nineteenth century and that it is unworkable for modern judicial review. Thayer's position is discussed in detail below, chap. 3 at nn. 49–52, and chap. 6 at nn. 37–48.

the English conception of fundamental law, particularly its amenability to unchecked legislative interpretation.[8] Although fundamental law was understood to bind ordinary legislation, it was also seen as different in kind from ordinary law and on that ground excluded from judicial implementation. In England, Wood indicated, fundamental law was "dependent on such a distinct conception of public law in contrast to private law as to be hardly enforceable in the regular court system"; fundamental law was "enforceable only by the people's right of revolution, a final sanction that dissolved the contract of government." "There was," Wood continued, "therefore no logical or necessary reason why the notion of fundamental law, so common to Englishmen for over a century, should lead to the American invocation of it in the ordinary courts of law."[9] Yet he concluded it was precisely this "implementation [of the American Constitution] in the ordinary courts of law"—and not its status as "a fundamental law superior to ordinary legislative acts"—that was "the most important source of the peculiarly effective nature of American constitutional restrictions on legislative power."[10]

Wood did not, however, account for the specific steps through which judicial implementation of the American Constitution took place; that is, how it lost its predominantly political and public law attributes to become the supreme law of the land, and on that ground to be implemented rightly and routinely in the ordinary courts of law. Indeed, Wood recognized that "the history of American law remains to be written."[11] In discussing early developments he too fell back on "ambiguity" and "confusion" in American thinking.[12] Certain ambiguities did exist, but they only help to explain how Marshall was able to succeed in the silent, unacknowledged transformation of fundamental law into supreme ordinary law. The decisive factor in the amenability of the American Constitution to routine judicial implementation was Marshall's single-minded purposive skill, one that,

8. Wood, *Creation of American Republic*, 274–75.
9. Ibid., 292.
10. Ibid., 291.
11. Ibid., 296.
12. Ibid., chap. 7, particularly pp. 291–305.

when fully understood, gives new meaning to the "statesmanlike deviousness" attributed to him by Alexander Bickel.[13]

Contemporary Implications

Loss of access to the original understanding of constitutional law and to Marshall's silent, unrecognized transformation of it is a central part of the perpetual controversy that has accompanied modern judicial review. As specific issues change with each generation, the terms of the controversy have been reformulated. But at its heart lies the inability of modern constitutional law to conform to all the requirements of law and to reconcile its legal and political components. On the one hand, Marshall's success has been so complete that constitutional law is now unintelligible outside a conventional legal framework. The Constitution is firmly established as a third branch or source of law, following common and statutory law, and judicial application and exposition of it have become part of the ordinary legal responsibility. On the other hand, the practice of constitutional law contains an irrepressible political component beyond that known and accepted in other branches of law. Judicial exposition of the law of the Constitution, operating as part of a legal check on unconstitutional legislation, generates a policy-making that, unlike that of ordinary law, conflicts with the requirements of democracy and opens judicial review to the charges of judicial supremacy and invasion of the legislative sphere. This political component is what Professor Bickel has called constitutional law's "counter-majoritarian difficulty."[14] While other branches of law necessitate judgments that blur the boundaries of separation of powers, only constitutional law has this particular problem.

Retrieval of the original understanding and of the distinction between fundamental law and ordinary law will not remove constitutional law's counter-majoritarian difficulty or end controversy over its

13. *Least Dangerous Branch*, 14.
14. Ibid., 16–23.

practice. Nor is it intended to reestablish the original distinctions. That is no longer possible or particularly desirable. It can, however, allow us to understand the modern practice and the contemporary debate more clearly than has yet been the case. If this account of intent is accurate, it indicates first that legalization of fundamental law was, and remains, a relatively superficial phenomenon achieved by application of ordinary law language and technique to it. However, language and technique cannot, and they did not, eliminate the fundamental law attributes that originally made the Constitution different in kind from ordinary law and judicial review a political act. More specifically, it has not changed the fact that restraints on sovereign power must be different in kind from those on individual behavior, and this remains true despite the substantial legalization of fundamental law now achieved.

Recognition of the precise origin of modern judicial review suggests that although in the acceptance and institutionalization of Marshall's innovations, constitutional law became a branch of law connected to common and statutory law, it is a new branch that departs in crucial ways from the common law tradition. Modern constitutional law evolved over the course of the nineteenth century by merging political components of fundamental law, as originally understood, with ordinary law attributes and technique. The result is a new legal-political institution that is unable to conform strictly to the requirements of either. Yet so exclusive is the ordinary law framework within which constitutional law operates—so deep the assumption that the Constitution is and somehow always was supreme ordinary law and that the framers contemplated something like the modern practice—that even when its unique attributes and political components are acknowledged, they are seen through the distorting lens of supreme ordinary law.

Dominance of ordinary law conceptions is visible, for example, in the repeated but futile search for ways to remove constitutional law's political or policy component, or at least to bring this component into conformity with that acceptable in ordinary law. This attempt was a central part of James Bradley Thayer's and Justice Frankfurter's doctrine of self-restraint, and of Justice Black's and John Hart Ely's

activism.[15] Thayer's and Frankfurter's self-restraint, however, w
remove judicial review's policy component only by so restricting a
occasions for judicial intervention as to keep the practice in name only; Black and Ely, in contrast, succeeded more in disguising constitutional law's value commitments than in providing a persuasive, value-free judicial review.

Dominance of ordinary law conceptions is also reflected in our failure to identify properly the function performed by modern constitutional law. On the one hand it has been recognized that courts cannot enforce the Constitution against sovereign power as routinely as they do ordinary law against individuals.[16] On the other hand we have not pursued this recognition thoroughly enough to ask precisely what function judicial review does fulfill if not enforcement against genuine violation. For the most part, thinking about constitutional law falls back on conceptions drawn from ordinary law and its inappropriate enforcement model.

There has been, in recent times, one major attempt to reexamine judicial review's function, that of Alexander Bickel in *The Least Dangerous Branch*. Responding simultaneously to inadequacies in the legal foundation of judicial review as expressed in *Marbury* and to deep and continuing public acceptance of the practice, Bickel argued that a principled foundation for judicial review could be found only by a reformulation of its function. He proceeded to identify this function as the defense of fundamental values or long-term principle. The historical analysis given here will show that this reconceptualiza-

15. See Thayer, "Doctrine of Constitutional Law"; Justice Frankfurter in *West Virginia Board of Education* v. *Barnette*, 319 U.S. 624, 646 (1943), dissenting opinion, and *Dennis* v. *United States*, 341 U.S. 494, 517 (1951), concurring opinion; Justice Black in *Adamson* v. *California*, 332 U.S. 46, 68 (1947), dissenting opinion; John Hart Ely, *Democracy and Distrust* (Cambridge: Harvard University Press, 1980).

16. See, e.g., Thayer, "Doctrine of Constitutional Law," 156, and Learned Hand, "The Contribution of an Independent Judiciary to Civilization," in *The Spirit of Liberty*, ed. Irving Dilliard (New York: Alfred A. Knopf, 1952), 181. See also Robert A. Dahl, "Decision-Making in a Democracy: The Supreme Court as a National Policy-Maker," *Journal of Public Law* 6 (Fall 1957): 279–95.

of the original and enduring elements of funda-
the process, allowed Bickel to explain much of
titutional law has in fact been. This accounts for
of Bickel's formulation despite sharply contend-
its proper implementation and for its centrality in the
recent statement of the perpetual controversy over judicial review's operation. One side in the current controversy supports a
general judicial implementation of fundamental values; the other
would restrict such implementation to those values identified in constitutional text or the intent of the framers.[17] I shall argue in more
detail later that despite the soundness of Bickel's discussion both he
and those who drew on it still relied, in different ways, on conceptions
derived from ordinary law, including its enforcement model, more
than is sustainable by constitutional law's history and dynamics. This
history also indicates how each position in the fundamental rights
controversy grows out of one of the two strands in the peculiar merger
of fundamental law and ordinary law that is modern constitutional
law. Beyond this, I believe that this history undermines some proffered
courses of action and conditions others.

17. For a good summary and critical analysis of this controversy as well as
sources on each side see Paul Brest, "The Fundamental Rights Controversy:
The Essential Contradictions of Normative Constitutional Scholarship," *Yale
Law Journal* 90 (April 1981): 1063.

CHAPTER TWO

Period 1

From Independence to *Federalist 78*

DISCUSSION OF judicial review in America must start with William Blackstone, the leading legal authority in the colonies and independent states. In turn, Blackstone must be understood from within the English context as defender of parliamentary supremacy in the aftermath of the English Revolution and in opposition to older judicial claims to declare legislation void.

English common law judges, most prominently Sir Edward Coke, had at one time claimed a right to reject legislation contrary to common reason, but this claim was not widely maintained after the revolutionary settlement of 1688.[1] By the time Blackstone's *Commentaries* appeared, support for judicial power over legislation was a distinctly minority position, and the *Commentaries* constituted an unchallenged statement of existing expectations.[2] Blackstone devoted considerable attention to parliamentary supremacy and parliamentary omnipotence but disposed of judicial claims over legislation in one paragraph in the introduction.[3]

Commentaries on the Laws of England, a defense of postrevolu-

1. For an analysis of English practice see Charles Howard McIlwain, *The High Court of Parliament and Its Supremacy* (New Haven: Yale University Press, 1910). McIlwain pointed out that the most extensive judicial claims were made before the revolutionary settlement and before establishment of the modern separation of powers between the legislative and judicial branches (ibid., 289–94).

2. McIlwain argued that Blackstone misconstrued the thrust of Coke's contentions but agreed that Blackstone's position represented the dominant English understanding (ibid., 308–10).

3. William Blackstone, *Commentaries on the Laws of England,* 4 vols; facsimile of the 1st ed., 1765–69 (Chicago: University of Chicago Press, 1979), 1:91.

tionary English law and institutions, accepted without question the natural rights doctrine vindicated in the English Revolution. The proper end of government, Blackstone agreed, was to safeguard natural liberty. However, natural liberty and the absolute rights that characterized the human condition in the state of nature comprised a notoriously insecure liberty. The natural liberty "of acting as one thinks fit" was therefore willingly exchanged for civil or political liberty, which "is no other than natural liberty so far restrained by human laws . . . as is necessary and expedient for the general advantage of the public."[4]

Human laws depended for their efficacy on stable political authority. In England political authority was lodged in Parliament, consisting of king, the House of Lords, and the House of Commons, and the doctrines of parliamentary supremacy and even parliamentary omnipotence were at the foundation of civil order:

> [Parliament] hath sovereign and uncontrolable authority in making, confirming, enlarging, restraining, abrogating, repealing, reviving, and expounding of laws, concerning matters of all possible denominations, ecclasiastical, or temporal, civil, military, maritime, or criminal: this being the place where that absolute despotic power, which must in all governments reside somewhere, is intrusted by the constitution of these kingdoms.[5]

To sanction any appeal from sovereign authority, including one to the judiciary, was to promote anarchy, and it was on this ground that Blackstone rejected the broad claim that "acts of parliament contrary to reason are void."

> If the parliament will positively enact a thing to be done which is unreasonable, I know of no power that can control it: and the examples usually alleged in support of this sense of the rule [that acts of parliament contrary to reason are void] do none of them prove, that where the main object of a statute is unreasonable the judges are at liberty to reject it; for that were to set the judicial

4. Ibid., 121.
5. Ibid., 156.

power above that of the legislature, which would be subversive of all government.[6]

Although Blackstone rejected this broad claim he did accept judicial authority over legislation in certain limited circumstances: "Acts of parliament that are impossible to be performed are of no validity; and if there arise out of them collaterally any absurd consequences, manifestly contradictory to common reason, they are, with regard to those collateral consequences, void."[7] But where legislative intent was clear, where there had been an unequivocal and deliberate expression of political will, judges could not place their assessment of unreasonableness over that of the legislature and refuse to put that will into effect. Blackstone left no doubt about his commitment to legislative omnipotence by choosing the widely used hypothetical example of a law making a man judge in his own cause as an illustration. Such a law was concededly unreasonable. Blackstone was concerned not with the determination of unreasonableness but with the proper judicial attitude toward a concededly unreasonable act.

Allowing a man to be judge of his own cause was so clearly contrary to established principle that Blackstone granted that judges could interpret a statute's general language to avoid such a result:

Where some collateral matter arises out of the general words, and happens to be unreasonable; there the judges are in decency to conclude that this consequence was not foreseen by the parliament, and therefore they are at liberty to expound the statute by equity, and only *quoad hoc* disregard it. Thus if an act of parliament gives a man power to try all causes, that arise within his manner of Dale; yet, if a cause should arise in which he himself is party, the act is construed not to extend to that, because it is unreasonable that any man should determine his own quarrel. [However], if we could conceive it possible for the parliament to enact, that he should try as well his own causes as those of other persons, there is no court that has power to defeat the intent of

6. Ibid., 91.
7. Ibid.

the legislature, when couched in such evident and express words, as leave no doubt whether it was the intent of the legislature or no.[8]

To contemporary American ears this sounds like an invitation to arbitrariness and a license to Parliament to overturn the very ends for which it was brought into being. It obviously did not to Blackstone, nor has it proved to be in English political life. The parliamentary omnipotence defended here related to a Parliament containing an effective system of internal checks and balances. Far from demonstrating absolutist arbitrariness, English government was then the acknowledged leading example of successfully limited government. Confident that the English system provided realistic checks against oppression,[9] Blackstone did not anticipate having to deal with willful violation of common right and reason. English politics generally has sustained Blackstone's expectations, and American politics has not been drastically different. In the decade following the American Revolution, however, many Americans were not at all sanguine about legislative adherence to established principle or the prospects for limited government in the new republics.[10] Fear of legislative willfulness and the absence of a working system of checks and balances in the American states under the Articles of Confederation were significant factors in an early American resistance to Blackstone's conclusions and support for a judicial check on unconstitutional legislation.

The Period 1 Cases

The early American resistance to Blackstone's ideas was manifested in the actual exercise of judicial review in some state courts and in the affirmation of judicial authority over legislation in cases where judges upheld challenged legislation. However, this early support for judicial

8. Ibid.

9. Ibid., 50–51 and 149–50.

10. For a good statement and analysis see Wood, *Creation of American Republic*, 403–25.

review was not accompanied by any uniform or coherent defense of the practice or by any systematic attempt to refute Blackstone's reasoning. Each period 1 case treated the problem somewhat differently, and in none was there any recognizable forerunner of arguments used today. Furthermore, in the act of repudiating Blackstone, period 1 judges still relied on a variety of English precedents and sources. In some cases they even drew on the *Commentaries* for support.

There were four period 1 cases in which judges either refused to execute a law or defended the power to refuse, for which we have some record of court reasoning.[11] The first, *Commonwealth v. Caton*, was decided in Virginia in 1782.[12] In 1776 the Virginia legislature enacted treason legislation that included a provision transferring the power of pardon from the executive to the legislature. Three individuals, including Caton, were convicted under the act, and in 1782 the House of Delegates granted them a pardon. The senate did not concur.

The defendants argued that the pardon voted by the house was valid and that the treason act's requirement that both houses concur was unconstitutional. These contentions were possible because the constitution also contained a provision under which the House of Delegates alone could assume the pardon power. The court rejected this argument as well as the validity of the pardon, denying that the case fell within the constitutional provision for a single house pardon.

Although no legislation was here held to be void, members of the court took the occasion to affirm that the judiciary did have the power to declare an unconstitutional act void. After praising the modern

11. *Commonwealth v. Caton*, 4 Call (Va.) 5 (1782); *Rutgers v. Waddington*, reproduced in *The Law Practice of Alexander Hamilton*, ed. Julius Goebel, Jr. (New York: Columbia University Press, 1964), 1:393–419; *Trevett v. Weeden*, Rhode Island (1786); *Bowman v. Middleton*, 1 Bay (S.C.) 252 (1792). For *Trevett* see brief of James M. Varnum, "The Case Trevett against Weeden" (1787), microprint, Early American Imprints Series, Charles Evans' American Bibliography no. 20825, American Antiquarian Society. For a discussion of other period 1 cases drawn from secondary material see Charles Grove Haines, *The American Doctrine of Judicial Supremacy* (New York: Macmillan, 1914), chap. 4.

12. 4 Call (Va.) 5 (1782).

"diffusion of knowledge" for its advancement of limited government
and promotion of general liberty, Judge George Wythe added:

> But this beneficial result attains to higher perfection, when those,
> who hold the purse and sword, differing as to the powers which
> each may exercise, the tribunals, who hold neither, are called
> upon to declare the law impartially between them. For thus the
> pretensions of each party are fairly examined, their respective
> powers ascertained, and the boundaries of authority peaceably
> established. . . . [I]f the . . . legislature . . . should attempt to
> overleap the bounds prescribed to them by the people, I, in
> administering the public justice of the country, will meet [it] at
> my seat in this tribunal; and, pointing to the constitution will say,
> to [the legislature], here is the limit of your authority; and hither,
> shall you go, but no further.[13]

This is the strongest and fullest defense of judicial authority over
legislation made by any of the judges in *Commonwealth v. Caton*. It is
similar in important ways to Coke's position asserted a century earlier
in England. Coke had attempted to make the common law courts the
balance of power between king and Parliament.[14] He worked before
full separation of legislative and adjudicative authority and before the
development of legislative supremacy. His judicial review was thus
very different from that visible at any time in America. Although
Wythe was not simply repeating Coke's position or contending with
the kinds of problems that faced seventeenth-century England, he did
defend judicial power over legislation as part of a political balance of
power. The legitimacy of a judicial check on legislation was connected
with the judiciary's purported disinterestedness and relative weakness—it held neither purse nor sword. Wythe did not mention a
written constitution or suggest any uniquely judicial obligation to the
law of the constitution; and he did not claim that judicial review was
part of the judiciary's legal responsibilities. Neither did he acknowl-

13. Ibid., 7–8.

14. See McIlwain, *High Court of Parliament*, 288–307, and Theodore F.
T. Plucknett, "Bonham's Case and Judicial Review," *Harvard Law Review* 40
(November 1926): 30–70.

edge Blackstone nor attempt to distinguish American from English circumstances.[15]

The second period 1 case was *Rutgers* v. *Waddington,* decided in New York in 1784.[16] It involved a statute, enacted immediately after the English army's evacuation from New York, to aid citizens who had fled the occupation and whose property had been confiscated and used by the English. The statute, which authorized victims to seek compensation through trespass actions in court and specifically barred a defense of military authority, was challenged on two grounds. It was argued first that the law of nations provided just such a defense and that this law was part of English common law, which in its applicable parts had been received by the state in the constitutional convention of 1777. Defense attorneys, including Alexander Hamilton, did not argue that the law of nations bound statutes the way it has since been argued that constitutions do. There was widespread acknowledgment that nations could legislate contrary to that law, and the defense in *Rutgers* argued that no state, but only the national government, had this power. The Trespass Acts were also said to be contrary to the Treaty of Peace, which contained an implied amnesty for the alleged trespass.

Judge James Duane, of the New York City Mayor's Court, was obviously sympathetic to the defense but wrote a carefully crafted opinion in which neither plaintiff nor defendant was fully vindicated.[17] The suit asked for compensation for property used by the English from 1777 to 1783. The court held that the law of nations was not applicable to the circumstances existing from 1777 to 1779 and thus that there was no bar to recovery for this period. For the remaining three years the law of nations was held to be applicable.

15. There were two other opinions in this case. For Judge Pendleton's see below, chap. 2 at n. 33. The other judges subscribed to Judge Blair's brief affirmation that "the court had power to declare any resolution or act of the legislature, or of either branch of it, to be unconstitutional and void": *Commonwealth* v. *Caton,* 4 Call (Va.) 5, 20 (1782).

16. *Law Practice of Hamilton,* ed. Goebel, 1:393–419. For commentary on *Rutgers* v. *Waddington* see ibid., 282–315.

17. Ibid., 393–419.

Duane did not rule, however, that the statute conflicted with the law of nations, nor did he declare it void. He subjected it instead to a construction that barred recovery while avoiding a direct conflict with the law of nations. In an obvious attempt to bring his action into conformity with Blackstone, Duane paraphrased the *Commentaries:*

> The Court is therefore bound to conclude, that such a consequence was not foreseen by the Legislature, to explain it by equity, and to disregard it in that point *only,* where it would operate thus unreasonably.
>
> The questions then, whether this statute hath in any respect revoked the law of nations, or is repealed by the definitive treaty of peace, are foreign to the circumstances of the case: neither will happen, nor ought to be apprehended.[18]

Duane's statutory construction and denial of full relief to the plaintiffs generated significant opposition in the legislature, which condemned his opinion with a resolution that also drew on Blackstone:

> That the adjudication aforesaid is in its tendency subversive of all law and good order, and leads directly to anarchy and confusion; because, if a Court instituted for the benefit and government of a corporation may take upon them to dispense with, an act in direct violation of a plain and known law of the state, all other Courts either superior or inferior may do the like; and therewith will end all our dear bought rights and privileges, and Legislatures become useless.[19]

Trevett v. *Weeden,* decided in Rhode Island in 1786, is probably the best known of the period 1 exercises of judicial review. The Rhode Island legislature had issued a large amount of paper money and had made it a criminal offense to refuse to accept that money on a par with silver and gold. It also denied those so accused the right to a jury trial. Weeden, a butcher, had been indicted under the statute. There is no

18. Ibid., 416–17. Emphasis in original.
19. Reprinted ibid., 312.

court opinion for *Trevett* v. *Weeden,* but an account of the case is available in a pamphlet written by the defendant's lawyer, James Varnum.[20]

Rhode Island at this time did not have a formal written constitution but was still governed under its colonial charter, as modified at independence. This charter did not include an explicit guarantee of trial by jury. Nevertheless Varnum maintained "that the trial by jury is a fundamental right, a part of our legal constitution: That the Legislature cannot deprive the citizens of this right: And that your Honours can, and we trust will, so determine."[21]

To make his case Varnum surveyed English history from Magna Charta through a variety of its reaffirmations. He marshaled three pages of evidence in support of the proposition that "the trial by jury was ever esteemed a first, a fundamental, and a most essential principle, in the English constitution. . . . [T]his sacred right," he continued, "was transferred [from England] to this country."[22] The colonial charter in its declaration that the colonists had "all liberties and immunities of free and natural subjects" was "declaratory of, and fully confirmed to the people the Magna Charta, and other fundamental laws of England," including trial by jury.[23] Nor did the break from England and the subsequent reconstitution of government affect rights already established: "The revolution hath made no change . . . so as to abridge the people of the means of securing their lives, liberty and property."[24]

In defending judicial authority to refuse to enforce the act, Varnum also turned to English sources. He cited Bacon, Coke, Hobart, and Plowden[25] and quoted Blackstone to the effect that "acts of Parliament that are impossible to be performed [are of no validity]; and if there arise out of them collaterally any absurd consequences, manifestly contrary to common reason, they are, with regard to those

20. "The Case Trevett against Weeden" (1787).
21. Ibid., 11.
22. Ibid., 14.
23. Ibid., 15.
24. Ibid., 23.
25. Ibid., 33.

collateral consequences, void."[26] Varnum ignored the fact that this passage was part of the same paragraph in which Blackstone rejected the claim of judicial authority over laws that explicitly violated common reason. The Rhode Island law challenged in *Trevett* was a deliberate expression of legislative will and, according to Blackstone, beyond judicial challenge. Varnum did not quote that part of Blackstone's argument and proceeded to claim that the law was both contrary to "common right or reason"[27] and "repugnant or impossible to be performed."[28] Like Wythe in *Caton* and Duane in *Rutgers*, Varnum simply did not acknowledge or address Blackstone's main contention.

Whether or not Varnum treated Blackstone properly, the Rhode Island court accepted his argument and refused to enforce the act. The judges, however, did not actually declare the legislation void but, by Varnum's account, ruled instead that "the information [was] not cognizable before them."[29] As in New York following *Rutgers* v. *Waddington,* the legislative reaction was strong. The judges were called before the legislature to explain their ruling and were threatened with removal. No immediate action was taken, but at the next judicial election all but one were removed.[30]

The last period 1 case, *Bowman* v. *Middleton,* belongs chronologically in period 2 but is so characteristic of period 1 and came so early in period 2 as to be properly classified with the earlier cases.[31] It was decided in 1792 in South Carolina and dealt with a disputed land title. One of the parties claimed title under a state law passed in 1712. By that act title had been transferred from one holder and his heirs to another. In *Bowman* the court declared the 1712 act void on the ground that in taking property from one individual and vesting it in another without trial by jury, the legislature violated "common right." The opinion, as reported, was very short:

26. Ibid., 30.
27. Ibid., 30–31.
28. Ibid., 31.
29. "The Case of the Judges," appended ibid., 38–39.
30. For details see ibid., 37–45, and Haines, *American Doctrine,* 204–06.
31. 1 Bay (S.C.) 252 (1792).

THE COURT, present, GRIMKE and BAY, Justices, who, after a full consideration on the subject, were clearly of opinion, that the plaintiffs could claim no title under the act in question, as it was against common right, as well as against magna charta, to take away the freehold of one man and vest it in another, and that, too, to the prejudice of third persons, without any compensation, or even a trial by the jury of the country, to determine the right in question. That the act was, therefore, ipso facto, void. That no length of time could give it validity, being originally founded on erroneous principles. That the parties, however, might, if they chose, rely upon a possessory right, if they could establish it.[32]

Bowman v. *Middleton* is the least argumentative and least self-conscious of the period 1 cases. It reads as though Blackstone did not exist and there was no controversy over the legitimacy of a judicial check on legislation. In its uncomplicated reliance on common right and Magna Charta it furnishes another example of the absence of any peculiarly American components in period 1 cases.

Explicit Social Contracts

The period 1 reliance on weak and inappropriate English sources fails to convey the extent to which differences between English and American circumstances, significant enough to undermine Blackstone's authority, were actually acknowledged. The only period 1 reference to such differences appeared in a second *Commonwealth* v. *Caton* opinion, that of Judge Edmund Pendleton. After asking whether the constitution or an act that violated it "shall prevail and be the rule of judgment," Pendleton observed:

The constitution of other governments in Europe or elsewhere, seem to throw little light upon this question, since we have a written record of that which the citizens of this State have adopted as their social compact; and beyond which we need not extend our researches. It has been very properly said, on all sides,

32. Ibid., 254–55.

that this act, declaring the rights of the citizens, and forming their government, divided it into three great branches, the legislative, executive, and judiciary, assigning to each its proper powers, and directing that each shall be kept separate and distinct, must be considered as a rule obligatory upon every department, not to be departed from on any occasion. But how far this court, in whom the judiciary powers may in some sort be said to be concentrated, shall have power to declare the nullity of a law, passed in its forms by the legislative power, without exercising the power of that branch, contrary to the plain terms of that constitution, is indeed a deep, important, and I will add, a tremendous question, the decision of which might involve consequences to which gentlemen may not have extended their ideas.[33]

This brief, unelaborated passage stated the shared assumptions of period 1. The starting point was the perception that American circumstances differed from those of Europe because there existed "a written record of [our] social compact." Written social contracts or constitutions were in fact instrumental in the widespread period 1 willingness to reject Blackstone. But, as evidenced by the absence of significant reliance on them in the cases, or of any attempt to refute Blackstone's argument or even to present a coherent defense of judicial authority over legislation, no systematic connection had yet been made between written constitutions and this judicial authority. Pendleton's is the only period 1 source even to allude to such a connection, and to understand its meaning, it will be necessary to draw on fuller, but still relatively sparse, period 2 sources.

During periods 1 and 2, written constitutions served first as evidence that political authority rested on real, explicit social contracts rather than on the imaginary or hypothetical ones relied upon elsewhere. Next, by virtue of being committed to writing, these contracts or constitutions had an explicit, publicly verifiable content, in contrast to the traditional, customary, and hence uncertain content of European fundamental law. Last, these social contracts or constitutions were of a status unquestionably superior to ordinary law and

33. 4 Call (Va.) 5, 17 (1782).

thus bound subsequent legislation in a way that European fundamental law, of entirely statutory status, could not. Written constitutions did not initially carry the meaning that was to be accorded them after *Marbury*. Specifically, commitment to writing in no way made fundamental law the kind of law rightly amenable to judicial application, interpretation, and enforcement; it was important only as a vehicle for fundamental law's explicitness and thereby for the certitude of its content and status.

Before we examine the precise relationship between explicit fundamental law and period 1 and 2 judicial review, it is necessary to demonstrate and to emphasize that the significance of the written constitution lay in its explicitness or certitude and not in its being law subject on that ground to judicial exposition and enforcement. The latter widely held but unjustifiable modern reading is reflected in Thayer's 1893 account of the period 2 understanding. According to Thayer, the courts "began by resting [judicial review] upon the very simple ground that the legislature had only a delegated and limited authority under the constitutions; that these restraints, in order to be operative, must be regarded as so much law; and, as being law, that they must be interpreted and applied by the court."[34] Only the first of these propositions can, in fact, be found in period 1 and 2 sources. The notion that American constitutions were "so much law" and, as such, to be interpreted and applied in court is characteristic of the unfounded modern practice of reading Marshall's legalization of fundamental law into eighteenth-century statements.

That the uniqueness of American fundamental law inhered in the explicitness and certitude of its content is reflected in Pendleton's comment that the existence of written social contracts precluded the need to "extend our researches" beyond it. Period 2 sources would make the same point more fully. The most complete statement is Judge St. George Tucker's in *Kamper v. Hawkins*, the leading period 2 exercise of judicial review in Virginia. After noting that written constitutions were unknown before the American Revolution, Tucker continued:

34. "Doctrine of Constitutional Law," 138.

What the *constitution* of any country *was* or rather *was supposed to be*, could only be collected from what the *government had at any time done;* what had been *acquiesced* in by the people, or other component parts of the government; or what had been *resisted* by either of them. Whatever the government, or any branch of it had *once done*, it was inferred they had a *right* to do *again.* . . . But, with us, the constitution is not an "ideal thing, but a real existence; it can be produced in a visible form": its principles can be ascertained from the living letter, not from obscure reasoning or deductions only.[35]

James Iredell made the same point in a letter to Richard Spaight: "The Constitution [is] not . . . a mere imaginary thing, about which ten thousand different opinions may be formed, but a written document to which all may have recourse."[36] In *VanHorne's Lessee* v. *Dorrance,* Justice William Paterson formulated the issue as follows:

It is difficult to say what the constitution of England is; because, not being reduced to written certainty and precision, it lies entirely at the mercy of the Parliament. . . . In England there is no written constitution, no fundamental law, nothing visible, nothing real, nothing certain, by which a statute can be tested. In America the case is widely different: Every State in the Union has its constitution reduced to written exactitude and precision.[37]

Although written constitutions were thus identified as the chief distinguishing characteristic of American fundamental law, they could not in fact carry all the weight ascribed to them or account by themselves for the willingness to reject Blackstone. For one thing, despite Paterson's assertion, not all the states had written constitutions, and period 1 judicial review was not confined to states that did. More important, commitment to writing was only one component in the explicitness of American fundamental law, and not the major one. Of greater importance were the American constitutions' perceived status

35. 1 Va. Cases 20, 78 (1793). Emphasis in original.
36. *Correspondence of Iredell,* ed. McRee, 2:174.
37. 2 U.S. (2 Dall.) 304, 308 (1795).

as real social contracts, in contrast to the fictional or imaginary ones of Europe. Tucker, Iredell, and Paterson in the quotations above all refer to the reality of American constitutions and contrast them with "ideal" or "imaginary" European counterparts. This reality was imparted to American social contracts not by being written but by circumstances approximating a state of nature following the revolutionary break from England and, consequently, by the concreteness and reality of the social contracts that ended it.

Virginia provided the clearest evidence of the importance of a real state of nature in establishing the concreteness of American fundamental law. At independence a convention produced both Virginia's first constitution and ordinary legislation. This convention had no specific mandate to draft a constitution, nor was the constitution submitted to popular ratification. This posed no particular difficulty until the consolidation of period 2 judicial review. At that point doubt about the constitution's superior status, generated by the absence of extraordinary authorization or ratification, threatened to undermine judicial claims to enforce it against legislation that was said to have violated it. In *Kamper v. Hawkins* all five participating judges addressed the question of the constitution's status before defending their decision not to execute the legislation before the court. All of them agreed that despite the absence of clarity about the convention's status, the constitution was binding fundamental law. It achieved this status, they claimed, by its function in bringing Virginia out of a state of nature, by its subject matter, and by its subsequent popular acceptance as a constitution.[38]

The most important factor in establishing the constitution's superior status was that the convention which framed it was convened in the absence of civil government and with no connection whatever to any previous government. In Judge John Tyler's words:

> To investigate this subject rightly, we need but go back to that awful period of our country when we were declared out of the protection of the then mother country—and take a retrospective

38. See 1 Va. Cases 20, 27–28, 36–38, 46–48, 57–58, and 69–74 (1793), for the discussions of Judges William Nelson, Spencer Roane, James Henry, John Tyler, and St. George Tucker, respectively.

view of our situation, and behold the bands of civil government
cut asunder, and destroyed:—No social compact, no system of
protection and common defence against an invading tyrant—in
a state of nature, without friends, allies, or resources:—In such a
case what was to be done?

Those eminent characters to whom so much gratitude is . . .
due . . . recommended a convention of delegates to be chosen . . .
who were to meet together for the express design of completely
protecting and defending the rights, both civil and religious, of
our common country. . . . What power had the people therefore
that was not confided to their representatives?

. . . And shall [the convention's] validity be now questioned?
for what purpose? To revert back to our former insignificancy? It
cannot be.[39]

Judge Spencer Roane made the same argument:

I consider that at the time of the adoption of our present Constitution, the British government was at an end in Virginia: . . .

The people were therefore at . . . the period of the election of
the Convention, which formed the Constitution, absolved from
the former kingly government, and free, as in a state of nature, to
establish a government for themselves. . . .

This convention was not chosen under the sanction of the
former government; it was not limited in its powers by it, if
indeed it existed, but may be considered as a spontaneous as-
semblage of the people of Virginia. . . . This constitution is sanctioned by the consent and acquiescence of the people for seven-
teen years; and it is admitted by the almost universal opinion of
the people, by the repeated adjudications of the courts of the
commonwealth, and by very many declarations of the legislature
itself, to be of superior authority to any opposing act of the
legislature.[40]

In addition to making these same points, Judge Tucker's opinion drew
the sharpest contrast between American and European circumstances:

39. Ibid., 57–58.
40. Ibid., 36–37.

Our case was much stronger than either [the English in 1688 or the French in 1789]. There was at least the shadow of legal, constitutional authority in the convention parliament of England in 1688, as the ordinary legislature; and the national assembly of France was constitutionally assembled under the authority of the government it subverted. The convention of Virginia had not the shadow of a legal, or constitutional form about it. It derived its existence and authority from a higher source; a power which can supersede all law, and annul the constitution itself—namely, the *people*, in their *sovereign, unlimited,* and *unlimitable* authority and capacity.[41]

What distinguished American from European fundamental law was not its technically correct existence as a written social contract but its role in bringing the American states out of a state of nature. The experience of having disavowed completely the existing government and of having self-consciously adopted a totally new set of institutions imparted a concreteness and reality to American fundamental law never before experienced. Participation in this experience and the shared public agreement of its significance made all the states, whether or not they had technically correct social contracts, more like one another than any was like England.

This unique American experience also explains how Rhode Island, which did not have a written constitution at all, nevertheless produced one of the major period 1 exercises of judicial review. Varnum, in dealing with Rhode Island circumstances, had to defend a judicial check on legislation in the absence of any state convention or separate written social contract. Yet he was as insistent as the *Kamper* judges that Rhode Island had a constitution that bound the legislature. In response to the argument that Rhode Island had no constitution, he proclaimed: "Constitution!—we have none:—Who dares to say that?"[42] As the *Kamper* judges were to do, he defended this assertion by appeal to common consent. Popular acceptance of legislation passed by the General Assembly demonstrated that the assembly could "meet, deliberate and enact, in virtue of a constitution." If

41. Ibid., 74. Emphasis in original.
42. Varnum, "Trevett against Weeden," 25.

there were no constitution, representatives of the towns could "only meet . . . to form a social compact." This constitution, Varnum also insisted, bound ordinary legislation: "[If the legislature] attempt to destroy, or in any manner infringe [the constitution] they violate the trust reposed in them, and so their acts are not considered as laws, or binding upon the people."[43]

Appeal to common consent, in the absence of properly ratified constitutions, seems a weak reliance by today's standards. In period 1, however, this appeal reflected the shared experience of every living adult of having passed through a state of nature and of having emerged with a completely new set of institutions whose leading principles were undisputed. This gave a historical reality and concreteness to American social contracts that to eighteenth-century Americans stood in decisive contrast to the fictional and imaginary ones of European analysis.[44] This concrete reality is the deepest component in the widely held perception that the uniqueness of American fundamental law lay in its explicitness. Commitment to writing was clearly important, but it reinforced rather than created this explicitness.

The Rejection of Legislative Omnipotence

The most important consequence of the reality and explicitness of American social contracts was that it overturned the doctrine of

43. Ibid., 25–26.

44. Thomas S. Grey has contrasted the American states' use of constitutional conventions with the eighteenth-century English practice of justifying "social and governmental institutions . . . by imaginative reconstruction from a state of nature through one or more actual or hypothetical contracts or agreements." In contrast to this imaginative reconstruction, Grey pointed out, the American conventions were the "practical embodiment" of "an extraordinary assembly of the whole people." The conventions did function in this capacity but, as the Rhode Island and Virginia experiences demonstrate, the uniqueness of American fundamental law and of its real, concrete, and literally binding status antedated institutionalization of the conventions. See Grey, "Origins of the Unwritten Constitution: Fundamental Law in American Revolutionary Thought," *Stanford Law Review* 30 (May 1978): 864.

legislative omnipotence. Despite the strength of the European fundamental law and social contract traditions and the emergence of meaningfully limited government in England, legislative omnipotence was still the rule. In the absence of anything comparable to the real, explicit American social contracts, the English had nothing tangible to hold up against the latest expression of parliamentary will, the sole embodiment of sovereignty. As Blackstone underscored, even a legislative act that concededly violated fundamental law was valid.

The real and explicit American social contracts, in contrast, provided precise, publicly stated boundaries for each of the branches and thus, for the first time, for literally limited government. In Pendleton's words, the Virginia constitution, which "assign[ed] to each [branch] its proper powers, and direct[ed] that each shall be kept separate and distinct, must be considered as a rule obligatory upon every department, not to be departed from on any occasion."[45] This unremarkable statement, easily overlooked today, initially carried with it enormous significance. The existence of explicit, publicly verifiable limits on each of the branches introduced the powerful idea that it was now, for the first time, possible to identify with certitude a legislative act that, in its violation of fundamental law, was on its face void, or not law. American legislatures could not violate fundamental law as it was conceded Parliament could violate English fundamental law. Statements comparable to Pendleton's are an integral part of period 1 and 2 discussions of judicial review. Among the clearest is Justice Paterson's in *VanHorne's Lessee v. Dorrance:*

> The constitution is the work or will of the people themselves, in their original, sovereign, and unlimited capacity. . . . The constitution fixes limits to the exercise of legislative authority, and prescribes the orbit within which it must move. . . . Whatever may be the case in other countries, yet in this there can be no doubt, that every act of the legislature, repugnant to the constitution, is absolutely void.[46]

45. *Commonwealth v. Caton*, 4 Call (Va.) 5, 17 (1782). The full quotation is given above, chap. 2 at n. 33.
46. 2 U.S. (2 Dall.) 304, 308 (1795). For other formulations of the same point see *Kamper v. Hawkins*, 1 Va. Cases 20, 25–30, 36–38, 59 (1793),

That written, explicit social contracts bound government in an unprecedented way was not disputed. As Pendleton indicated, it was agreed to "on all sides."[47]

The ideas that legislative omnipotence was inapplicable to American circumstances and that an act which violated the constitution was void have been so thoroughly accepted for over two centuries that statements to this effect seem too trivial to be noticed. In the absence of controversy over these propositions at the time of independence it has also been assumed, to the extent it was ever even considered, that members of the founding generation shared the same assessment of their triviality. But precisely the opposite was the case. At independence the end of legislative omnipotence and the capacity, literally, to identify an unconstitutional act were new and immensely powerful ideas. They set the stage for the period 1 and 2 battle over judicial review, one whose terms were very different from subsequent controversy.

Period 1 and 2 judicial review was composed of two distinct questions. The first was, "Can the legislature violate the constitution?" As we have just seen, the answer to this question was, universally, no. This answer reflected agreement on the inapplicability of legislative omnipotence under explicit social contracts and was manifested in the repeated, uncontested assertion that an unconstitutional act was void. The second question was, "May the judiciary refuse to enforce an unconstitutional act?" There was no comparable agreement on the answer to this question. It constituted the central controversy of period 1 and was the issue resolved in period 2. The widespread period 1 willingness to reject Blackstone and to support a judicial check on legislation, coupled with the absence of any uniform or coherent defense, indicates that supporters of judicial review moved

---

Judges Nelson, Roane, and Tyler, respectively; James Iredell, "To the Public," and Iredell to Spaight, in *Correspondence of Iredell*, ed. McRee, 2:145–46 and 172–73, quoted and discussed below, chap. 3 at nn. 6–7; Alexander Hamilton, *The Federalist, No. 78*, Modern Library (New York: Random House, n.d.), 505–06, quoted and discussed below, chap. 3 at n. 72.

47. *Commonwealth* v. *Caton*, 4 Call (Va.) 5, 17 (1782).

directly from the agreed end of legislative omnipotence, and the invalidity of an act that violated the constitution, to support for judicial refusal to execute such an act.

Opponents of a judicial check on legislation accepted without reservation the period 1 premise that an unconstitutional act was void. Nevertheless, they denied that this innovation conveyed to the judiciary authority to refuse to enforce a properly enacted piece of legislation. The key proposition of period 1 opposition to judicial review maintained that although legislative omnipotence no longer obtained, legislative supremacy did.

The concrete expression of legislative supremacy was the statement that the Constitution was "a rule to the *legislature only*"[48] and could not be invoked by the judiciary to overturn a legislative determination. Although American legislatures, unlike the English Parliament, were bound by the explicit content of a concrete fundamental law and although an act that violated fundamental law was void, judges still could not refuse to enforce a duly enacted piece of legislation. As Pendleton suggested in *Commonwealth* v. *Caton*,[49] such action went beyond any known boundary of legitimate judicial power and compounded the wrong done by the legislature. Others denounced judicial review in stronger terms. No matter "what law they have declared void," judicial refusal to enforce a properly enacted law was a "usurpation" of power, "an absolute negative on the proceedings of the Legislature, which no judiciary ought ever to possess."[50] The remedy for legislative violation of fundamental law—even under a real social contract of explicit content—remained what it had always been, popular action and, ultimately, revolution.[51]

---

48. This is a part of Tucker's formulation of the period 1 opposition to judicial review, which he summarized before rebutting in his *Kamper* opinion: *Kamper* v. *Hawkins*, 1 Va. Cases 20, 77 (1793). Emphasis in original. His full statement is given below, chap. 3 at n. 18.

49. 4 Call (Va.) 5, 17 (1782). See the full quotation above, chap. 2 at n. 33.

50. Richard Spaight to James Iredell, August 12, 1787, *Correspondence of Iredell*, ed. McRee, 2:169.

51. Ibid., 169–70.

The Concededly Unconstitutional Act

As the structure of the period 1 debate indicates, the judicial power contemplated by both sides was confined to the concededly unconstitutional act, to circumstances where it was agreed that the legislature had "in fact" violated the constitution. This point was most clearly expressed by James Iredell in his statement of the period 1 opposition to judicial review:

> The great argument is, that though the Assembly have not a *right* to violate the constitution, yet if they *in fact* do so, the only remedy is, either by a humble petition that the law may be repealed, or a universal resistance of the people. But that in the mean time, their act, whatever it is, is to be obeyed as a law; for the judicial power is not to presume to question the power of an act of Assembly.[52]

The concededly unconstitutional act has not been the subject of judicial review since Marshall. As a result, despite substantial evidence that period 1 and 2 judicial review was so confined, modern scholarship has not taken this proposition seriously and has considered the concededly unconstitutional act to be trivial and irrelevant. During periods 1 and 2, however, the issue was at the center of theoretical and practical interest. Theoretically it touched the claim of legislative omnipotence and legislative supremacy as defended by Blackstone, who had deliberately couched his argument in terms of a concededly unconstitutional act, one that made a man judge of his own cause. Judicial refusal to enforce parliamentary will, he argued, would undermine political authority. Those Americans who followed Blackstone applied this position to American circumstances and denied that judges had any authority whatever over duly enacted legislation. The Constitution, they insisted, was "a rule to the legislature only," and even when the legislature "*in fact*" violated it, the judiciary could not question legislative authority. Refutation of Blackstone's position and establishment of the proposition that the courts could

---

52. "To the Public," ibid., 147. Emphasis in original.

refuse to execute a concededly unconstitutional act were not, in the years following independence, a trivial undertaking.

The limitation of judicial review to the concededly unconstitutional act was as important practically as it was theoretically. Period 1 judicial review developed in contemplation of a legislative record in many states that included enough clearly unconstitutional measures to make debate in these terms meaningful. One leading source of concededly unconstitutional legislation was the "revolutionary justice" that accompanied the American Revolution.[53] Although milder than that of many other revolutions, it shared the familiar feature of deliberate violation of established principle. In the American context it consisted largely of confiscation of Loyalist property without jury trial.

The debtor relief legislation and what Madison called the "multiplicity and mutability of laws"[54] in many of the states also contributed to making the concededly unconstitutional act a serious practical issue. Although little debtor relief legislation reached the courts, the states' political records generated widespread fear of an unchecked legislative supremacy capable of willful violation of long-standing principle.[55]

53. Five period 1 and 2 cases grew out of wartime legislation, but in only two did courts actually refuse to enforce challenged legislation. These were *Holmes v. Walton* (New Jersey, 1780) and *Bayard v. Singleton*, 1 N.C. 5 (1787). There is no record of the court opinion in *Holmes v. Walton*. For an account see Austin Scott, "*Holmes v. Walton*: The New Jersey Precedent," *American Historical Review* 4 (April 1899): 456–69. Two other cases were *Commonwealth v. Caton*, 4 Call (Va.) 5 (1782), and *Rutgers v. Waddington* (New York, 1784), discussed above, chap. 2 at nn. 12–15 and 16–19, respectively. The fifth was *Cooper v. Telfair*, 4 U.S. (4 Dall.) 14 (1800), discussed below, chap. 3 at nn. 42–48. In *Cooper* the U.S. Supreme Court upheld legislation which had been passed during the war under a state constitution that had already been superseded.

54. See James Madison, "Vices of the Political System of the United States," April 1787, in *The Writings of James Madison*, ed. Gaillard Hunt, 9 vols. (New York: G. P. Putnam's Sons, 1900–1910), 2:365–67.

55. *Trevett v. Weeden* was the only debtor relief case to reach the courts. The legislation in this case explicitly denied trial by jury, the central issue in period 1 and 2 judicial review.

We have been so used to examining period 1 and 2 judicial review as a forerunner of modern practice that we have neglected to look at it in its own setting, as a reply to Blackstone's specific arguments and to the political conditions of the 1770s and 1780s. The major response to the aggressive legislative supremacy of the 1780s was the movement for a stronger national government that would assume much of the legislative authority then lodged in the states. Period 2 judicial review was another response. It developed before the new Constitution was functioning and reflected the fear that the unmixed republicanism of the new American states threatened limited government in a way that it was no longer threatened in England. For as we have noted, despite parliamentary omnipotence, the English had achieved a working limited government through internalized acceptance of fundamental law restraints and an effective system of checks and balances. The assumption that American state legislatures had a poorer record than the English Parliament was a visible part of period 2 judicial review. Justice Paterson, in the course of invalidating state legislation in *VanHorne's Lessee* v. *Dorrance,* complained:

> The English history does not furnish an instance of the kind; the Parliament, with all their boasted omnipotence, never committed such an outrage on private property. . . .
>
> Shame to American legislation! That in England, a limited monarchy, where there is no written constitution, where the Parliament is omnipotent, and can mould the constitution at pleasure, a more sacred regard should have been paid to property, than in America, surrounded as we are with a blaze of political illumination; where the Legislatures are limited; where we have republican governments, and written constitutions, by which the protection and enjoyment of property are rendered inviolable.[56]

Finally, the actual practice of judicial review during periods 1 and 2 confirms that it was in fact reserved for the concededly unconstitutional act. There were eight cases for which records indicate judges

56. 2 U.S. (2 Dall.) 304, 310, and 314 (1795).

refused to enforce legislation. Six involved legislative interference with trial by jury.[57] The other two involved legislation dealing with the organization and exercise of judicial power, an area touching the doctrine of concurrent review.[58] By this doctrine it was agreed that each branch could determine the constitutionality of legislation dealing with its own operation.

This extraordinary consensus governing the use of judicial review indicates that it was in fact reserved for legislation regarded as clear violation of fundamental law. This record also points to another crucial aspect of period 1 and 2 judicial review. Determinations of unconstitutionality were not then legal acts but public or political ones. This was so even when made by the judiciary. As *Trevett* and *Bowman* suggested, and as period 2 cases will confirm, determinations of unconstitutionality did not follow from interpretation of written law but consisted of the reaffirmation of first principles contained in explicit fundamental law. Judicial authority to enforce fundamental law was made possible by its reality and explicitness—that is, by the public verifiability of its existence and content, not by its legal quality as understood in ordinary law.

The most succinct expression of period 1 and 2 assumptions appears in the defense of judicial review made in *Marbury*. But because we have been so misled by Marshall's diversion of the original issues, we have been unable to recognize this or understand its significance. Marshall began by structuring *Marbury* on the standard two questions of period 1 and 2 judicial review: "whether an act, repugnant to the constitution, can become the law of the land"; and "if an act of the

57. These were *Holmes* v. *Walton* (New Jersey, 1780); *Trevett* v. *Weeden* (Rhode Island, 1786); *Bayard* v. *Singleton*, 1 N.C. 5 (1787); *Bowman* v. *Middleton*, 1 Bay (S.C.) 252 (1792); *VanHorne's Lessee* v. *Dorrance*, 2 U.S. (2 Dall.) 304 (1795); and *Stidger* v. *Rogers*, 2 Ky. Decisions 52 (1801). There were altogether about a dozen cases in which the issue of judicial review was raised. In some, judicial authority over legislation was asserted but not exercised in the particular case; in others, judges avoided implementing legislation through statutory interpretation. For a review of the most significant cases see Haines, *American Doctrine*, chaps. 4, 5, and 7.

58. *Hayburn's Case*, 2 U.S. (2 Dall.) 409 (1792), and *Kamper* v. *Hawkins*, 1 Va. Cases 20 (1793).

legislature, repugnant to the constitution, is void, does it, notwithstanding its invalidity, bind the courts, and oblige them to give it effect?"[59] Bickel is surely correct in pointing out that *Marbury* begs the real question of the judicial review we know, namely, who decides in the first place whether an act is repugnant to the Constitution.[60] But *Marbury* only begs the real question of the judicial review Marshall had yet to put into place. In 1803 the issue was precisely as Marshall stated it. He posed the two questions as they had been posed repeatedly during the preceding decades and gave the answers that had been given successfully during the 1790s. Next, Marshall discussed judicial review in terms of the unambiguous, conceded violation of fundamental law. The clear-cut cases that Marshall used as examples and that are dismissed today as trivial and irrelevant were then at the center of controversy. They were the kinds of examples uniformly given in defenses of judicial review in the 1790s.[61] Unless we are to conclude that leading judges and public figures carried on a trivial and irrelevant debate for over twenty years, we have to understand that it was initially directed at a different order of question from that which developed later.

Judicial Review at the Constitutional Convention

The successful period 2 defense of judicial authority over unconstitutional legislation was developed coincidentally in time with the drafting of the Constitution of 1787. However, this defense was not articulated at the convention, which reflected instead the last expression of period 1 conceptions.

There was no comprehensive discussion of judicial review at the Constitutional Convention, only a series of comments made in debate

59. *Marbury* v. *Madison*, 5 U.S. (1 Cr.) 137, 176, and 177 (1803).
60. *Least Dangerous Branch*, 2 and 3.
61. See Iredell to Spaight, August 26, 1787, *Correspondence of Iredell*, ed. McRee, 2:174; Judge Tucker in *Kamper* v. *Hawkins*, 1 Va. Cases 20, 79–81 (1793); and Justice Paterson in *VanHorne's Lessee* v. *Dorrance*, 2 U.S. (2 Dall.) 304, 309 (1795).

on related questions. A proposal for a council of revision, a joint executive-judicial veto over legislation, provided the context for the largest number of these comments.

The convention rejected the council of revision in favor of the qualified executive veto. The council was opposed on a variety of grounds: it was said that policy judgments inherent in the veto were foreign to judicial expertise; that uniting the executive and judiciary against the legislature would overwhelm the latter; and that as judges would eventually have to expound the laws, they should have no hand in their original passage.[62] In addition, several delegates argued that specific inclusion of the judiciary in the veto power was unnecessary, as judges would have a check on legislation in their capacity to pass on constitutionality.

It was in the course of discussing this last point that the most direct statements were made, both supporting and opposing the judicial power to refuse to execute laws. Elbridge Gerry referred with obvious approval to the fact that "in some States, the Judges had actually set aside laws as being against the Constitution."[63] Luther Martin argued that "as to the Constitutionality of laws, that point will come before the Judges in their proper official character. In this character, they have a negative on the laws."[64] John Mercer, on the other hand, "disapproved of the Doctrine that Judges as expositors of the Constitution should have authority to declare a law void,"[65] and John Dickinson "thought no such power ought to exist."[66] Of those who addressed themselves to the question, more delegates supported judicial power over legislation than denied it.

It was not always clear, however, whether speakers endorsing judi-

---

62. *The Records of the Federal Convention of 1787*, ed. Max Farrand, 4 vols. (New Haven: Yale University Press, 1937; reprint ed., 1966), 1:97–98, 138–40, and 2:73–80, 298–300.

63. Ibid., 1:97.

64. Ibid., 2:76. Gouverneur Morris commented that "he could not agree that the Judiciary which was part of the Executive, should be bound to say that a direct violation of the Constitution was law" (ibid., 299).

65. Ibid., 298.

66. Ibid., 299.

cial review were supporting a general power over legislation or one limited to defense of the courts' constitutional sphere. Gerry's observation was immediately preceded by the remark that the judiciary "will have a sufficient check against encroachments on their own department by their exposition of the laws, which involved a power of deciding on their Constitutionality."[67] Wilson, in reference to an earlier invocation of judicial power over legislation, described that power as follows: "It has been said that the Judges, as expositors of the Laws would have an opportunity of defending their constitutional rights."[68]

Whatever the precise scope of the power contemplated by particular speakers, this difference of opinion expressed at the convention mirrored period 1 differences of opinion in the country as a whole. There was more support than opposition for judicial authority over legislation in the convention, and this was probably an accurate reflection of the strength of the contending sides outside the convention.

The convention debates also documented the recognition that explicit and extraordinary popular ratification of a constitution was necessary in order to remove all doubt about its control over subsequent legislation. But this discussion took place exclusively in the context of federalism. In urging ratification of the new Constitution by conventions rather than the legislature, Madison argued:

The articles of Confederation themselves were defective in this respect, resting in many of the States on the Legislative sanction only. Hence, in conflicts between acts of the States, and of Congress, especially where the former are of posterior date, and the decision is to be made by State Tribunals, an uncertainty must necessarily prevail, or rather perhaps a certain decision in favor of the State authority.[69]

This is the only discussion of the Constitution's status as binding law made at the convention, and it occurred in the context of assuring

67. Ibid., 1:97.
68. Ibid., 2:73.
69. Ibid., 1:122.

supremacy of national over state laws. There was no comparable discussion of the relationship between the Constitution and national legislation. Also, the supremacy clause, which identifies the Constitution as the supreme law of the land, was discussed exclusively in the context of federalism. The first version of the clause was taken from the Paterson Plan and identified national legislation and treaties as the "supreme law of the respective States."[70] On August 23 the convention, without debate, adopted Rutledge's amendment to include the Constitution as part of the "supreme law of the several States."[71] The final wording, referring to the Constitution as the supreme law of the land, appeared in the report of the Committee on Style, which sat at the end of the convention.[72]

The relative inattention to establishment of the Constitution's superior and binding status over national legislation reflected the fact that the concept of a legally binding constitution controlling subsequent legislation was not yet fixed in American constitutional thinking as it was soon to be. Such an idea was not alien to American thinking, but it was not a routine part of it either.

Next, the debates reflected the understanding that judicial power over legislation was confined to the concededly unconstitutional act. This was demonstrated in the distinction drawn by James Wilson and George Mason between the wisdom and constitutionality of legislation, and the reservation of a judicial check for the latter. After noting the judiciary's power to protect its constitutional rights, Wilson continued: "This power of the Judges did not go far enough. Laws may be unjust, may be unwise, may be dangerous, may be destructive; and yet not be so unconstitutional as to justify the Judges in refusing to give them effect."[73] Mason made the same point:

It had been said . . . that if the Judges were joined in this check on the laws, they would have a double negative, since in their expository capacity of Judges they would have one negative. He would reply that in this capacity they could impede in one case

70. Ibid., 245.
71. Ibid., 2:389.
72. Ibid., 603.
73. Ibid., 73.

only, the operation of laws. They could declare an unconstitutional law void. But with regard to every law however unjust oppressive or pernicious, which did not come under this description, they would be under the necessity as Judges to give it a free course.[74]

The distinction between the wisdom and constitutionality of legislation has long been unserviceable and is often little more than a partisanly inspired rationalization for opposition to the substance of particular Supreme Court determinations. It became unworkable only when determinations of constitutionality became legal ones, derived from exposition of the written constitution. In period 1 the distinction was intelligible and workable. It reflected the common understanding that determinations of unconstitutionality were public ones following unambiguous legislative violation of publicly acknowledged principles of explicit fundamental law. Mason's formulation constituted the precise expression of that understanding: the judicial authority was one of "declar[ing] an unconstitutional law void."

The convention debates also indicate that in 1787 fundamental law was understood to bind morally and politically, not legally. This was demonstrated in the discussion of enforcing specific constitutional prohibitions on legislative power. In response to a motion to include in the Constitution a prohibition on bills of attainder and ex post facto laws, Oliver Ellsworth remarked that "there was no lawyer, no civilian who would not say that ex post facto laws were void of themselves. It cannot then be necessary to prohibit them." Wilson supported Ellsworth, arguing "against inserting anything in the Con-

74. Ibid., 78. Madison did not draw this distinction at the convention but he did later in the debate on the Alien and Sedition Acts. See James Madison, "Report on the Virginia Resolutions," in *The Debates in the Several State Conventions on the Adoption of the Federal Constitution*, ed. Jonathan Elliot, 2d ed. 5 vols. (Philadelphia: J. B. Lippincott, 1836), 4:568. See also Madison to Spencer Roane, September 2, 1819, in *Writings of Madison*, ed. Hunt, 8:449, quoted and discussed below, chap. 4 at n. 17, and Alexander Hamilton, *Federalist 78*, 509–10, quoted and discussed below, chap. 3 at n. 82.

stitution as to ex post facto laws. It will bring reflections on the Constitution—and proclaim that we are ignorant of the first principles of Legislation, or are constituting a Government which will be so."[75] Daniel Carroll replied that despite this universal understanding, state legislatures had passed such laws and they had taken effect, leading Wilson to conclude that as provisions in the state constitutions barring such acts had proved useless, a similar provision would likely be useless in the U.S. Constitution. "Besides," he added, "both sides will agree to the principle and will differ as to its application."[76]

Here two of the leading lawyers of the day accepted the notion of a law void in itself, unconnected with any judicial determination to that effect. Unconstitutionality, at the end of period 1 and in the very act of writing the national Constitution, was thought not to be determined by judicial exposition of written supreme law but to consist of violation of long-standing and publicly acknowledged first principles of fundamental law, written or unwritten. There was, in addition, no expectation of or reliance on routine judicial enforcement of constitutional provisions or judicial resolution of conflicting interpretations of those provisions. The convention's rejection, two weeks later, of a motion to prepare a bill of rights reflected the same underlying presumptions. Whatever the precise reasons for rejection of a bill of rights, it would not have been as easily done had there then existed the strong link that now exists between written constitutional limits and a regular system of judicial enforcement of those limits.[77]

Finally, the discussions of state ex post facto laws provide additional evidence that the concededly unconstitutional act was then a serious political issue. It was the problem that generated the search for, and openness to, judicial enforcement of constitutional principle. Period 2 was to bring near universal support for judicial enforcement, but that remedy was still conceived of as directed to laws void in

75. *Records of the Federal Convention*, 2:376.
76. Ibid.
77. For the discussion and vote on the Bill of Rights see ibid., 587–88. For Madison's discussion of his reasons for not including a bill of rights in the new constitution see Madison to Jefferson, October 17, 1788, in *Writings of Madison*, ed. Hunt, 5:271–75, and discussed below, chap. 4 at nn. 1–10.

themselves, unconnected with judicial exposition of the written text. This was to remain the operative conception of unconstitutionality, for the purposes of judicial refusal to execute a law, through period 2 and into period 3.

CHAPTER THREE

Period 2
From *Federalist 78* to *Marbury*

THE EXCHANGE between Ellsworth and Wilson on ex post facto laws at the convention was actually the bridge between the first two periods in the evolution of American judicial review. In direct reply to Wilson's observation on the unenforceability of a prohibition on ex post facto laws, Hugh Williamson of North Carolina observed: "Such a prohibitory clause is in the Constitution of North Carolina, and tho it has been violated, it has done good there and may do good here, because the Judges can take hold of it."[1] With little additional discussion a prohibition of ex post facto laws and bills of attainder was added to the Constitution.

North Carolina's experience with judicial enforcement of the Constitution had greater consequences than this brief exchange suggests. In 1786 James Iredell, a North Carolina lawyer, was representing a client whose property had been confiscated during the Revolution. A state statute provided that subsequent claims on behalf of such property were to be dismissed upon presentation of an affidavit that the property had been purchased from the commissioner of forfeited estates. The right to trial by jury, specifically mentioned in the North Carolina constitution, had been denied.

Iredell's client's case, *Bayard v. Singleton*,[2] had been pending for some time, and in 1786 Iredell published in a North Carolina newspaper a defense of the judicial authority to refuse to execute an unconstitutional act.[3] When the case was heard the following year the court declared the act that denied trial by jury void.

Iredell repeated and reformulated his defense of the judicial refusal

1. *Records of the Federal Convention*, ed. Farrand, 2:376.
2. 1 N.C. 5 (1787).
3. "To the Public," in *Correspondence of Iredell*, ed. McRee, 2:145–49.

to enforce an unconstitutional act in a letter to James Spaight, one of the North Carolina delegates to the Constitutional Convention.[4] This letter was dated August 26, 1787, while the convention was still sitting. I do not know when, or even if, this letter arrived in Philadelphia, but from the totality of the evidence I have concluded that both Hamilton and Wilson became familiar with Iredell's defense of judicial review at this time. Each proceeded to make major restatements of Iredell's argument within the next few years, Hamilton in *Federalist 78* and Wilson in *Lectures on the Law,* delivered in 1790–91. *Federalist 78,* although varying the emphasis given to specific points, repeated in striking detail most of those made by Iredell and added no new ones. Wilson's discussion of a constitutional prohibition of ex post facto laws at the convention indicated no expectation of any judicial role in its enforcement, yet *Lectures on the Law* made the standard period 2 defense of judicial review.[5]

Iredell's 1786 statement, "To the Public," took up the standard period 1 concerns. It opened with a strong expression of the rejection of legislative omnipotence by the American states and of the novelty of this rejection:

> In forming the constitution . . . [we] were not ignorant of the theory *of the necessity of the legislature being absolute in all cases,* because it was the great ground of the British pretensions. . . . When we were at liberty to form a government as we thought best . . . we decisively gave our sentiments against it, being willing to run all the risks of a government to be conducted on the principles then laid as the basis of it. The instance was new

4. Ibid., 172–76.
5. Edward S. Corwin noted a change in Wilson's attitude toward judicial review between the Constitutional Convention, which disbanded in September 1787, and the Pennsylvania Ratifying Convention, which convened in November 1787. At the Constitutional Convention, Corwin said, Wilson's "tone . . . is that of a man weighing a novel idea," whereas at the Ratifying Convention he was "no longer in doubt." Corwin did not offer any explanation for this change nor did he capture properly Wilson's position at the Constitutional Convention: Corwin, "The Supreme Court and Unconstitutional Acts of Congress," *Michigan Law Review* 4 (June 1906): 620.

in the annals of mankind. No people had ever before deliberately met for so great a purpose. Other governments have been established by chance, caprice, or mere brutal force. Ours . . . sprang from the deliberate voice of the people. . . .

I have therefore no doubt, but that the power of the Assembly is limited and defined by the constitution. It is a *creature* of the constitution. (I hope this is an expression not prosecutable.) The people have chosen to be governed under such and such principles. They have not chosen to be governed, or promised to submit upon any other; and the Assembly have no more right to obedience on other terms, than any different power on earth has a right to govern us; for we have as much agreed to be governed by the Turkish Divan as by our own General Assembly, otherwise than on the express terms prescribed.[6]

That it was explicit fundamental law and real social contracts that ended legislative omnipotence is more concisely stated in Iredell's letter to Spaight:

Without an express Constitution the powers of the Legislature would undoubtedly have been absolute (as the Parliament in Great Britain is held to be), and any act passed, *not inconsistent with natural justice* (for that curb is avowed by the judges even in England), would have been binding on the people. The experience of the evils which the American war fully disclosed, attending an absolute power in a legislative body, suggested the propriety of a real, original contract between the people and their future Government, such, perhaps, as there has been no instance of in the world but in America.[7]

As already noted in my examination of period 1 material, the end of legislative omnipotence has never been considered an event of par-

6. *Correspondence of Iredell,* ed. McRee, 2:145–46. Emphasis in original.
7. Ibid., 172–73. Emphasis in original. In 1798, after establishment of period 2 judicial review, Iredell denied that American judges could refuse to execute an act on the ground that it violated natural justice. See *Calder* v. *Bull,* 3 U.S. (3 Dall.) 386, 399 (1798), and discussion below, chap. 3 at nn. 61–65.

ticular importance in American historical analysis. But it obviously
was to Iredell. He drew attention to its novelty and even betrayed a
mild apprehension that it entailed some risk. At the same time, Iredell
recognized that despite its novelty and importance, it was universally
accepted and uncontroversial. Immediately following his statement
on the American disavowal of legislative omnipotence in "To the
Public," Iredell went on to say: "These are consequences that seem so
natural, and indeed so irresistable, that I do not observe they have
been much contested."[8] This echoes Pendleton's remark that it was
said "on all sides" that written social contracts established literally
binding limits on all the branches. Having thus stated the uncontroversial first component of the period 1 debate, that the legislature
could not violate the Constitution, Iredell moved to its second, contentious part: "The great argument is, that though the Assembly have
not a *right* to violate the constitution, yet if they *in fact* do so, the only
remedy is, either . . . petition . . . or . . . universal resistance."[9] He
proceeded to reject petition as demeaning to a self-governing people,
and revolution as too extreme to be useful. He then inquired "whether
the judicial power hath any authority to interfere in such a case," and
answered with what was to be the successful period 2 defense of
judicial authority to refuse to enforce an unconstitutional act:

> The [judicial] duty . . . I conceive, in all cases, is to decide accord-
> ing to the *laws of the State*. It will not be denied, I suppose, that
> the constitution is a *law of the State,* as well as an act of Assem-
> bly, with this difference only, that it is the *fundamental* law, and
> unalterable by the legislature, which derives all its power from it.
> One act of Assembly may repeal another act of Assembly. For
> this reason, the latter act is to be obeyed, and not the former. An
> act of Assembly cannot repeal the constitution, or any part of it.
> For that reason, an act of Assembly, inconsistent with the consti-
> tution is *void*, and cannot be obeyed, without disobeying the su-
> perior law to which we were previously and irrevocably bound.

8. *Correspondence of Iredell,* ed. McRee, 2:147.
9. Ibid. Emphasis in original. The full quotation is given above, chap. 2 at
n. 52.

The judges, therefore, must take care at their peril, that every act of Assembly they presume to enforce is warranted by the constitution, since if it is not, they act without lawful authority. This is not a usurped or a discretionary power, but one inevitably resulting from the constitution of their office, they being judges *for the benefit of the whole people,* not *mere servants of the Assembly.*[10]

This is the core of Iredell's defense of judicial authority over legislation. On first reading it could easily be taken as part of a single line of reasoning leading to *Marbury* and the doctrine we accept today. As represented in Thayer's formulation,[11] under this modern doctrine judicial authority over legislation is said to flow from the fact that the Constitution, as supreme law, is subject like other law to judicial application and enforcement. The *Marbury* doctrine assumes no difference in kind between the two that would preclude authoritative judicial application and interpretation of fundamental law.

Iredell, in this passage, held no such assumption and made no such argument, implicitly or explicitly. He did assert that the judicial obligation was to decide according to the laws of the state, and he included the constitution as a law of the state, cognizable in court. In so doing he introduced a major period 2 innovation, but he was neither contemplating nor implying that the constitution and ordinary law were cognizable in the same way or that the judicial responsibility to them was comparable. In arguing that fundamental law was cognizable in court, he was only rejecting the proposition that the constitution was a rule limited to the legislature. In its explicitness, the constitution was a rule to each branch equally, and the judiciary as well as the legislature was bound by and answerable directly to it. The judicial duty to decide according to the laws of the state meant that the judiciary was precluded from enforcing legislation that by violating the constitution was void or not law. This was the central proposition of period 2 judicial review and it followed from the judiciary's dual responsibility: to fundamental law, equally with and on the same terms as the other branches of government, and uniquely to ordinary

10. Ibid., 148. Emphasis in original.
11. "Doctrine of Constitutional Law," 138, quoted above chap. 2 at n. 34.

law under its common law obligation to fix the meaning of ordinary law.

Iredell was here rejecting Blackstone's contention that the judiciary could not take cognizance of the constitution at all, even when confronting a concededly unconstitutional act. This passage followed Iredell's reaffirmation of the uniquely American phenomenon of the end of legislative omnipotence and the absence of any legislative authority to violate the constitution. It was in rebuttal to "the great argument" that the judiciary could not act even if the legislature has "in fact" violated the constitution. It was made in contemplation of an act that denied trial by jury to those whose property had been confiscated during the war. This was an unambiguously unconstitutional act comparable to Blackstone's hypothetical example of legislation that made a man judge of his own cause.[12]

The judicial responsibility over unconstitutional legislation, defended in "To the Public," derived furthermore from the judiciary's responsibility to "the whole people," and not from any uniquely judicial relationship to fundamental law, as hinted at in *Marbury*. Enforcement of fundamental law was a political act, a peaceful substitute for revolution presented as a superior alternative to petition or universal resistance.[13] Judicial determination of a law's unconstitu-

12. In his letter to Spaight, Iredell used the hypothetical examples of acts abolishing trial by jury and acts passed after the legislature had abrogated previously established elections (*Correspondence of Iredell*, ed. McRee, 2:174).

13. Varnum's brief in *Trevett v. Weeden* also presented judicial review as a substitute for revolution. After insisting that the Rhode Island legislature was bound by the Rhode Island constitution, Varnum acknowledged the period 1 claims of legislative supremacy and of popular responsibility for constitutional enforcement: "But as the Legislative is the supreme power in government, who is to judge whether they have violated the constitutional rights of the people?—I answer . . . the people themselves will judge, as the only resort in the last stages of oppression." He added, however, what was to develop into one of the key contentions of period 2 judicial review: "But when [the legislature] proceed no farther than merely to enact what they may call laws, and refer those to the Judiciary Courts for determination, then, (in discharge of the great trust reposed in them, and to prevent the horrors of a civil war, as

tionality was also a public, or political, not a legal act. The force of a real social contract and publicly verifiable limits on legislative power made an act void. Identification of this invalidity could therefore be made by any of the branches.[14]

The most important implication of Iredell's argument was that judicial enforcement of fundamental law, unlike enforcement of ordinary law, carried with it no assumption of or sanction for judicial interpretation or exposition of fundamental law. The judiciary's common law responsibility to ordinary law necessitated authoritative determination of whether that law was violated in particular cases, which in turn necessitated exposition of ordinary law. Enforcement of fundamental law, in contrast, limited to the publicly verifiable, concededly unconstitutional act, required neither authoritative determination of fundamental law's violation in particular cases nor authoritative exposition of that law. On the contrary, uncertainty over whether an act violated fundamental law marked the limit of judicial power over legislation.

Assumption of judicial authority to expound or interpret the law of the Constitution was to be the distinguishing characteristic of period 3 judicial review. Because interpretation is the vehicle through which policy considerations enter the act of judging, this is the source of period 3's controversial assertion of judicial supremacy. Period 2 judicial review, in contrast, was an expression of the equality of the branches under explicit fundamental law made in reply to the legislative supremacy of period 1. It neither needed nor contemplated authority to expound or interpret the Constitution. It was, simply but significantly, legitimation and regularization of the judicial refusal to execute a concededly unconstitutional act. It was rejection of the view that judicial refusal to enforce such an act was a "usurped or a

---

in the present case) the Judges can, and we trust your Honours will, decide upon them" ("Trevett against Weeden," 26).

14. This point is made more clearly by Tucker, who specifically included the executive along with the judiciary as a branch that could make determinations of unconstitutionality: *Kamper v. Hawkins*, 1 Va. Cases 20, 77 (1793). Tucker's formulation is given below, chap. 3 at n. 18.

discretionary power."[15] Far from that, Iredell demonstrated that it was an inescapable obligation under a constitution of fixed and explicit limits. This sense of judicial obligation growing out of a real social contract was more forcefully expressed in Iredell's letter to Spaight: "It really appears to me, the exercise of the power is unavoidable, the Constitution not being a mere imaginary thing, about which ten thousand different opinions may be formed, but a written document to which all may have recourse, and to which, therefore, the judges cannot wilfully blind themselves."[16]

Two aspects of modern judicial review long thought to depend on the Constitution's status as supreme ordinary law were also originated by Iredell and expressed in his letter to Spaight. These are an insistence that judicial review can be exercised only as part of a regular lawsuit, and the conflict of laws analogy. As with "To the Public," the conclusion that Iredell was here contemplating the modern practice is based on an unwarranted reading of contemporary assumptions into period 2 material. Iredell's statement of these points is as follows:

> As no article of the Constitution can be repealed by a Legislature . . . it follows either that the *fundamental unrepealable* law must be obeyed, by the rejection of an act . . . inconsistent with it, or you must obey an act founded on an authority not given by the people, and to which, therefore, the people owe no obedience. It is not that the judges are appointed arbiters, and to determine as it were upon any application, whether the Assembly have or have not violated the Constitution; but when an act is necessarily brought in judgment before them, they must, unavoidably, determine one way or another. If it is doubted whether a subsequent law repeals a former one, in a case judicially in question, the judges must decide this; and yet it might be said, if the Legislature meant it a repeal, and the judges determined it otherwise, they exercised a *negative* on the Legislature. . . . This kind of objection, if applicable at all, will reach all judicial power

15. "To the Public," *Correspondence of Iredell*, ed. McRee, 2:148.
16. Ibid., 174.

whatever, since upon every abuse of it (and there is no power but what is liable to abuse) a similar inference may be drawn.[17]

Restriction of judicial review to a lawsuit underscored the point that the judicial check on unconstitutional legislation grew out of the judiciary's exclusive responsibility to expound ordinary law. Responsibility to reject an act made void by its violation of fundamental law was analogous to judicial responsibility in a conflict of laws situation in that in both circumstances the judiciary had to establish what the ordinary law is. But identification of unconstitutional legislation under explicit fundamental law still did not require exposition of that law.

The Development of Iredell's Argument

The most instructive period 2 restatement of Iredell's argument was Judge Tucker's, which was made in the course of refusing to enforce legislation in *Kamper v. Hawkins*. Tucker's statement began, as had Iredell's, with a summary of the period 1 position. Opponents of judicial review argued, according to Tucker, that "the constitution of a state is a rule to the *legislature only*, and not to the *judiciary*, or the *executive*: the legislature being bound not to transgress it; but that neither the executive nor judiciary can resort to it to enquire whether they do transgress it, or not."[18] Tucker began his reply by pointing out that the ground for this conclusion had been repudiated by the explicitness of the real, written American constitutions; he then proceeded to defend judicial authority to refuse to enforce an act that violated this real, explicit constitution:

> This sophism could never have obtained a moment's credit with the world, had such a thing as a written Constitution existed before the American revolution. . . . [W]ith us, the constitution is not an "ideal thing, but a real existence: it can be produced in a visible form": its principles can be ascertained from the living

17. Ibid., 173. Emphasis in original.
18. *Kamper v. Hawkins*, 1 Va. Cases 20, 77 (1793). Emphasis in original.

letter, not from obscure reasoning or deductions only. The government, therefore, and all its branches must be governed by the constitution. Hence it becomes the first law of the land, and as such must be resorted to on every occasion, where it becomes necessary to expound *what the law is.* This exposition it is the duty and office of the judiciary to make; our constitution expressly declaring that the legislative, executive, and judiciary, shall be separate and distinct, so that neither exercise the powers properly belonging to the other. Now since it is the province of the legislature to make, and of the executive to enforce obedience to the laws, the duty of expounding must be exclusively vested in the judiciary. But how can any just exposition be made, *if that which is the supreme law of the land be withheld from their view?* . . .

But that the constitution is a rule to all the departments of the government, to the judiciary as well as to the legislature, may, I think, be proved by references to a few parts of it.

Tucker then examined several provisions of the constitution, including those protecting trial by jury and the free exercise of religion. He conjured up hypothetical examples of unambiguous violation of these provisions and argued that the judiciary was not obliged to enforce such violations. He then concludes: "From all these instances it appears to me that this deduction clearly follows, viz. that the *judiciary* are *bound* to take notice of the constitution, *as the first law of the land;* and that whatsoever is contradictory thereto, is *not* the law of the land."[19]

Tucker's statement, even more than Iredell's, appears on first reading to be a simple precursor of *Marbury.* But like "To the Public," it differed decisively from it. First, the significance of the written constitution lay in its reality and explicitness, not in any presumed attribute as supreme ordinary law.[20] Next, Tucker did not in this passage make

---

19. Ibid., 77–81. Emphasis in original.

20. This point is most clearly expressed in that part of Tucker's opinion between the first and second sentences, omitted here but given above, chap. 2 at n. 35.

any claim, implicitly or explicitly, to judicial authority to expound the constitution or to say what the law of the constitution is. For Tucker the judicial authority is to expound ordinary law, and more clearly than had Iredell, he insisted that to make a "just exposition" of the ordinary law judges had to "resort to" and "take notice of the constitution." The constitution could not be "withheld from [judicial] view." As were all period 2 formulations, Tucker's argument was a response to the contention of Blackstone and his period 1 followers that judges must not consider fundamental law at all, even when confronted with a conceded violation of it, but were obliged to close their eyes to the constitution and see only the statute. Tucker insisted that it was necessary for judges to regard the constitution if they were to fulfill properly their common law responsibility to expound (ordinary) law. To fail to resort to the constitution was to risk putting into effect that which, in its violation of the constitution, was void or "not the law of the land."

The judiciary could legitimately take notice of the constitution because in its reality and explicitness it was "a rule to all . . . departments, to the judiciary as well as to the legislature." Period 2 judicial review derived from an equality of the branches under explicit fundamental law and not, as in *Marbury*, from a uniquely judicial relationship to supreme written law. The only exclusively judicial responsibility was to expound ordinary law.

Tucker's statement is the clearest formulation of period 2 judicial review. It is also close to but not identical with crucial passages in *Marbury*. These are read today to support judicial authority to expound the Constitution, even though it is freely admitted that neither *Marbury*'s text nor the logic of a written constitution can support such a reading. Moreover, long familiarity with the modern reading of *Marbury* has not only obscured the meaning and internal clarity of Tucker's straightforward analysis but has made modern readers more comfortable with *Marbury*'s inconsistency than with Tucker's consistency.[21]

21. The *Kamper* opinions of Judges Nelson and Roane provide two other formulations of Iredell's argument. Each argued first that the legislature may

The last major formulation of the period 2 argument, other than those of Wilson and Hamilton, was Justice Paterson's in *VanHorne's Lessee* v. *Dorrance*.[22] Paterson began with the familiar contrast between the written, real, and certain American constitutions and the unwritten and hence uncertain English constitution.[23] He then drew from this the standard two points of period 2 judicial review: an act that violated the Constitution was void; and judges were not obliged to enforce such an act. Paterson too supported his argument with examples of unambiguous constitutional violations:

> Whatever may be the case in other countries, yet in this there can be no doubt, that every act of the legislature, repugnant to the constitution, is absolutely void. . . .
>
> Could the legislature have annulled [the] articles [of the constitution] respecting religion, the rights of conscience, and elections by ballot? Surely, no. . . . If the legislature had passed an act declaring, that, in future, there should be no trial by jury, would it have been obligatory? No: It would have been void for want of jurisdiction, or constitutional extent of power. . . . I take it to be a clear position; that if a legislative act oppugns a constitutional

---

not violate the constitution (*Kamper* v. *Hawkins,* 1 Va. Cases 20, 23–30 and 36–38 [1793] respectively). Nelson then used the conflict of laws analogy to defend judicial refusal to execute an act that did: "If one man claim under an act contrary to the Constitution, that is, under what is *no* law . . . a court [must] give judgment against him" (ibid., 30–31; emphasis in original). Roane's defense of judicial authority over unconstitutional acts also relied on the conflict of laws analogy and it repeated Tucker's argument that the judiciary had to consider the constitution in order properly to expound ordinary law: "In expounding laws, the judiciary considers *every* law which relates to the subject: would you have them to shut their eyes against that law which is of the highest authority of any, or against a part of that law, which either by its words or by its spirit, denies to any but the people the power to change it?" (ibid., 38–39; emphasis in original).

22. 2 U.S. (2 Dall.) 304 (1795). Wilson's and Hamilton's defenses of judicial review are more profitably discussed later in this chapter (at nn. 66–67 and 71–82) as part of the consideration of the natural and positive law features of period 2 judicial review.

23. This part of Paterson's argument was given above, chap. 2 at n. 37.

principle, the former must give way, and be rejected on the score of repugnance. I hold it to be a position equally clear and sound, that, in such case, it will be the duty of the court to adhere to the constitution, and to declare the act null and void. The constitution is the basis of legislative authority; it lies at the foundation of all law, and is a rule and commission by which both legislators and judges are to proceed. It is an important principle, which, in the discussion of questions of the present kind, ought never to be lost sight of, that the judiciary in this country is not a subordinate, but co-ordinate branch of the government.[24]

Paterson's discussion adds nothing to that of Iredell and Tucker, but his insistence that the judiciary was "not a subordinate, but co-ordinate branch of the government" was the clearest period 2 statement of the dependence of judicial review on an equality of the branches. Paterson's references to the constitution as "principle," "rule," and "commission" instead of law are also instructive. Such usage was common in periods 1 and 2 and lasted into period 3.[25] When the Constitution was referred to as law it was usually as part of the phrase "fundamental law," or "supreme" or "first law of the land," and it carried the meaning of explicit fundamental law, not supreme written law.[26] This usage reflected the universal recognition

24. 2 U.S. (2 Dall.) 304, 308–09 (1795).

25. On the use of rule see Pendleton in *Commonwealth* v. *Caton*, 4 Call (Va.) 5, 17 (1782); James Wilson in *Lectures on the Law* in *The Works of James Wilson*, ed. Robert G. McCloskey, 2 vols. (Cambridge: Harvard University Press, Belknap Press, 1967), 1:329 and 330; and Tucker in *Kamper* v. *Hawkins*, 1 Va. Cases 20, 77, and 79 (1793). On the use of principle see Iredell, "To the Public," in *Correspondence of Iredell*, ed. McRee, 2:146; Tyler in *Kamper* v. *Hawkins*, 1 Va. Cases 20, 59 (1793); and Gibson in *Eakin* v. *Raub*, 12 Sergeant & Rawles (Pa.) 330, 354 (1825). On the use of regulation see Nelson in *Kamper* v. *Hawkins*, 1 Va. Cases 20, 27 (1793). On the use of charter see Roane, ibid., 36.

26. See Wilson in *Lectures on the Law* in *Works of Wilson*, ed. McCloskey, 329, and 330; Iredell to Spaight, *Correspondence of Iredell*, ed. McRee, 2:172 and 173; Tyler in *Kamper* v. *Hawkins*, 1 Va. Cases 20, 59 (1793); Tucker, ibid., 81; and Chase in *Whittington* v. *Polk*, 1 H. & J. (Md.) 236, 244 (1802).

of a difference in kind between fundamental law and ordinary law and the absence of any habit of thinking about fundamental law in the same terms as ordinary law.

Tucker's language, particularly his claim of a judicial authority to "resort to," "regard," and "take notice of" the constitution, is even more instructive. This language was uniformly used in period 2 cases and commentary to the exclusion of any judicial claim to apply, interpret, or expound the Constitution. The North Carolina court used it in *Bayard* v. *Singleton:* "Consequently, the Constitution (which the judicial power was bound *to take notice of* as much as of any other law whatever), standing in full force as the fundamental law of the land, notwithstanding the act on which the present motion was grounded, the same act must of course . . . stand as abrogated and without any effect."[27] So did Spencer Roane in his *Kamper* opinion: "In expounding [ordinary] laws, the judiciary *considers* every law which relates to the subject: would you have them *to shut their eyes against* that law which is the highest authority of any?"[28] Iredell in his letter to Spaight said: "The Constitution, therefore, being a fundamental law, and a law in writing of the solemn nature I have mentioned . . . the judicial power, in the exercise of their authority, must *take notice of it* as the groundwork of that as well as of all other authority."[29] And in a 1802 Maryland case in which the challenged legislation was upheld, the court defended judicial review in these terms: "To do right and justice according to the law, the judge must determine what the law is, which necessarily involves in it *the right of examining the constitution* (which is the supreme or paramount law, and under which the legislature derive the only authority they are invested with, of making laws) and considering whether the act passed is made pursuant to the constitution."[30] The uniformity of this language, as well as the absence of any attempt to call attention to the distinction between expounding ordinary law and considering, re-

27. 1 N.C. 5, 7 (1787). Emphasis added.
28. 1 Va. Cases 20, 38 (1793). Emphasis added.
29. *Correspondence of Iredell,* ed. McRee, 2:173. Emphasis added.
30. *Whittington* v. *Polk,* 1 H. & J. (Md.) 236, 244 (1802). Emphasis added.

garding, examining, or taking notice of the Constitution, is testimony to the depth and pervasiveness of the period 1 and 2 recognition of a difference in kind between fundamental law and ordinary law, and thus of the utter inappropriateness of judicial exposition of the former.

Period 2 Practice

A judicial authority to take notice of the Constitution and to refuse to enforce concededly unconstitutional acts still remained open to the charge that this authority could be abused. Iredell answered this objection by conceding the possibility. "There is no power," he agreed, "but what is liable to abuse."[31]

The period 2 record does not, however, reveal abuse. During the 1790s there was both great receptivity to Iredell's claim of judicial authority over unconstitutional legislation and very little actual use of this authority. Iredell's success was manifested by the widespread adoption of his argument, the absence of counterargument, and the disappearance of the kind of controversy that had accompanied period 1 exercises of judicial review. Legislative resistance such as that following *Rutgers* and *Trevett* disappeared as opposition became a minority position, increasingly on the defensive, without the self-confident assertiveness it had during period 1.

The ease with which the period 1 opposition was overcome owed much to the universal agreement that real, explicit social contracts ended legislative omnipotence and that an unconstitutional act was void. This agreement had already stripped much of the force from the contention that judges must enforce such acts. Nevertheless, the period 1 doctrine of legislative supremacy was still a serious one, requiring effective rebuttal. Iredell provided that rebuttal and it succeeded in quieting most opposition.

Despite this success, there were few period 2 cases in which judges actually declared legislation void. The only legislation that the U.S. Supreme Court refused to enforce touched the exercise of judicial

31. Iredell to Spaight, *Correspondence of Iredell*, ed. McRee, 2:173.

power.[32] This subject matter made Court action part of the relatively uncontroversial practice of concurrent review. In three other cases the constitutionality of legislation was challenged, but the U.S. Supreme Court upheld the acts.[33] Justice Paterson, in the U.S. Circuit Court for Pennsylvania, however, did overturn a state law in *VanHorne's Lessee v. Dorrance.*[34]

There was only slightly greater use of judicial review in the state courts. In addition to *Bayard* v. *Singleton,* which opened period 2 in 1787,[35] there were three state cases in which judges refused to enforce an act. Two of these, however, were not, strictly speaking, exercises of judicial review. One, *Kamper* v. *Hawkins,* overturned legislation dealing with judicial organization and was thereby also an exercise of concurrent review.[36] The other two, decided in South Carolina, were *Bowman* v. *Middleton* and *Lindsay* v. *Commissioners.*[37] In *Lindsay,* however, the Court was evenly divided and the legislation upheld.

The absence of active judicial review during period 2 reflected the understanding that this power was confined to the concededly unconstitutional act. This understanding was expressed on the U.S. Supreme Court by repeated use of the doubtful case rule. Under this rule legislation could be overturned only if there was no doubt about its unconstitutionality. The rule was invoked in all three cases in which the Court considered and upheld legislation. Extensive reference to the doubtful case rule in the state courts did not begin until the early 1800s, although it was visible before.[38] However, the ends served by the rule were achieved in the states by the same disinclination to use judicial power over legislation that was visible on the Supreme Court.

32. *Hayburn's Case,* 2 U.S. (2 Dall.) 409 (1792), discussed below, chap. 3 at nn. 91–94.

33. *Hylton* v. *United States,* 3 U.S. (3 Dall.) 171 (1796); *Calder* v. *Bull,* 3 U.S. (3 Dall.) 386 (1798); *Cooper* v. *Telfair,* 4 U.S. (4 Dall.) 14 (1800).

34. 2 U.S. (2 Dall.) 304 (1795) discussed below, chap. 3 at nn. 55–57.

35. 1 N.C. 5 (1787), discussed below, chap. 3 at n. 54.

36. 1 Va. Cases 20, (1793), discussed below, chap. 3 at nn. 83–90.

37. 1 Bay (S.C.) 252 (1792), discussed above, chap. 2 at nn. 31–32, and 2 Bay (S.C.) 38 (1796), discussed below, chap. 3 at nn. 58–60.

38. For state court use of the doubtful case rule see Thayer, "Doctrine of Constitutional Law," 140–42.

The first reference to the doubtful case rule on the Supreme Court was in *Hylton v. United States,* decided in 1796. Here it was argued that a national tax on carriages was a direct tax, which in its failure to be apportioned according to the census violated the U.S. Constitution. In the course of upholding the law Justice Samuel Chase remarked: "I think [the unconstitutionality of the law] may be *doubted; and if I only doubted, I should affirm the judgment of the circuit court. The deliberate decision of the national legislature . . . would determine me, if the case was *doubtful,* to receive the construction of the legislature. . . . I will never exercise [the power of review] *but in a very clear case.*"[39]

Calder v. Bull, the next case in which the rule was invoked, upheld a Connecticut law that set aside a probate court decree and granted the litigants a new hearing. The act was challenged as an ex post facto law prohibited by the U.S. Constitution. In sustaining the act, the Supreme Court held unanimously that the constitutional prohibition reached only criminal actions. Chase's opinion repeated what he had said in *Hylton:* "I will not decide *any law to be void, but in a very clear case.*"[40] Iredell made the same point: "The Court will never resort to [its] authority [over legislation] but in a clear and urgent case."[41]

Cooper v. Telfair, the last period 2 Supreme Court case in which judicial review was discussed, grew out of legislation passed in Georgia during the Revolutionary War.[42] It provided for banishment of individuals declared guilty of treason and confiscation of their property. The individuals so affected were named in the legislation that was freely conceded to be a bill of attainder. There was no express prohibition of bills of attainder in the Georgia constitution under which the law had been passed. Cooper, who was named in the bill, argued that the act violated that constitution's provision declaring that the legislative, executive, and judicial branches should be separate and distinct, and its provision safeguarding trial by jury.

39. 3 U.S. (3 Dall.) 171, 173, and 175 (1796). Emphasis in original.
40. 3 U.S. (3 Dall.) 386, 395 (1798). Emphasis in original.
41. Ibid., 399.
42. 4 U.S. (4 Dall.) 14 (1800).

Here too the Supreme Court refused to overturn the act and in the process drew on the doubtful case rule more extensively than it had in the other cases. The several opinions noted the absence of a specific prohibition of bills of attainder in the Georgia constitution and argued that the jury trial provision was inapplicable as it only reached offenses committed within Georgia. Cooper, it was pointed out, had not established that the acts with which he was charged had been committed in the state.

It was the separation of powers argument, however, that drew forth the greatest reliance on the doubtful case rule. Justice Paterson concluded: "It never was imagined, that [the general principles of separation of powers] applied to a case like the present; and to authorise this Court to pronounce any law void, it must be a clear and unequivocal breach of the constitution, not a doubtful and argumentative implication."[43] Chase agreed: "The general principles contained in the constitution are not to be regarded as rules to fetter and controul; . . . for, even in the constitution itself, we may trace repeated departures from the theoretical doctrine, that the legislative, executive, and judicial powers, should be kept separate and distinct."[44] Justice Bushrod Washington, who did not address the separation of powers issue, nevertheless affirmed his commitment to the doubtful case rule: "The presumption . . . must always be in favour of the validity of laws, if the contrary is not clearly demonstrated."[45]

That the bill of attainder challenged in *Cooper* had been passed under a state constitution no longer in operation, and before adoption of the U.S. Constitution, may have contributed to the Court's reluctance to overturn it.[46] Chase's opinion, however, suggested other reasons for the Court's response and also provided a good summary of the status of judicial review at the end of period 2.

Chase noted both the widespread acceptance of a judicial check on legislation and the absence of Court use of this power: "It is . . . a

43. Ibid., 19.
44. Ibid., 18–19.
45. Ibid., 18.
46. See David P. Currie, "The Constitution in the Supreme Court: 1789–1801," *University of Chicago Law Review* 48 (Fall 1981): 878–79.

general opinion," he pointed out, "it is expressly admitted by all this bar, and some of the Judges have, individually, in the Circuits, decided, that the Supreme Court can declare an act of Congress to be unconstitutional, and, therefore, invalid; but there is no adjudication of the Supreme Court itself upon the point."[47] In an earlier passage in *Cooper* Chase had suggested the reasons behind this absence of adjudication: "There is . . . a material difference between laws passed by the individual states, during the revolution, and laws passed subsequent to the organization of the federal constitution. Few of the revolutionary acts would stand the rigorous test now applied."[48]

The declining interest in using judicial review during the 1790s paralleled the disappearance of the political atmosphere that had given rise to the practice. Revolutionary justice had ended with the war and was, by the late 1790s, a self-contained historical episode. In addition, the sense of insecurity originally associated with state legislatures receded with the establishment of the Constitution of 1787. Fear that limited government would not survive amidst deliberate legislative disregard of established principle was no longer a prominent part of public discourse. Period 2 judicial review had owed as much to this fear as to specific legislation that met its standard of unconstitutionality. As this fear declined, judicial review seemed increasingly unnecessary and was thus unused. At the same time, however, Iredell's defense of judicial authority to refuse to enforce unconstitutional acts became firmly established. By the end of the 1790s this authority was almost beyond dispute.

The Significance of the Doubtful Case Rule

As already noted, modern scholarship has acknowledged the period 2 reliance on the doubtful case rule, but it has not taken this reliance seriously, because the rule can neither account for the modern practice nor provide a practical standard for its operation.

47. 4 U.S. (4 Dall.) 14, 19 (1800).
48. Ibid.

At the root of the modern difficulty is our failure to understand the discontinuity between period 2 and 3 judicial review. As part of period 2's enforcement of fundamental law—a political responsibility to the "whole people" devised in a period of revolutionary instability—the doubtful case rule marked an intelligible and practical limit on judicial power. As part of the application of supreme ordinary law under conditions of basic political stability, as judicial review became during period 3, the rule is in fact unworkable.

This problem is highlighted in the contrasting assessments of the doubtful case rule made by Judge John Gibson in 1825 and Thayer in 1893. Gibson, in the first decades of the nineteenth century, had a unique position from which to observe the evolution of American judicial review.[49] He was still in touch with the original political understanding of fundamental law at the same time that he was observing its legalization, and he rejected this legalization as unwarranted. But by 1825 he had already lost touch with the conditions that had given rise to period 1 and 2 judicial review, particularly the urgency that had then been connected with checking the concededly unconstitutional act.[50] Accordingly, he rejected all judicial authority over legislation, including that limited to "cases that are free from doubt or difficulty." In so doing he pointed out that if power over legislation were in fact a necessary part of judicial responsibility, then refusal to determine constitutionality in cases of doubt would constitute an evasion of judicial responsibility. No judge, he indicated, would refuse to give authoritative interpretation of ordinary law because of the difficulty or doubt entailed.[51]

---

49. See *Eakin* v. *Raub,* 12 Sergeant & Rawles (Pa.) 330, 343 (1825). For additional discussion of Gibson's position see below, chap. 3 at nn. 68–70, chap. 4 at nn. 39–44, and chap. 6 at nn. 6–21.

50. See ibid., 356, quoted and discussed below, chap. 3 at n. 69.

51. Ibid., 352. Gibson's statement of the point is as follows: "[If the] existence [of the power of judicial review] be conceded, no considerations of policy, arising from the obscurity of the particular case, ought to influence the exercise of it. The judge would have no discretion; but the party submitting the question of constitutionality would have an interest in the decision of it, which could not be postponed to motives of deference for the opinion of the

Thayer, writing in 1893, attempted to revive the doubtful case rule as a standard for modern judicial review.[52] By this time legalization of fundamental law was complete and the original distinctions were totally inaccessible. For Thayer and his contemporaries there was no other conception of the Constitution except as "so much law," a part of that law rightly amenable to judicial application and interpretation. However, as part of such a conception, the doubtful case rule, as Gibson had recognized, *did* partake of an evasion of legal responsibility. It was, among other reasons, because it was so perceived that Thayer's and Frankfurter's attempt to implement it failed. In period 2, in contrast, the doubtful case rule was not an evasion of legal responsibility because constitutional enforcement was no part of that responsibility to begin with. As a new political responsibility it had its own properties and limits. Precisely because it was understood to be beyond the boundaries of the judiciary's common law responsibility it needed the doubtful case rule, or some equivalent, to confine it within acceptable limits.

Natural Law and Positive Law in Period 2 Judicial Review

Period 2 judicial review contained elements of positive law and natural law but was not a direct manifestation of either tradition. As a new responsibility judicial control over unconstitutional legislation combined features of both in a novel way. The preeminent positive law feature of period 2 judicial review was its connection to a written constitution. Its positive law side was bolstered by the conflict of laws analogy, its confinement to regular lawsuits, and its insistence that

---

legislature; his rights would depend, not on the greatness of the supposed discrepancy with the constitution, but on the existence of any discrepancy at all; and the judge would, therefore, be bound to decide this question, like every other in respect to which he may be unable to arrive at a perfectly satisfactory conclusion; but he would evade the question, instead of deciding it, were he to refuse to decide in accordance with the inclination of his mind."

52. "Doctrine of Constitutional Law," 138–56. See also discussion below, chap. 6 at nn. 37–48.

judicial enforcement of the Constitution was a necessary part of the judiciary's common law responsibility to ordinary law. Nevertheless, period 2 judicial review drew its main ideas from the natural law tradition. Despite the fairly widespread invocation of written constitutions, their status as concrete social contracts was more important than their commitment to writing per se. It was this status that ended legislative omnipotence, established the invalidity of laws that violated the constitutions, and authorized judicial refusal to enforce such acts. The notion of a social contract establishing and limiting government was, furthermore, unintelligible outside the natural law tradition. Judicial enforcement of them was a political act, a peaceful substitute for revolution, and the legitimacy of revolution, whether carried out popularly or judicially, was established by governmental invasion of natural rights.

The relative unimportance of the written constitution was reflected in the absence of any mention of or reliance on it in the three leading period 2 defenses of judicial review: Iredell's "To the Public," Hamilton's *Federalist 78*, and Wilson's *Lectures on the Law*. More important than this eloquent silence, however, was that despite period 2 reliance on an explicit text, the precise content of fundamental law restraints in particular cases was not established through textual interpretation or exposition. That content, as we shall see in examining period 2 and 3 cases, inhered rather in first principles of government identified by the existence of explicit fundamental law. Reflecting the English legacy, its specific content was a mixture of a few natural law principles and common law precedents, constituting a consensus on the meaning of fundamental law. The U.S. Constitution was the supreme law of the land, but judicial enforcement of it was not the application and interpretation of written law but the defense of first principle committed to writing.

This peculiar merger of natural and positive law elements is visible in the casual judicial attitude toward constitutional text in period 2 cases. Although judges drew on relevant text, they did so in an offhand way. They did not regularly cite or quote the particular provisions of the state constitutions upon which they were relying, and in no case did determinations of constitutionality rest on the kind of textual exposition familiar then and now in ordinary law and in constitutional law today.[53] In *Bayard* v. *Singleton* the North Carolina court declared void a law that dispensed with trial by jury for claims involving property confiscated during the war. Although jury trial was explicitly protected in the North Carolina constitution, the opinion did not quote or cite this provision directly. The relevant part of the opinion read: "That by the Constitution every citizen had undoubtedly a right to a decision of his property by a trial by jury." The court went on to discuss limited government in general:

> For that if the Legislature could take away this right, and require him to stand condemned in his property without a trial, it might with as much authority require his life to be taken away without a trial by jury, and that he should stand condemned to die, without the formality of any trial at all: that if the members of the General Assembly could do this, they might with equal authority, not only render themselves the Legislators of the State for life, without any further election of the people, from thence transmit the dignity and authority of legislation down to their heirs male forever.[54]

In *VanHorne's Lessee* v. *Dorrance,* Justice Paterson rejected Pennsylvania's attempt to settle disputed property claims without provision for either trial by jury or mutual choice of referee. Paterson held that in the absence of agreement by the parties, only one of these alternate methods was allowable. In defending his decision Paterson drew minimally on constitutional text. The *VanHorne's Lessee* opinion was initially a jury charge, and Paterson's entire discussion of constitutional text consisted of a reference to "certain parts of the late bill of rights and constitution of Pennsylvania, which I shall now read."[55] The *Reports* then indicated, in parenthesis, that Paterson read three articles of the Declaration of Rights and two sections of the Constitution of Pennsylvania and referred the reader to a source for

53. The only textual exegesis anticipating modern practice in a period 1 or 2 case is to be found in *Kamper* v. *Hawkins,* 1 Va. Cases 20 (1793). Even here it was scanty by modern standards. See discussion below, chap. 3 at nn. 87–90.

54. 1 N.C. 5, 7 (1787).

55. 2 U.S. (2 Dall.) 304, 310 (1795).

the precise text. The provisions referred to were not reproduced in the *Reports*.[56]

Paterson did, however, make a lengthy statement of the natural law basis of property rights:

> The right of acquiring and possessing property, and having it protected, is one of the natural, inherent, and unalienable rights of man. Men have a sense of property: Property is necessary to their subsistence, and correspondent to their natural wants and desires; its security was one of the objects, that induced them to unite in society. No man would become a member of a community, in which he could not enjoy the fruits of his honest labor and industry. The preservation of property then is a primary object of the social compact, and, by the late constitution of Pennsylvania, was made a fundamental law. . . . The legislature, therefore, had no authority to make an act divesting one citizen of his freehold, and vesting it in another, without a just compensation. It is inconsistent with the principles of reason, justice, and moral rectitude; it is incompatible with the comfort, peace, and happiness of mankind; it is contrary to the principles of social alliance in every free government; and lastly, it is contrary both to the letter and spirit of the constitution. In short, it is what every one would think unreasonable and unjust in his own case.[57]

The disproportionate attention given natural law principles over constitutional text is also mirrored in Paterson's wording at the end of this paragraph. Reason, justice, and the principles of social alliance in every free government took precedence over the letter and spirit of the constitution. Public consensus on the former gave meaning to the latter and provided the deepest level of support for the judicial check on legislation then being sanctioned.

Lindsay v. *Commissioners*, decided in South Carolina in 1796,

56. The references were to a statement of the inherent and inalienable right to property, a provision protecting trial by jury, a statement that the Declaration of Rights was part of the Constitution, and a prohibition against legislative interference with any part of the Constitution.

57. 2 U.S. (2 Dall.) 304, 310 (1795).

revealed the same merger of natural and positive law elements. It considered whether the city of Charleston had to compensate property holders in taking private property to build a street. The state constitution provided that "no freeman shall be divested of his property, but by the judgment of his peers, or the law of the land." Members of the court were unanimous in recognizing a right of eminent domain which was bound by "the law of the land." They were evenly divided on what the law of the land demanded in this case. Judges on each side discussed the issue in terms of common law precedent, and in the course of his opinion Judge John Grimke remarked: "The 2d section of the 9th article of our state constitution, confirms all the before mentioned principles. It was not declaratory of any new law, but confirmed all the ancient rights and principles, which had been in use in the state, with the additional security, that no bills of attainder, nor ex post facto laws, or laws impairing the obligation of contracts, should ever be passed in the state."[58]

In his reliance on common law precedent and in his indication that the constitution "was not declaratory of any new law, but confirmed . . . ancient rights and principles," Grimke captured the merger of principle and text that characterized period 2 judicial review and, as we shall see, remained in the judicial review of Marshall's Supreme Court colleagues. The constitutional text was important as indisputable evidence of limited government and, generally, for identification of those principles that bound governmental power. However, the meaning of those principles for the purposes of judicial review was not to be found by textual exegesis but by appeal to a preexisting established content.

Lindsay is also interesting incidentally as a measure of the successful spread of the period 2 argument. It was decided by the same court which in 1792 had overturned an act on the ground that it was "against common right [and] magna charta."[59] In 1796 the judges discussed the validity of the challenged legislation in light of the South

---

58. 2 Bay (S.C.) 38, 57 (1796).
59. See *Bowman* v. *Middleton*, 1 Bay (S.C.) 252, 254 (1792), discussed above, chap. 2 at nn. 31–32.

Carolina constitution, as well as common law principles, and one of
the judges voting to overturn the legislation paraphrased key parts of
Federalist 78.[60]

The famous debate between Justices Chase and Iredell in *Calder v.
Bull* is still another indication of the merger of natural and positive
law elements in period 2 judicial review. In *Calder,* Chase asserted
that in a government established "on *express compact, and on republican principles*" judges could invalidate legislation that contra-
vened "the *great first principles* of the *social compact*" whether or not
these principles were "expressly" included in the Constitution.[61] Iredell disagreed, arguing that there was no "fixed standard" for the "abstract principles of natural justice," and consequently no justification
for a judicial refusal to enforce laws particular judges had determined
violated these principles. However, a law that violated the "marked
and settled boundaries" of legislative power "define[d] with precision" in the American constitutions was "unquestionably void."[62]

This was a debate between two strands of the period 2 understanding, not one between a natural and positive law conception of judicial
review as understood today. Chase's position reflected the view that
the key phenomena in American constitutional development were the
reality or concreteness of the American social contracts and the general consensus on their main animating principles and substantive
content. The most important substantive agreement was that any
contract formed on republican principles, by definition, barred government from invading property rights.[63] In this view express or
explicit compacts themselves made possible the idea of an invalid act,
gave invalidity substantive meaning, and allowed judges to refuse to
enforce such acts. This position is represented in Varnum's defense of

60. 2 Bay (S.C.) 38, 61–62 (1796).

61. 3 U.S. (3 Dall.) 386, 388 (1798). Emphasis in original.

62. Ibid., 399.

63. The centrality of property rights in early American republicanism is
discussed in G. Edward White, *The Marshall Court and Cultural Change,
1815–35, The Oliver Wendell Holmes Devise History of the Supreme Court
of the United States,* vols. 3, 4 (New York: Macmillan, 1988), chap. 1
(particularly 48–61) and chap. 9.

judicial review in the absence of a written constitution, supported by the *Kamper* judges' acceptance of a consensus on fundamental law as sufficient to establish the binding quality of the Virginia constitution, and reflected in Paterson's disproportionate emphasis on natural law principles over constitutional text in *VanHorne's Lessee* v. *Dorrance*.

Iredell's reliance on the "marked and settled boundaries" of the Constitution located the explicitness of American social contracts in the specific provisions of which they were composed rather than in the contracts themselves or in a consensus on their content. Nevertheless, even for Iredell, the crucial factor in authorizing judicial enforcement of fundamental law was the "precision" of the constitutional provisions that ended legislative omnipotence and established limited government, not any presumed positive law attributes attached to the Constitution as written law. The content of constitutional provisions in particular cases came from their "settled" character, not from judicial exposition. This in turn meant the extratextual sources of natural law principle and common law precedent, backed up by the doubtful case rule.[64]

Edward S. Corwin, writing in 1914, argued that although Iredell's position triumphed in "appearance" Chase's was actually the dominant one in American constitutional law, at least until the Civil War.[65] Corwin's judgment of the initial dominance of natural law was correct, but it was based on incomplete understanding. It did not appreciate the significance initially attached to "express compacts," and it attributed to Iredell's written constitution both positive law and ordinary law features that prevailed only in the aftermath of Marshall's success. For Iredell, as for all of period 2 practice, judicial review was a novel responsibility merging natural and positive law in which the natural law elements were stronger. We shall see in detail in chapter 5 how Marshall introduced textual exposition into judicial review without openly challenging or displacing the period 2 understanding.

64. It was in connection with this reference to the marked and settled boundaries of the American constitutions that Iredell invoked the doubtful case rule: 3 U.S. (3 Dall.) 386, 399 (1798).

65. "The Basic Doctrine of American Constitutional Law," *Michigan Law Review* 12 (February 1914): 250–51.

Marshall's judicial review, triumphant as it was to become, in his own time was indeed only the appearance of the modern form.

The Natural Law Strand:
Wilson and *VanHorne's Lessee* v. *Dorrance*

The mixture of natural and positive law in Iredell's work was a feature of all period 2 judicial review. It was not through Iredell's formulation, however, but those of James Wilson and Alexander Hamilton that defense of judicial review reached its widest audience. Period 2 Court cases either quoted or paraphrased one of these two leading sources. Of the two, Wilson's was closer to Iredell in that it displayed both the natural and positive law components of the original. Hamilton, on the other hand, ignored the natural law elements in and underlying Iredell's analysis and expanded the positive law ones. Marshall leaned totally on this positive law strand, and the *Marbury* text drew heavily and freely from *Federalist 78* and *Kamper* v. *Hawkins*, the leading period 2 case that followed Hamilton as well as Iredell. Marshall also extended and transformed the positive law side beyond that displayed in *Federalist 78* and in the process gave judicial review its modern form.

The clearest expression of the natural law components in Wilson's judicial review appeared not in his specific defense of the practice but in his comparison of the English and American constitutions made in an earlier part of *Lectures on the Law:*

> You will be surprised on being told, that . . . no such thing as a constitution, properly so called, is known in Great Britain. What is known, in that kingdom, under that name, instead of being the controller and the guide, is the creature and the dependent of the legislative power. The supreme power of the people is a doctrine unknown and unacknowledged in the British system of government. The omnipotent authority of parliament is the dernier resort, to which recourse is had in times and in doctrines of uncommon difficulty and importance. The natural, the inherent, and the predominating rights of the citizens are considered as so dangerous and so desperate a resource, as to be

inconsistent with the arrangements of any government, which does or can exist.[66]

Wilson did not identify the written constitution as the distinguishing feature of American constitutionalism or as the basis for the end of legislative omnipotence. He did not, in fact, provide any evidence at all to support the assertion that legislative omnipotence did not apply in the United States. This discussion not only reflected the initial importance of the rejection of legislative omnipotence but suggested that for Wilson, as for Chase, the most significant factor in this rejection was the consensus on the meaning of events that reconstituted political life after the break from England. In particular it suggested that "express compacts and republican principles" were more basic than written constitutions per se in ending legislative omnipotence and, in the process, creating the possibility of invalid acts.

Wilson's identification of the Constitution with the "natural, the inherent, and the predominating rights of the citizens" and as a "desperate and dangerous resource" also conveyed the period 2 understanding that constitutional enforcement was an extraordinary political act, not a legal one. It underscored the character of judicial review as a substitute for revolution rather than a part of legal process. Iredell conveyed this same sense when, in *Calder* v. *Bull*, he referred to the judicial check on legislation as a "delicate and awful" authority.[67] Although we still refer to judicial review as delicate, it is no longer comprehensible as being awful. With the triumph of Marshall's judicial review it has become a part of law enforcement, albeit a special part.

The most graphic expression of the way in which period 2 judicial review functioned as a substitute for revolution was provided in Judge Gibson's opinion in *Eakin* v. *Raub*. Near the beginning of this opinion Gibson noted that there existed two judicial pronouncements defending judicial authority over legislation—Paterson's in *VanHorne's Lessee* and Marshall's in *Marbury*. He dismissed the former as "meta-

66. *Works of Wilson*, ed. McCloskey, 1:309.
67. 3 U.S. (3 Dall.) 386, 399 (1798).

phorical illustration" rather than "argument"[68] and devoted his opinion to a critique of *Marbury.* Toward the end of *Eakin* v. *Raub* Gibson returned briefly to Paterson's opinion. As we have seen and as Gibson's criticism confirms, *VanHorne's Lessee* had drawn heavily on the same natural law strands that animated *Lectures on the Law:*

> In *VanHorne* v. *Dorrance* . . . the right is preemptorily asserted, and examples of monstrous violations of the constitution are put in a strong light, by way of example; such as taking away the trial by the jury, the elective franchise, or subverting religious liberty. But any of these would be such a usurpation of the political rights of the citizens, as would work a change in the very structure of the government; or, to speak more properly, it would itself be a revolution, which, to counteract, would justify even insurrection; consequently, a judge might lawfully employ every instrument of official resistance within his reach. By this, I mean, that while the citizen should resist with pike and gun, the judge might co-operate with *habeas corpus* and *mandamus.* It would be his duty, as a citizen, to throw himself into the breach, and if it should be necessary, perish there; but this is far from proving the judiciary to be a *peculiar organ,* under the constitution, to prevent legislative encroachment on the powers reserved by the people; and this is all that I contend it is not.[69]

These comments captured and conveyed period 2 judicial review's character as a substitute for revolution. However, as Gibson was no longer in touch with the period 1 and 2 fear of legislative irresponsibility, Paterson's position seemed to him irrelevant if not somewhat hysterical. Gibson's formulation also underscored the differences between Paterson's period 2 position and the legalized form of judicial review then developing. The conceded judicial obligation to defend first principles against revolutionary attack did not mean that the

68. 12 Sergeant & Rawles (Pa.) 330, 346 (1825). Gibson was either unaware of or ignored the *Kamper* opinions' defenses of judicial review.

69. 12 Sergeant & Rawles (Pa.) 330, 356 (1825). Emphasis in original.

judiciary was the appointed arbiter of conflict over constitutional interpretation.[70]

Wilson's specific defense of judicial authority over legislation, in *Lectures on the Law,* did not display the political character or natural law foundations of this power as openly as did his more general discussion of American constitutionalism. Nor did he spell out the steps in the period 2 position quite as clearly as had Tucker. His statement, however, is pure period 2 judicial review. Reading it as an expression of the modern *Marbury* doctrine is possible only by an unjustifiable attribution of period 3 assumptions to it.

As Wilson is a major period 2 authority it is important to reproduce his full statement, despite its length:

> From the constitution, the legislative department, as well as every other part of government, derives its power: by the constitution, the legislative, as well as every other department, must be directed; of the constitution, no alteration by the legislature can be made or authorized. In our system of jurisprudence, these positions appear to be incontrovertable. The constitution is the supreme law of the land: to that supreme law every other power must be inferiour and subordinate.
>
> Now, let us suppose, that the legislature should pass an act, manifestly repugnant to some part of the constitution; and that the operation and validity of both should come regularly in question before a court, forming a portion of the judicial department. In that department, the "judicial power of the United States is vested" by the "people," who "ordained and established" the constitution. The business and the design of the judicial power is, to administer justice according to the law of the land. According to two contradictory rules, justice, in the nature of things, cannot possibly be administered. One of them must, of necessity, give place to the other. Both, according to our supposition, come regularly before the court, for its decision on their operation and validity. It is the right and it is the duty of the court

70. The transitional character of judicial review in the first part of the nineteenth century is discussed below (chap. 6).

to decide upon them: its decision must be made, for justice must be administered according to the law of the land. When the question occurs—What is the law of the land? it must also decide this question. In what manner is this question to be decided? The answer seems to be a very easy one. The supreme power of the United States has given one rule: a subordinate power in the United States has given a contradictory rule: the former is the law of the land: as a necessary consequence, the latter is void, and has no operation. In this manner it is the right and it is the duty of a court of justice, under the constitution of the United States, to decide.

This is the necessary result of the distribution of power, made, by the constitution, between the legislative and judicial departments. The same constitution is the supreme law to both. If that constitution be infringed by one, it is no reason that the infringement should be abetted, though it is a strong reason that it should be discountenanced and declared void by the other. . . .

This regulation is far from throwing any disparagement upon the legislative authority of the United States. It does not confer upon the judicial department a power superiour, in its general nature, to that of the legislature; but it confers upon it, in particular instances, and for particular purposes, the power of declaring and enforcing the superiour power of the constitution—the supreme law of the land.[71]

Wilson started, as did all period 2 sources, with a statement of the end of legislative omnipotence. This took the form of an insistence on legislative subordination to the Constitution. He also insisted, as had Iredell, that the Constitution as well as ordinary law was cognizable in court. This was Wilson's rejection of the period 1 claim that the Constitution was a rule to the legislature only. Although Wilson referred to the Constitution as the "supreme law of the land," there is no necessary implication that it was supreme ordinary law and on that ground subject to judicial application and interpretation. Wilson made no reference whatever to the written constitution, and his argu-

71. *Works of Wilson*, ed. McCloskey, 1:329–30.

ment contained no suggestion of any uniquely judicial relationship to the law of the Constitution. On the contrary, this supreme law of the land was, for Wilson, "the natural, the inherent, and the predominating rights of the citizens," which bound politically, not legally, as a desperate and dangerous resource. The judicial cognizability of the Constitution followed from an equality of the branches under the Constitution: "The same constitution is the supreme law to both." So, too, Wilson's disavowal of any imputation of judicial supremacy was totally defensible as part of period 2 judicial review. The movement from legislative to judicial supremacy was not completed until the judiciary overturned legislation on the basis of its own exposition of the constitutional text. Wilson's judicial review was the refusal to abet a constitutional violation; it was the power of "declaring and enforcing the superiour power of the constitution" against an act "manifestly repugnant" to it. This was the familiar period 2 claim of judicial authority to refuse to enforce a concededly unconstitutional act.

The Positive Law Strand:
Hamilton and *Kamper* v. *Hawkins*

It was, among other reasons, to strip judicial review of its "awful" quality as a "dangerous and desperate resource" that Marshall set out to transform judicial authority over legislation from the enforcement of explicit fundamental law, anchored in natural rights, into routine application and enforcement of supreme written law. In so doing he followed the positive law strain of period 2 judicial review as expressed in *Federalist 78*. For reasons I shall give below, I think that Hamilton was not contemplating transformation of the Constitution into supreme ordinary law but was concerned primarily with strengthening acceptance of the power defended by Iredell. His analysis, however, was highly suggestive to Marshall.

Federalist 78 differed from "To the Public" in tone and emphasis rather than substance. Hamilton dropped Iredell's argumentativeness, which in itself had acknowledged that fundamental law had not previously been considered the kind of law cognizable in court. The theme of *Federalist 78* was actually the independent judiciary, and the defense of judicial review was part of Hamilton's case for an independent judiciary. This subordination of the issue of judicial review also conveyed the impression that it was a routine and unexceptional power and that there existed greater agreement on this point than was in fact the case at the beginning of the 1790s.

Federalist 78 also relied heavily on the conflict of laws analogy, using it, as had Iredell, to show that judicial refusal to enforce particular acts was not unprecedented. Hamilton discussed the analogy more extensively than had Iredell, but with no suggestion and no necessary implication that judicial identification of an unconstitutional act required exposition of fundamental law. Hamilton's extensive discussion of the analogy did, however, emphasize the positive law component of period 2 judicial review. This emphasis was highlighted by his omission of all parts of Iredell's argument that revealed its reliance on natural rights. Hamilton did not speak of the Constitution as a social contract, of the natural law basis of limited government, or of judicial enforcement as a substitute for revolution. There is no hint in *Federalist 78* that the American Constitution constituted public acknowledgment of any "dangerous and desperate" resource or that judicial enforcement of it was the exercise of an "awful" power.

Beyond this, Hamilton's presentation, although following the familiar period 2 form, introduced a significant new element into the positive law conception of judicial review. *Federalist 78* started with a statement of the period 1 agreement that an act that violated the Constitution was void:

> There is no position which depends on clearer principles, than that every act of a delegated authority, contrary to the tenor of the commission under which it is exercised, is void. No legislative act, therefore, contrary to the Constitution, can be valid. To deny this, would be to affirm, that the deputy is greater than his principal; that the servant is above his master; that the representatives of the people are superior to the people themselves: that men acting by virtue of powers, may do not only what their powers do not authorize, but what they forbid.[72]

72. *Federalist 78*, 505–06.

However, in dealing with the contentious second question of the period 1 debate, whether judges could refuse to enforce an unconstitutional act, Hamilton suggested, as had no one else, that the judiciary's relationship to fundamental law was comparable to its relationship to ordinary law:

> If it be said that the legislative body are themselves the constitutional judges of their own powers, and that the construction they put upon them is conclusive upon the other departments, it may be answered, that this cannot be the natural presumption, where it is not to be collected from any particular provisions in the Constitution. It is not otherwise to be supposed, that the Constitution could intend to enable the representatives of the people to substitute their *will* to that of their constituents. It is far more rational to suppose, that the courts were designed to be an intermediate body between the people and the legislature, in order, among other things, to keep the latter within the limits assigned to their authority. The interpretation of the laws is the proper and peculiar province of the courts. A constitution is, in fact, and must be regarded by the judges, as a fundamental law. It therefore belongs to them to ascertain its meaning, as well as the meaning of any particular act proceeding from the legislative body. If there should happen to be an irreconcilable variance between the two, that which has the superior obligation and validity ought, of course, to be preferred; or, in other words, the Constitution ought to be preferred to the statute, the intention of the people to the intention of their agents.[73]

This paragraph includes the most sweeping claim of period 2 judicial review. Not only was fundamental law cognizable in court, but as a consequence of its attributes as law it belonged to the judges "to ascertain its meaning." It is likely that Marshall's assimilation of fundamental law into ordinary law owed much to this passage. The conclusion that Hamilton was here anticipating or contemplating modern judicial review or that he was claiming authority for authori-

73. Ibid., 506. Emphasis in original.

tative judicial exposition of the constitutional text as we know it today would, however, be premature. When read from within the period 2 context, Hamilton's claim is no more than a stronger version of the period 2 contention that judges could identify and refuse to enforce a concededly unconstitutional act. Following the standard format, the paragraph defending judicial review assumed the existence of an unconstitutional act—that "no legislative act . . . contrary to the Constitution, can be valid."[74] It addressed the period 1 contention that the legislators were nevertheless "the constitutional judges of their own powers." Hamilton repeated Iredell's insistence that this expression of legislative omnipotence or even supremacy was untenable. The Constitution was cognizable in court and subject, rightly, to judicial enforcement. In claiming a judicial right to ascertain the Constitution's meaning, Hamilton was reinforcing this point and the judicial right to identify an unconstitutional act.

It is important to note in evaluating Hamilton's position that none of the period 2 statements that relied heavily on it interpreted *Federalist 78* as a sanction for judicial exposition of the Constitution. All defended judicial authority to "take notice of" the Constitution in the course of expounding ordinary law.[75] Supreme Court justices before and through Marshall's tenure who sanctioned judicial authority over legislation routinely coupled this sanction with enunciation of the doubtful case rule,[76] a rule that is a denial of judicial authority to expound the Constitution. Marshall himself, while developing this idea suggested by Hamilton in *Federalist 78*, held back from making a claim to judicial application and interpretation of the Constitution in language even as direct as that of *Federalist 78*.[77] Nor was there any acknowledgment of judicial authority to expound the Constitution,

---

74. Ibid., 505, and quoted above, chap. 3 at n. 72.

75. See above, chap. 3 at nn. 19, 28, and 30.

76. See *Hylton v. United States*, 3 U.S. (3 Dall.) 171, 173, 175 (1796); *Calder v. Bull*, 3 U.S. (3 Dall.) 386, 395, 399 (1798); *Cooper v. Telfair*, 4 U.S. (4 Dall.) 14, 18, 19 (1800); *Ogden v. Saunders*, 25 U.S. (12 Wheat.) 213, 270, 294 (1827); and *Craig v. Missouri*, 29 U.S. (4 Pet.) 410, 443, 446, 458 (1830).

77. See the discussion of *Marbury v. Madison*, 5 U.S. (1 Cr.) 137 (1803) below, chap. 5 at nn. 1–8.

as judges routinely expound ordinary law, by any of Marshall's Supreme Court colleagues.[78] Every source save *Federalist 78* reflected, unambiguously, the period 2 understanding whereby the judicial refusal to execute an unconstitutional act was the defense of first principle stated in fundamental law, not the exposition of supreme ordinary law. Even if Hamilton intended something more, this statement in *Federalist 78* by itself did not achieve it.

Additional differences between *Federalist 78* and Marshall's judicial review have convinced me that whatever Hamilton's precise intent (and I am not confident that this can be identified as surely as can the intent of others), he was not anticipating modern judicial review but seeking to augment judicial control of legislation within period 2 terms. The first, and most important, difference is the absence of any mention of or reliance on the written constitution in *Federalist 78*. Hamilton's argument rested entirely on the need for judicial power to enforce the explicit limits contained in the Constitution. His defense of judicial review opened with the following statement:

> The complete independence of the courts of justice is peculiarly essential in a limited Constitution. By a limited Constitution, I understand one which contains certain specified exceptions to the legislative authority; such, for instance, as that it shall pass no bills of attainder, no *ex-post-facto* laws, and the like. Limitations of this kind can be preserved in practice no other way than through the medium of courts of justice, whose duty it must be to declare all acts contrary to the manifest tenor of the Constitution void. Without this, all the reservations of particular rights or privileges would amount to nothing.[79]

In a summary statement toward the end of the central part of *Federalist 78* he used the same language: "If, then, the courts of justice are to be considered as the bulwarks of a limited Constitution against legislative encroachments, this consideration will afford a strong argu-

78. See the discussion below, chap. 5 at nn. 50–145.
79. *Federalist 78*, 505.

ment for the permanent tenure of judicial offices."[80] And in a brief reference to judicial review in a related context in *Federalist 81* Hamilton argued: "The Constitution ought to be the standard of construction for the laws, and . . . wherever there is an evident opposition, the laws ought to give place to the Constitution. [T]his doctrine is not deducible from any circumstances peculiar to the plan of the convention, but from the general theory of a limited Constitution; and as far as it is true, is equally applicable to most, if not to all the State governments."[81] In *Marbury* judicial review is traced to the theory of a written constitution, and the written constitution, understood as supreme ordinary law, remains to this day a necessary condition for its submission to judicial exposition. Hamilton's exclusive and consistent reliance on the limited constitution reflected the dominance of period 2 ideas.

The second difference between Hamilton's and Marshall's judicial review is Hamilton's acceptance of restriction of judicial authority over legislation to unconstitutional as distinguished from unjust laws. In the concluding part of *Federalist 78*, in contemplation likely of the debtor relief legislation of the 1780s, Hamilton wrote:

> But it is not with a view to infractions of the Constitution only, that the independence of the judges may be an essential safeguard against the effects of occasional ill humors in the society. These sometimes extend no farther than to the injury of the private rights of particular classes of citizens, by unjust and partial laws. Here also the firmness of the judicial magistracy is of vast importance in mitigating the severity and confining the operation of such laws.[82]

The distinction between unjust and unconstitutional laws was blurred irrevocably in Marshall's treatment of the Constitution. But as we have repeatedly seen, it was an essential and totally intelligible part of period 1 and 2 judicial review, and Hamilton treated it in these terms. He confined judicial authority over legislation to "infractions of the

80. Ibid., 508.
81. *Federalist 81*, 524.
82. *Federalist 78*, 509.

Constitution"; for unjust and partial laws the judges can only "miti-gat[e their] severity and confin[e their] operation." This easy accep-tance of the distinction between unjust and unconstitutional laws and the absence of any mention of or reliance on the written constitution indicate that whatever the precise scope of the judicial review Hamil-ton was contemplating, it lacked the crucial elements of Marshall's.

Hamilton's assertion that the courts' proper and peculiar province to interpret the laws included ascertaining the meaning of fundamen-tal law was nevertheless of great significance. It was the second major step in the transformation of fundamental law into supreme ordinary law after the assertion of its cognizability in court. It was obviously of great significance for Marshall, who drew on this language in *Mar-bury*. But in 1788 there existed no conception of the Constitution as supreme ordinary law and none was likely intended here. Clearly, none of Hamilton's contemporaries so interpreted *Federalist 78*, and Marshall did not effectuate the transformation of fundamental law into supreme ordinary law by simple repetition of this contention. The full assimilation of fundamental law into ordinary law and the development of the judicial authority to expound the Constitution were forged in the doing, in Marshall's great opinions in the decades after *Marbury*.

Kamper v. *Hawkins*, decided in the Virginia General Court in 1793, was the leading period 2 case emphasizing judicial review's positive law components.[83] It was as important as *Federalist 78* in its suggestiveness to Marshall. As was to be the case in *Marbury* the legislation declared void in *Kamper* dealt with judicial organization. The Virginia court opposed this legislation on the grounds that it violated the Virginia constitution's provisions for judicial appoint-ment and the principle of judicial independence. *Kamper* was the only pre-Marshall exercise of judicial review in which judges refused to execute a law on the ground that it violated a particular constitutional provision rather than long established common or natural law princi-ple.

Kamper v. *Hawkins* marked the second major confrontation within

83. 1 Va. Cases 20 (1793).

five years between the Virginia court and the Virginia legislature over legislative reorganization of the judiciary. The first had taken place in 1788 before the emergence of the period 2 defense of judicial review and had been resolved in a conspicuously different manner. In 1788, members of the Virginia Court of Appeals had objected on constitutional grounds to a new law that assigned judges of the Court of Appeals to sit in newly created district courts. The judges argued that this additional assignment without additional salary constituted an actual diminution of salary in violation of the constitutional provision that judicial salaries be adequate and fixed, and of the general principle of judicial independence.

Under the 1788 law the judges' first responsibility would have been to appoint clerks in the newly created district courts. The judges refused to do so and issued a public remonstrance addressed to the legislature in which they outlined their opposition to the law, defended their refusal to comply with it, and resigned en masse. The remonstrance included a public appeal to the legislature to rectify its error and concluded by indicating that should the legislature fail to do so there would be no alternative but an appeal to the people, who would judge between legislature and judiciary.[84] The crisis was resolved with compromise legislation that avoided the constitutional issue and with requalification of the same judges.

The remonstrance controversy revealed that although there was an expectation in 1788 that the judiciary could defend its constitutional sphere, the idea was not yet available that judges could intervene in constitutional issues as part of their assigned responsibility to resolve ordinary lawsuits. Defense of the constitution was still a directly political act and, ultimately, an appeal to the people. Five years later, when the Virginia court again objected on constitutional grounds to legislative reorganization of the judiciary, the confrontation took place through an ordinary lawsuit. These were precisely the five years during which the period 2 defense of judicial review was established, and the constitution, or fundamental law, was accepted as the kind of

84. The full text of the remonstrance can be found in an appendix to *Kamper* v. *Hawkins*, ibid., 98–108.

law that judges could take notice of in court. Three of the five *Kamper* judges commented on and rejected what they now depicted as the irregularity of the course followed in the remonstrance controversy. Judge Henry's remarks were typical:

> This question has heretofore been alleged as one of the reasons of the high court of appeals for declining to execute a very important law of the land;—without saying any thing about the propriety or impropriety of that business, it is sufficient for my present purpose to observe, that the question did not then come before the court in a judicial manner,—it was taken up as a general proposition, and when published, contained an appeal to the people; this looked like a dissolution of the government.[85]

The legislation challenged in *Kamper* assigned equity jurisdiction to common law judges in the district courts. This assignment, it was argued, violated provisions of the Virginia constitution requiring judges to be appointed by joint ballot of both Houses followed by an executive commission for good behavior. The act was challenged in the course of responding to a petition for an injunction entered in a common law court under the new law. The district court adjourned the case to the General Court for judgment on the questions of whether courts had the right to refuse to execute an unconstitutional act and, if so, whether this act was unconstitutional.

Kamper contained three emphatic affirmations of period 2 judicial review, of which Tucker's, examined above, was the most extensive.[86] Each of the opinions also considered the constitutionality of the legislation in light of the Virginia constitution's requirements for judicial appointment. Assignment of equity jurisdiction to common law judges, it was argued, bypassed these requirements and created new judgeships by ordinary legislation. As judges so appointed could be as easily dismissed, the legislation violated not only the specific

85. Ibid., 50.
86. For Tucker's statement see above, chap. 3 at nn. 18–19. For Roane's and Nelson's see above, chap. 3, n. 21. Judges Henry and Tyler accepted judicial authority over legislation but neither made particularly clear statements of his position on this point. See 1 Va. Cases 20, 47–48, 58–61 (1793).

provisions of the constitution but the principle of judicial independence as well.[87] Judge Nelson argued, in addition, that two other
constitutional provisions—those dealing with the impeachment of
the governor and the judges, respectively—demonstrated an intent
that judges in chancery and in common law be different individuals.[88]
The *Kamper* holding was thereby the first and only period 2 determination of unconstitutionality that rested in textual construction.

Although the *Kamper* reliance on constitutional text stands in
marked contrast to all other period 2 judicial review, it may be
inappropriate to characterize this reliance as textual construction in
the modern sense. Doubt about the applicability of modern categories
is suggested by Judge Roane's opinion, which began with the following statement:

> This great question was adjourned by me from the district
> court in Dumfries. . . .
>
> My opinion then was, upon a short consideration, that the
> district court ought to execute this law; for I doubted how far the
> judiciary were authorized to refuse to execute a law, on the
> ground of its being against the spirit of the Constitution.
>
> My opinion, on more mature consideration, is changed in this
> respect, and I now think that the judiciary may and ought not
> only refuse to execute a law expressly repugnant to the Constitu-
> tion; but also one which is, by a plain and natural construction,
> in opposition to the fundamental principles thereof.[89]

Roane's initial position, especially the denial of judicial authority
over legislation that violated the spirit of the constitution, seems to be
identical with Iredell's as stated in *Calder* v. *Bull*. Judicial power is
limited to violations of express provisions and, presumably, to violations established without need for constitutional construction. But
even after Roane was willing to accept determinations of unconstitutionality based on construction, he saw this construction as establishing a violation of principle, not text. This reflected the period 2

87. See ibid., 35, 52–53, 63–65, and 87–93.
88. Ibid., 33–34.
89. Ibid., 35–36.

understanding that a constitutional violation was one of established principle committed to writing, not one of written law.

The rest of Roane's *Kamper* opinion maintained this subordination of text to principle. He argued that legislative assignment of equity jurisdiction to common law judges invaded the principle of independence of the judiciary and concluded that "the clause in question, is repugnant to the fundamental principles of the Constitution, in as much as the judges of the general court have not been balloted for and commissioned as judges in chancery, pursuant to the fourteenth article of the Constitution."[90]

All the *Kamper* judges agreed that the legislation violated the constitution's provisions on judicial appointment and the principle of judicial independence. It is impossible to determine precisely how each understood the relationship between the two. None, however, subordinated text to principle as sharply as did Roane. In the process their arguments that legislative reorganization of the judiciary violated the Virginia constitution's provisions on judicial appointment remain a major building block of Marshall's judicial review.

The importance of the *Kamper* discussions becomes clearer when contrasted with those in *Hayburn's Case,* another period 2 example of concurrent review, which was decided in the federal circuit courts in 1792.[91] In *Hayburn* U.S. Supreme Court justices declined to carry out a law that made federal judges arbiters of disputes over government pensions and that provided appeal from the judges' determinations to the secretary of war and Congress. Judges in three circuit courts argued that these duties were not judicial in nature and could not, under the Constitution, be assigned to the judiciary. The provision for appeal, they also insisted, violated the Constitution by allowing executive and legislative officers to review judicial determinations.[92]

To support these conclusions the New York Circuit Court relied on

90. Ibid., 42.

91. 2 U.S. (2 Dall.) 409 (1792).

92. For the opinion of the Circuit Court for the District of New York see ibid., 410. The circuit courts for the Districts of Pennsylvania and North Carolina stated their positions in a letter to the president (ibid., 411–14).

the principle of separation of powers, as established by the U.S. Constitution: "That by the Constitution of the United States, the government thereof is divided into *three* distinct and independent branches, and that it is the duty of each to abstain from, and to oppose, encroachments on either. That neither the *Legislative* nor the *Executive* branches, can constitutionally assign to the *Judicial* any duties, but such as are properly judicial, and to be performed in a judicial manner."[93] The only reference to specific constitutional provisions in *Hayburn's Case* occurred in the statement from the court for the Pennsylvania district, and this reference was incidental to a primary reliance on principle. Wilson, Blair, and Peters argued that the challenged legislation violated the "important principle" of judicial independence as well as that of separation of powers. As evidence of the Constitution's commitment to judicial independence they cited its provisions guaranteeing judicial tenure during good behavior and protection against diminution of salary.[94]

In *Hayburn's Case,* thus, judges invoked general principles included in the Constitution whose meanings were established by common agreement. Constitutional text, if invoked at all, was called upon to reinforce those principles. The impact *of Hayburn's Case* on *Marbury,* and the course of American judicial review, was thus negligible. *Kamper,* in contrast, contained all the key elements that were to reappear in *Marbury.* First, it merged the existing expectation that judges would defend their constitutional sphere with the period 2 innovations: legitimation and regularization of the judicial refusal to enforce unconstitutional laws generally, and inclusion of this power as part of its responsibility to adjudicate ordinary lawsuits. Next, *Kamper* established a precedent for declaring the unconstitutionality of an act on the basis of its violation of constitutional text as judicially construed. Finally, Marshall's reliance on *Kamper* is visible in the carefully crafted similarities and differences between the key paragraph of *Marbury* and Tucker's defense of the judicial authority to refuse to enforce an unconstitutional act.

93. Ibid., 410. Emphasis in original.
94. Ibid., 411.

For all its innovativeness and suggestiveness to Marshall, however, *Kamper* remained a period 2 case. For one thing, its constitutional construction was not extensive by modern standards and, for Roane at least, this construction was subordinate to defense of constitutional principle. *Kamper,* in addition, not only fell within the bounds of concurrent review but was part of an ongoing feud between the Virginia legislature and judiciary. More important, despite the textual construction of *Kamper,* other parts maintained the period 2 understanding that judicial review was a new political responsibility and not part of a conventional legal one. The constitution here being enforced was repeatedly depicted as a social contract and its enforcement as the defense of first principle.[95] Judicial review, for the *Kamper* judges, rested on the judicial responsibility to expound ordinary law under a real and explicit social contract.[96] And for none was the written constitution per se the key factor in its submission to judicial enforcement. Three of the five *Kamper* opinions defended judicial control over legislation without any mention of the written constitution. Tucker's comparatively full discussion revealed more clearly than did any other period 2 source that the significance of the written constitution was as a vehicle for its explicitness.[97]

95. See 1 Va. Cases 20, 36–38, 40, 57–59, 67–69, and 70–74 (1793).
96. See, in particular, Tucker and Roane, ibid., 78–81 and 38–39.
97. Ibid., 77–78. Nelson's reference to the written constitution in *Kamper* is too brief to sustain any definitive interpretation. It is, however, wholly compatible with the period 2 meaning and likely an expression of it. "The difference between a free and an arbitrary government I take to be—that in the former limits are assigned to those to whom the administration is committed; but the latter depends on the will of the departments or some of them. Hence the utility of a written constitution" (ibid., 23).

CHAPTER FOUR

Enforcing and Expounding
the Constitution

THE ASSUMPTION made today that the founding generation supported some form of judicial review is clearly correct. The additional assumption that it was characterized by ambiguity and inconsistency is not, and stems from our misreading of the period 2
understanding. The ambiguities in American judicial review, in fact,
belong overwhelmingly to period 3 and beyond. One large part of this
ambiguity revolves around our conception of constitutional "enforcement." In period 3, constitutional enforcement was disassociated
from the genuine violation; today the term is applied to any judicial
determination of unconstitutionality. It involves what in period 2 was
called the wisdom or expediency of legislation in contrast to its
constitutionality.

This change in usage is one part of our failure to take seriously
commitment in period 2 to the doubtful case rule. It has also facilitated our loss of contact with the dynamics of true constitutional
enforcement. We now think of that enforcement as a routine judicial
activity, an extension of ordinary law enforcement. We ignore what in
period 2 was unspoken common ground and at the foundation of the
difference in kind between fundamental law and ordinary law—
namely, that only sovereign power can violate fundamental law and
that it is, by definition, the strongest force in the community. Sovereign power thus cannot be made to obey fundamental law as individuals can be made to obey ordinary law. Courts, in confronting
constitutional violations are not the agents of society's collective
power, bringing that power to bear against an individual violator;
they are, rather, the agents of a constitutional principle that the
strongest force in the community has violated. Courts thus lack sufficient power to enforce fundamental law routinely.

The period 2 understanding that judicial defense of the Constitution was a substitute for revolution, a political action different in kind from its assigned function as enforcer of ordinary law, was the major expression of this shared understanding. The only systematic articulation of this difference, and of the character and dynamics of genuine constitutional enforcement, was made by Madison in the course of explaining to Jefferson why he had not included a bill of rights in the new Constitution. Madison gave Jefferson four reasons, the last of which was the most significant: "because experience proves the inefficacy of a bill of rights on those occasions when its controul is most needed."[1] The experience to which Madison referred, that of the state governments under the Articles of Confederation, had taught Madison that a bill of rights could not protect private and minority rights: "Repeated violations of these parchment barriers have been committed by overbearing majorities in every State."[2]

In defending this position, Madison argued that a bill of rights was an instrument devised for a monarchy, where it could and did protect private rights. In a republic, he insisted, it could not achieve this end. Monarchies, Madison pointed out, contained a force stronger than the sovereign, that of the people themselves. Should the sovereign violate the bill of rights, this force could be mobilized to enforce it: "In a monarchy the latent force of the nation is superior to that of the Sovereign, and a solemn charter of popular rights must have a great effect, as a standard for trying the validity of public acts, and a signal for rousing and uniting the superior force of the community."[3] For Madison, as for all participants in the period 2 debate, revolution, or the threat of revolution, enforced fundamental law. However, Madi-

---

1. James Madison to Thomas Jefferson, October 17, 1788, in *Writings of Madison*, ed. Hunt, 5:272. Madison's other reasons were that the structure of the federal government as one of enumerated powers provided protection for individual rights; that submitting some rights, particularly those of conscience, to public definition could actually narrow desired protection; and that the existence of the state governments provided a check against abuse of power by the federal government that was unavailable elsewhere (ibid., 271–72).

2. Ibid.

3. Ibid., 273.

son continued to argue that in a republic, revolution—and by implication its substitute—could not in fact succeed.

Republics lodged sovereign power in the people or, more precisely, in a majority. Should a majority abuse its power, Madison pointed out, there was no force in the community strong enough to counter it: "In a popular government, the political and physical power may be considered as vested in the same hands, that is in a majority of the people, and, consequently the tyrannical will of the Sovereign is not [to] be controuled by the dread of an appeal to any other force within the community."[4]

Madison recognized that strategically placed or entrenched minorities could also threaten the constitutional order, but he did not believe they presented a fatal threat. Whatever their capacity for oppression or disruption, by the very principle of majority rule they could eventually be defeated.[5] There was, however, no available force capable of stopping an abusive majority, and it remained republican government's most serious danger: "Wherever the real power in a Government lies, there is the danger of oppression. In our Governments the real power lies in the majority of the Community, and the invasion of private rights is *chiefly* to be apprehended, not from acts of Government contrary to the sense of its constituents, but from acts in which the Government is the mere instrument of the major number of the Constituents."[6]

Although Madison here concluded that a bill of rights could not be enforced in the absence of a societal force stronger than a majority, he did not oppose amending the Constitution to include one. But the uses that Madison contemplated for a bill of rights were very different from those that we think of today. For one thing, his support was largely, and perhaps entirely, tactical. During the campaign for ratification of the Constitution the Federalists agreed to support a bill of rights in return for unconditional ratification. Madison accepted this

4. Ibid.
5. *Federalist No. 10, 57.*
6. Madison to Jefferson, October 17, 1788, in *Writings of Madison*, ed. Hunt, 5:272. Emphasis in original.

compromise and told Jefferson: "I have never thought the omission [of a bill of rights] a material defect, nor been anxious to supply it even by *subsequent* amendment, for any other reason than that it is anxiously desired by others."[7] In sponsoring the Bill of Rights Madison was fulfilling his part of this agreement.

Beyond this, Madison did agree that a bill of rights could do no harm and might do some good. It was possible, he noted, that oppression might some time come from "usurped acts of the government" rather than "interested majorities of the people." Still worse, "artful and ambitious rulers" could thoroughly subvert the republican regime. In these instances "a bill of rights will be a good ground for an appeal to the sense of the community."[8] And at all times a bill of rights could bolster popular commitment to minority rights: "The political truths declared in that solemn manner acquire by degrees, the character of fundamental maxims of free Government, and as they become incorporated with the national sentiment, counteract the impulses of interest and passion."[9]

This assessment, written in 1788, demonstrated Madison's adherence to period 2 conceptions and assumptions as described in the last chapter. Fundamental law and a bill of rights were "political truths" and "fundamental maxims of free Government," not law. They achieved their end by rallying the force of society against usurpation or by reinforcing popular self-restraint. Madison here did not betray the slightest expectation that a bill of rights could or would function as a legal restraint. This analysis indicates how period 2 judicial review, as a substitute for revolution, was expected to function. In upholding stipulated limits against the legislature, courts were not enforcing law but were rallying and reasserting a previously established self-restraint.

Madison's discussion, it is also worth noting, provided additional evidence of the immediacy of concern in period 2 with the concededly unconstitutional act and the genuine constitutional violation. Madi-

7. Ibid., 271. Emphasis in original.
8. Ibid., 273.
9. Ibid.

son discussed the efficacy of a bill of rights on "those occasions where its controul is needed most." His leading example was Virginia, where, he claimed, religious establishment would have taken place despite a constitutional provision for rights of conscience, if there had existed a popular majority of the same sect.[10] This was precisely the kind of concededly unconstitutional act used in all period 2 discussions of constitutional violation.

"A Legal Check in the Hands of the Judiciary"

Much of the ground for the charges of inconsistency and ambiguity in period 2 judicial review grows out of Jefferson's reply to this letter of Madison's. In his reply Jefferson suggested that a bill of rights would put a "legal check . . . into the hands of the judiciary." He coupled this suggestion with praise for the judiciary's "learning and integrity" and its capacity to withstand popular passion.[11] Madison in turn used this argument on the floor of the House as he led the bill of rights toward passage: "If [these provisions] are incorporated into the constitution, independent tribunals of justice will consider themselves in a peculiar manner the guardians of those rights; they will be an impenetrable bulwark against every assumption of power in the legislative or executive; they will be naturally led to resist every encroachment upon rights expressly stipulated for in the constitution by the declaration of rights."[12]

Subsequently, however, both Jefferson and Madison opposed judicial review. This change, it is alleged, was motivated by partisan

10. Ibid., 272.

11. Thomas Jefferson to James Madison, March 15, 1789, in *The Papers of Thomas Jefferson*, ed. Julian P. Boyd (Princeton: Princeton University Press, 1958), 14:659. Jefferson prefaced this reference to the legal check by indicating, "Your thoughts on the subject of the Declaration of rights in the letter of Oct. 17 I have weighed with great satisfaction. Some of them had not occurred to me before, but were acknowledged just in the moment they were presented to my mind."

12. *The Debates and Proceedings in the Congress of the United States*, compiled by Joseph Gales (Washington, D.C.: Gales & Seaton, 1834), 1:457.

opposition to Marshall's substantive policies rather than by a consistent, principled position on judicial review. It is thus necessary to inquire whether Madison, in adopting Jefferson's argument, changed his mind about the efficacy of a bill of rights or its functioning as a legal check; and, in general, whether Jefferson and Madison can rightly be charged with inconsistency. As suggested by the analysis of period 1 and 2 judicial review and for additional reasons to be given in the rest of this chapter, I do not believe that either man was inconsistent or that Madison changed his position on the dynamics of constitutional enforcement in a republican regime.

The first question is precisely what Jefferson and Madison were contemplating in 1788 when they identified the judiciary as a "legal check" and "guardian" of the Bill of Rights. All available evidence indicates that it was the check accepted in period 2. For them judicial review remained an extraordinary, not a routine, judicial act, confined to defense of the Bill of Rights against conceded violation and without authority to expound the Constitution. Marshall's judicial review moved beyond the concededly unconstitutional act and introduced authoritative judicial exposition of the Constitution. It is thus not inconsistent to support period 2 judicial review and oppose Marshall's.

That Madison and Jefferson accepted the period 2 understanding is indicated, first, by the fact that their only statement supporting a legal check against constitutional violation was the one cited above, made in the context of enforcing the Bill of Rights. This part of the Constitution was most readily identifiable as first principle with known preexisting content.

Second, both consistently denied any judicial authority to expound the Constitution or to resolve conflicting interpretations of it. These denials antedated the partisan conflicts of the 1790s and 1800s and thus cannot be attributed to them. One of the earliest appears in *Federalist 49*, where Madison considered a proposal for constitutional enforcement that Jefferson had made earlier: "Whenever any two of the three branches of government shall concur in opinion, each by the voices of two thirds of their whole number, that a convention is necessary for . . . *correcting breaches of [the Constitution]*, a convention shall be called for the purpose."[13] This proposal is unintelligible if Jefferson had any expectation that judicial enforcement of the Constitution went beyond the conceded violation of established principles, such as those contained in the Bill of Rights. When, as here, he contemplated legitimate differences over constitutional interpretation Jefferson turned for resolution of that conflict to the people, not the courts.

Madison's reply to this proposal indicated that he too did not expect that the judiciary would or should resolve conflict over constitutional interpretation:

> The several departments being perfectly coordinate by the terms of their common commission, none of them, it is evident, can pretend to an exclusive or superior right of settling the boundaries between their respective powers; and how are the encroachments of the stronger to be prevented, or the wrongs of the weaker to be redressed, without an appeal to the people themselves, who, as the grantors of the commission, can alone declare its true meaning, and enforce its observance?[14]

Madison in *Federalist* 49 identified the people, not the courts, as expounders of the Constitution. He did so, moreover, with the same casualness with which period 2 judges distinguished between "taking notice of" the Constitution and expounding ordinary law. Nevertheless, Madison rejected Jefferson's proposal that popular conventions be used to enforce the Constitution. He did so, however, only for practical reasons. Madison pointed out that the legislature would most likely be the branch accused of violating the Constitution, and that popular conventions would most likely reflect the same forces represented in the legislature. Conventions would thus be unable to judge dispassionately the charges brought against the legislature.[15] Madison's own solution for resolving constitutional conflict was a different political mechanism, the familiar system of checks and balances and the extended republic as outlined in *Federalist* *51* and *10*.

13. *Federalist No. 49*, 327. Emphasis in original.
14. Ibid., 328.
15. Ibid., 330–31. For discussion of additional objections made by Madison to Jefferson's proposal see below, chap. 5 at nn. 25–30.

Madison's most direct denial of judicial authority to expound the Constitution was made in 1788, a year after the Constitutional Convention disbanded. In the course of commenting on a council of revision in a draft constitution for Kentucky, he stated: "In the state Constitution and indeed in the Federal one also, no provision is made for the case of a disagreement in expounding them; and as the courts are generally the last in making the decision, it results to them by refusing or not refusing to execute a law, to stamp it with its final character. This makes the Judiciary Department paramount in fact to the Legislature, which was never intended and can never be proper."[16] Again, this position is not inconsistent with Madison's support for Court defense of the Bill of Rights. It would be so only if such defense reached circumstances where there was "a disagreement in expounding" constitutional provisions.

Madison also accepted the distinction between the expediency and constitutionality of legislation, a distinction that underscored the importance of the doubtful case rule and the inappropriateness of judicial exposition of the Constitution. In 1819, in the course of criticizing the scope of Marshall's opinion in *McCulloch* v. *Maryland*, Madison made the following argument:

> Does not the Court also relinquish by their doctrine [of implied powers] all controul on the Legislative exercise of unconstitutional powers? According to that doctrine, the expediency and constitutionality of means for carrying into effect a specified power are convertible terms; and Congress are admitted to be Judges of the expediency. The Court certainly cannot be so; a question, the moment it assumes the character of mere expediency or policy, being evidently beyond the reach of Judicial cognizance.[17]

Madison was here using the doctrine of judicial review as then understood to challenge Marshall's broad interpretation of the necessary and proper clause. In so doing he assumed that there was no controversy over the nature and limits of judicial review. It was limited to

16. *Writings of Madison*, ed. Hunt, 5:294.
17. Ibid., 8:449.

"controul on the Legislative exercise of [concededly] unconstitutional powers" as reflected in the then intelligible distinction between the expediency and constitutionality of legislation.[18]

The absence of any mechanism for authoritative exposition of the Constitution meant that differences among the branches would have to be resolved by some form of concurrent review. As has been widely observed, both Madison and Jefferson accepted this solution, even though it entailed practical difficulties.

In 1793, writing under the pseudonym Helvidius, Madison explicitly supported concurrent review: "It may happen . . . that different departments . . . may, in the exercise of their functions, interpret the constitution differently, and thence lay claim to the same power. This difference of opinion is an inconvenience not entirely to be avoided. It results from what may be called . . . a *concurrent* right to expound the constitution."[19]

Madison reaffirmed this position in 1834 with an argument identical to that which he had made almost fifty years earlier in *Federalist* 49. The branches of the national government, he argued, were "coordinate," and "each must, in the exercise of its functions, be guided by the text of the Constitution according to its own interpretations of it." In cases of disagreement "the prevalence of the one or the other department must depend on the nature of the case, as receiving its final decision from the one or the other." He went on to urge that the departments respect each other's opinions.[20]

Jefferson's support for concurrent review went hand in hand with a lifelong search for some effective method of resolving differences over constitutional interpretation. In 1809, in the course of evaluating a draft for a state constitution, Jefferson praised a provision whereby two branches could overrule a third.[21] This solution was similar to his

18. Madison made the same point in arguing against congressional authority to pass the Alien and Sedition Acts. See "Report on the Virginia Resolutions," in *Debates on Adoption of Federal Constitution,* ed. Elliott, 4:568.

19. "Helvidius No. II," in *Writings of Madison,* ed. Hunt, 6:155. Emphasis in original.

20. Madison to ?, 1834, *Letters and Other Writings of James Madison,* 4 vols. (Philadelphia: J. B. Lippincott, 1865), 4:349.

21. Jefferson to Don Valentine deForonda, October 4, 1809, *The Writings*

own proposal as discussed in *Federalist* 49. In 1809 he added: "Our constitution has not sufficiently solved this dilemma."[22] In 1815 he addressed the same problem and indicated that each branch was, rightfully, judge of the constitutionality of measures for which it had authority "to act ultimately, and without appeal."[23] Recognizing that concurrent review could create difficulties, Jefferson trusted to "the prudence of the public functionaries, and authority of public opinion [to] produce accommodation," adding that there were necessarily inconveniences in human proceedings.[24] In 1820 he attacked the notion that judges were to be the "ultimate arbiters of all constitutional questions" as a "very dangerous doctrine indeed, and one which would place us under the despotism of an oligarchy."[25] Only the people, he concluded, could be trusted to exercise "the ultimate powers of the society."[26] In contemplation, likely, of the Federalist judiciary Jefferson also declared that judges were as partisan as other officials. Although his confidence in the dispassionate judgment of the judiciary may have changed over time, rejection of authoritative judicial exposition of the Constitution remained constant.

Enforcing Republican Constitutions

As indicated both by Madison's adoption of Jefferson's argument on Court enforcement of the Bill of Rights and by his acceptance of judicial "controul on the Legislative exercise of unconstitutional powers," Madison never opposed period 2 judicial review. If the judiciary, by refusing to enforce a concededly unconstitutional act, could rein-

---

of Jefferson, ed. Paul Leicester Ford, 10 vols. (New York: G. P. Putnam's Sons, 1892–99), 9:259.

22. Ibid.

23. Jefferson to W. H. Torrance, June 11, 1815, ibid., 9:518. In this same letter Jefferson acknowledged the legitimacy of an alternate solution, that "the legislature alone is the expounder of the sense of the constitution, in every part of it whatever."

24. Ibid.

25. Jefferson to William C. Jarvis, September 28, 1820, in *Writings of Jefferson*, ed. Ford, 10:160.

26. Ibid., 161.

force acknowledged restraints and gain popular support for them, so much the better. But there is no evidence that he ever placed significant reliance on it as an instrument of constitutional maintenance or that by supporting judicial guardianship of the Bill of Rights on the House floor he repudiated his original assessment of the "inefficacy of a Bill of Rights on those occasions where its controul is needed most." For the long run the judiciary was no match for the forces that threatened constitutional integrity in a republic. In a regime where "the physical and political power were united in the same hands," the judicial reassertion of principle had insufficient force behind it to counter a determined majority. As constitution maker Madison provided more effective restraint, which for him remained the primary mechanism of constitutional enforcement in a republic.

Madison built his restraints into the institutional structure of the new national government. They consisted of the familiar system of checks and balances among the branches, as described in *Federalist 51*, and the extended republic, as described in *Federalist 10*. Checks and balances were designed to curb abuse of power by government officials. A properly designed system required that "the provision for defense . . . be made commensurate to the danger of attack. Ambition must be made to counteract ambition."[27] Attacks on the constitutional order came from the ambition of officials who were willing to subvert the regime in order to augment their power. Defense, consequently, was to come through the personal ambition of other officials. If protected by separate, independent, and powerful branches of government, officials could safely challenge and expose the wrongdoing of others. While motivated by their own desire for advancement—a reliable force in human nature—these officials would simultaneously be maintaining the system. As Madison summarized the argument, "The interest of the man must be connected with the constitutional rights of the place."[28]

The remedy for abuse of power by a majority was the extended republic.[29] Because an abusive majority could not be checked once it

27. *Federalist No. 51*, 337.
28. Ibid.
29. *Federalist No. 10*, 53–62.

had been formed, constitutional enforcement necessitated prevention of its formation in the first place. That was to be achieved, consistently with the principles of republicanism, by enlarging the geographic area within which republican government and the majority principle would operate. In the American context, it meant abandoning the Articles of Confederation and shifting significant power from the states to the national government. In this much analyzed "republican remedy for the diseases most incident to republican government,"[30] Madison pointed out that a majority drawn from a larger geographic area would necessarily contain more interests than one drawn from a smaller one. By virtue of its internal diversity, such a majority would be "less probable . . . [to] have a common motive to invade the rights of other citizens; or if such a common motive exists, it will be more difficult for all who feel it to discover their own strength, and to act in unison with each other."[31] National majorities would thus be less likely to abuse power than local ones.

Both sets of political devices—checks and balances and the extended republic—were defenses "commensurate with the danger of attack." If these failed, the judiciary could still attempt to uphold the Constitution but Madison did not have great confidence that it would be effective. In a comment to Spencer Roane in 1821, Madison explicitly indicated that he had not in fact abandoned the analysis of constitutional enforcement made in 1788. He commiserated with Roane about what both regarded as Marshall's unjustified aggrandizement of both judicial power and the power of the national government. Madison, however, was not as alarmed as was Roane. The judiciary, he remarked, was too weak to inflict serious harm:

> It is not probable that the Supreme Court would long be indulged in a career of usurpation opposed to the decided opinions and policy of the legislature. . . .
> But what is to control Congress when backed, and even pushed on by a majority of their constituents . . . ? Nothing within the pale of the constitution but sound arguments and

30. Ibid., 62.
31. Ibid., 61.

conciliatory expostulations addressed both to Congress and to their constituents.[32]

In 1821, as in 1788, an abusive majority remained the greatest danger to constitutional maintenance in a republic. For the same reason that the judiciary could not inflict danger, it could not repel it. Once the extended republic was in place there was no solution to majority abuse of power other than exhortation—"sound arguments and conciliatory expostulations."

Constitutional Enforcement: The Modern Record

More important than whether Madison changed his mind about the enforceability of constitutional limits is whether subsequent experience has vindicated his analysis or proved it wrong. I shall depart from the chronological order followed until now to examine this question now. This departure is necessary because the counterpart to our failure to understand period 1 and 2 judicial review is a partial and distorted understanding of constitutional enforcement since that time.

There has been, at least since Thayer, awareness of the enduring validity of Madison's argument and of the judicial weakness in the face of genuine constitutional violation.[33] The classic formulation is that of Learned Hand: "A society so riven that the spirit of moderation is gone, no court *can* save; . . . a society where that spirit flourishes, no court *need* save."[34] At the same time, we have never confronted directly enough the full implications of this awareness. Loss of access to the original meaning of fundamental law has left us with no conception of the Constitution but that of supreme ordinary law. We have as a result applied, inappropriately, the latter's enforcement model to modern judicial review. We focus on leading constitutional

32. Madison to Spencer Roane, May 6, 1821, in *Writings of Madison*, ed. Hunt, 9:58–59.

33. "Doctrine of Constitutional Law," 156.

34. *The Spirit of Liberty*, 181. Emphasis in original. See also Dahl, "Supreme Court as Policy-Maker."

decisions and major Court achievements and regard these as "enforcement" of the Constitution. By period 2 standards and by any strict definition of enforcement, however, modern judicial review cannot be understood in these terms. Moreover, in the process we have ignored the genuine constitutional violations in American political life and the Court's utter incapacity to deal with them. We think of constitutional enforcement in terms of *Brown* v. *Board of Education* and its condemnation of racial segregation in public schools rather than the more serious violations of black rights over the preceding century. These include denials of basic physical protection, of meaningful due process, and of voting rights. This racial injustice was, without doubt, this country's most massive and sustained constitutional violation, and it was not rectified in court. By the same token, we think about "enforcing" the First Amendment in terms of Court decisions upholding rights of demonstrators in the 1960s, or narrowing the definition of libel, but we ignore the legal system's incapacity to end the unambiguous First Amendment violation constituted by the suppression of black protest from the end of Reconstruction until the 1950s. After these, our most serious constitutional violations, I suggest, came the Japanese-American relocations of World War II and the excesses of McCarthyism in the 1950s as well as its earlier manifestations. These too were never checked in court. One of the major consequences of the legalization of fundamental law has been a forgetting of the areas and periods within which the Constitution has simply gone unenforced. And it has gone so for precisely the reason identified by Madison—by virtue of the violations' command of active or tacit majority support.

What we now call constitutional enforcement has been for the most part judicial resolution of conflict over contending valid interpretations of the Constitution; it is what in period 2 was understood to involve the expediency or policy rather than the constitutionality of legislation. Some of these circumstances were closer than others to the genuine violation. This is most clearly so for *Brown* v. *Board of Education,* which in addressing public racial segregation touched the area of our most serious constitutional violation. So, too, incorporation of most of the Bill of Rights provisions into the Fourteenth

Amendment and heightened scrutiny for these procedural requirements and individual rights guarantees ended a good deal of arbitrariness by local officials.[35] Nevertheless, neither public segregation nor the local arbitrariness rectified by incorporation constituted unambiguous constitutional violation as did the willful denial of basic black rights and protections from Reconstruction through the 1960s.

These achievements, moreover, cannot properly be described as vindication of minority rights *against* the majority. Judicial defense of black rights and incorporation did not take place until the middle of the twentieth century. These constitutional programs were initiated by a Court that reflected the strength of the New Deal coalition of the locally powerless that had taken power at the national level.[36] However, no matter how often constitutional law's dependence on a receptive public environment is acknowledged, we persist unthinkingly in bringing to the Constitution the inappropriate enforcement conceptions of ordinary law. This is reflected, for example, in John Ely's description of judicial review as the "protec[tion of] minorities from the unchecked exercise of the majority's will."[37] Similarly, despite acknowledgment of the problems of constitutional enforcement, it is still often assumed that these do not intrinsically differ from those connected with the selective enforcement of ordinary law. There is, however, a basic unbridgeable difference between the two. Selective enforcement of ordinary law can be remedied with a change of executive policy or administration. Enforcement of fundamental law, on

35. There would likely be little dissent today from Judge Hans Linde's judgment about the salutary quality of this adjudication. Before incorporation, he pointed out, "most state courts had a poor record of taking seriously the individual rights and fair procedures promised in their states' bills of rights. Those guarantees rarely seemed to demand anything other than the familiar and accepted practices in the local communities and courthouses" (Hans A. Linde, "E Pluribus—Constitutional Theory and State Courts," *Georgia Law Review* 18 [Winter 1984], 174).

36. See Peter Railton, "Judicial Review, Elites, and Liberal Democracy," in J. Roland Pennock and John W. Chapman, eds., *Nomos XXV: Liberal Democracy* (New York: New York University Press, 1983), 164–65.

37. *Democracy and Distrust*, 69.

the other hand, requires the voluntary cooperation of the potential violator.

This discussion of constitutional enforcement is not a quibble over terminology. Rather, it is intended to lay bare the differences in kind between fundamental law and ordinary law that before Marshall were understood with a directness and immediacy that we have since lost. Sovereign power, in period 1 and 2 as now, cannot be restrained against its will as is individual behavior or even delegated power.[38] There simply is insufficient force to do so. Thus period 1 and 2 references to the supreme, paramount, and fundamental law carried with them none of the connotations of ordinary law. When the judiciary attempted to enforce fundamental law against what was thought to be a threat to the very survival of limited government, it was universally understood that the judiciary was acting in a political capacity. It was reinforcing popular self-restraint, not carrying out its routine assigned responsibility for law enforcement. The political character of judicial enforcement of fundamental law was also reflected in the fact that a change of regime from the Articles of Confederation to the Constitution of 1787, not judicial review, ended the constitutional violations that had given rise to period 2 judicial review.

Last, this discussion of constitutional enforcement is not meant to denigrate the achievements of modern judicial review. It is of course the case that the judiciary played an important role in combating the racial injustice that constituted this country's worst constitutional violation. But that role was not literally one of enforcement. Nor can the vast majority of constitutional decisions that make up constitutional law be understood in these terms. I shall return to this issue of the precise function fulfilled by modern judicial review in the last chapter. Here I want to focus on the enduring soundness of Madison's reasoning and of the distinction between fundamental law and ordinary law on which it rested. Without an understanding of that distinc-

---

38. When the judiciary acts as a check on delegated power it acts, as in ordinary law, as society's designated agent. It thus has societal power behind it.

tion there can be no proper understanding of period 2 judicial review, of Marshall's transformation of it, or of the modern practice which emerged from that transformation.

Gibson on Constitutional Enforcement

We have turned before to Gibson's discussion in *Eakin* v. *Raub* to bring us in touch with the unarticulated assumptions of period 2 judicial review. Gibson's analysis of constitutional enforcement serves the same end.

By 1825, when Gibson wrote, Marshall had already achieved significant success in blurring the distinction between fundamental law and ordinary law and along with it the concept of constitutional enforcement. Gibson's was a dissenting voice that challenged the emerging new conceptions on the basis of the period 2 understanding.

At one point in *Eakin* v. *Raub* Gibson considered Marshall's suggestion that judicial invalidation of legislation was necessary to enforce the Constitution: "It has been said that [denial of a judicial check on legislation] would deprive the citizen of the advantages which are peculiar to a written constitution, by at once declaring the power of the legislature, in practice, to be illimitable." He replied: "The principles of a written constitution are more fixed and certain, and more apparent to the apprehension of the people, than principles which depend on tradition and the vague comprehension of the individuals who compose the nation, and who cannot all be expected to receive the same impressions or entertain the same notions on any given subject."[39] Twenty-two years after *Marbury,* the period 2 understanding that the significance of the written constitution lay in its explicitness, not in any legal character, was still alive.

Gibson continued:

> But there is no magic or inherent power in parchment and ink, to command respect, and protect principles from violation. In the business of government, a recurrence to first principles answers

39. 12 Sergeant & Rawles (Pa.) 330, 354 (1825).

the end of an observation at sea, with a view to correct the dead-reckoning; and for this purpose, a written constitution is an instrument of inestimable value. It is of inestimable value also, in rendering its principles familiar to the mass of the people.[40]

For Gibson, as for Madison, constitutional provisions were political principles, not law. They were like "an observation at sea . . . to correct the dead reckoning," or "fundamental maxims of free Government." They were a few moral-political restraints that functioned as rallying grounds and general guides for public action or in an educative capacity, not as legal provisions to be applied and enforced in court.

Moreover, as these principles were directed at sovereign power, when it came to enforcement they were "parchment and ink."[41] According to Gibson, enforcement did not depend on the judiciary but on an uncorrupted public opinion. He pointed out that it was in fact public opinion that had maintained the Pennsylvania constitution over the preceding thirty years while it was experiencing "the shocks of strong party excitement." During this time, he continued, "the judiciary has constantly asserted a right to [declare laws unconstitutional] in clear cases," but it never exercised the power. This legislative respect for the constitution, Gibson argued, was the result of the "responsibility of the legislature to the people," not of "an apprehension of control by the judiciary." In his judgment, the latter conclusion would be "absurd."[42] This judicial record in Pennsylvania, it should also be noted, duplicated that of the Supreme Court during period 2. It provided additional evidence of the centrality of the doubtful case rule and the concededly unconstitutional act in period 2 and into

40. Ibid.

41. Madison used the same terminology in his letter to Jefferson explaining the absence of a bill of rights in the original Constitution (quoted above, chap. 4 at n. 2). He did so also in *Federalist 48* in concluding that "a mere demarcation on parchment of the constitutional limits of the several departments is not a sufficient guard against . . . encroachments (326). *Federalist 48* was prelude to the argument of *Federalist 51* that checks and balances was the only effective enforcement mechanism for the Constitution.

42. 12 Sergeant & Rawles (Pa.) 330, 355.

period 3, and of the atrophy of judicial review between the ending of the revolutionary era and Marshall's reinvigoration of the practice.

Gibson's reliance on pubic opinion rather than the courts to enforce constitutional principle was not, it must be emphasized, the expression of his preference or choice of enforcement mechanisms. It was instead a statement of fact, of the unavailability in a republic of any force stronger than public opinion: "For, after all, there is no effectual guard against legislative usurpation, but public opinion, the force of which, in this country, is inconceivably great."[43] Should the people fail to respect constitutional limits, courts would be too weak to be able to do anything about it: "Once let public opinion be so corrupt, as to sanction every misconstruction of the constitution, and abuse of power, which the temptation of the moment may dictate, and the party which may happen to be predominant, will laugh at the puny efforts of a dependent power to arrest it in its course."[44]

This conclusion duplicated that of Madison, as stated in his letters to Jefferson and Roane and as validated over the course of American history. Written half a century before the Civil War amendments, it is an eloquent anticipation of the American courts' inability to enforce these amendments, for close to a century, in the face of the corruption of American public opinion by racism.

43. Ibid., 354–55.
44. Ibid., 355.

CHAPTER FIVE

Period 3
The Marshall Court

MARBURY OPENED period 3 in the evolution of judicial review, but it did so with a restatement of the period 2 argument. In form, substance, and wording it repeated what had already received widespread support. It is thus not surprising that there was no particular response to *Marbury*'s assertion of judicial authority over unconstitutional acts.

In *Marbury*, Marshall divided the issue of judicial review into its standard two parts. The first was "whether an act, repugnant to the constitution, can become the law of the land."[1] This inquiry into the status of legislative omnipotence was the starting point for the period 1 rejection of Blackstone. By 1803 the argument against legislative omnipotence hardly had to be made, but Marshall made it nevertheless. The opening paragraphs of the defense of judicial review in *Marbury* repeated the period 1 agreement that explicit fundamental law ended legislative omnipotence and that "an act of the legislature, repugnant to the constitution, is void."[2] Marshall's only innovation was to stress the written character of the "superior," "paramount," and "fundamental" law that bound the branches.

The period 1 and 2 rejection of legislative omnipotence had always been asserted in contemplation of a concededly unconstitutional act, as it was in *Marbury*. Marshall inquired whether an unconstitutional act could be valid law only after declaring void a section of the Judiciary Act of 1789. He did so, following the precedent established in *Kamper*, for a law dealing with organization of the judiciary. Marshall did reverse the order followed in *Kamper* and declared the act void before inquiring into judicial authority to do so. Neverthe-

---

1. *Marbury v. Madison*, 5 U.S. (1 Cr.) 137, 176 (1803).
2. Ibid., 177.

less, in making the standard period 2 defense of judicial review, Marshall was under no more obligation to discuss who should determine the constitutionality of legislation than was any period 2 source.[3]

The second inquiry, as stated in *Marbury,* was, "Does [an act which is void] notwithstanding its invalidity, bind the courts, and oblige them to give it effect?"[4] This was the standard second question of period 1 and 2 debate. In answering, Marshall drew on the period 2 answers, particularly on Hamilton's and Tucker's formulations. The key paragraphs of *Marbury* read as follows:

> It is emphatically the province and duty of the judicial department to say what the law is. Those who apply the rule to particular cases, must of necessity expound and interpret that rule. If two laws conflict with each other, the courts must decide on the operation of each.
>
> So if a law be in opposition to the constitution: if both the law and the constitution apply to a particular case, so that the court must either decide that case conformably to the law, disregarding the constitution; or conformably to the constitution, disregarding the law; the court must determine which of these conflicting rules governs the case. This is of the very essence of judicial duty.
>
> If then the courts are to regard the constitution; and the constitution is superior to any ordinary act of the legislature; the constitution, and not such ordinary act, must govern the case to which they both apply.[5]

The first sentence in this formulation combined key phrases from *Federalist 78* and Tucker's *Kamper* opinion. In Tucker's opinion the word *law* referred to ordinary law, not the Constitution. For at least the last century the law mentioned in this first sentence, as in the third,

---

3. Failure to discuss this point is, of course, the now classic modern criticism of *Marbury.* See, e.g., Bickel, *Least Dangerous Branch,* 3, and Archibald Cox, *The Role of the Supreme Court in American Government* (London: Oxford University Press, 1976), 14.

4. *Marbury v. Madison,* 5 U.S. (1 Cr.) 137, 177 (1803).

5. Ibid., 177–78.

has been read to include the Constitution. I am convinced that none of Marshall's contemporaries read the words that way.[6] In context, following the assertion that an unconstitutional act was void, this paragraph introduced the conflict of laws analogy as used in period 2 to support the argument that the judicial responsibility to expound ordinary law precluded enforcement of an act that, in its invalidity, was not law.

The second sentence of this key paragraph used the word *rule* rather than *law* or *constitution*. In period 2 usage *rule* was widely used to refer to the Constitution,[7] but Wilson also used it to refer to legislative acts.[8] In this same second sentence Marshall described the judicial function as it applied to ordinary law. In the next paragraph Marshall included both the Constitution and ordinary legislation within the term *rule* and spoke of the Constitution and ordinary law as applying to the same case. This is as close as Marshall ever came to a direct assertion that applying, expounding, and interpreting the Constitution was part of the province and duty of the judicial department. There is only the barest support for such a reading of *Marbury*, and that only because of subsequent events. These key paragraphs, aside from the enigmatic second sentence, are pure period 2 judicial review. They linked the judiciary's authority over legislation to its responsibility to expound ordinary law, used the conflict of laws analogy to justify refusal to enforce a concededly unconstitutional act, and reaffirmed Court authority "to regard" the Constitution and thereby the key period 2 innovation, the rejection of Blackstone.

The rest of *Marbury* maintained the period 2 analysis and language. Marshall asserted the right of courts "to regard," "to look into," and "to examin[e]" the Constitution.[9] In asserting that "the

6. See chap. 6 for discussion of the evolution of the *Marbury* doctrine during the nineteenth century.

7. See Pendleton in *Commonwealth* v. *Caton*, 4 Call (Va.) 5, 17 (1782); Wilson, *Lectures on the Law,* in *Works of Wilson,* ed. McCloskey, 1:330; Tucker in *Kamper* v. *Hawkins,* 1 Va. Cases 20, 77 (1793); and Paterson in *VanHorne's Lessee* v. *Dorrance,* 2 U.S. (2 Dall.) 304, 309 (1795).

8. *Lectures on the Law,* in *Works of Wilson,* ed. McCloskey, 330.

9. *Marbury* v. *Madison,* 5 U.S. (1 Cr.) 137, 178, and 179 (1803).

constitution is to be considered, in court, as a paramount law,"[10] Marshall was only denying that the Constitution was a rule to the legislature only. His examples of clear constitutional violations practically duplicated a section of Tucker's *Kamper* opinion.[11] Reference to "the supreme law of the land" echoed James Wilson's usage,[12] and the statement that the invalidity of an act repugnant to the Constitution is a principle not "to be lost sight of" was taken directly from Paterson in *VanHorne's Lessee.*[13] Marshall's argument on the judicial oath was intended to demonstrate that "the framers of the constitution contemplated that instrument, as a rule for the government of *courts,* as well as of the legislature."[14] The inability of the judicial oath to sustain the judicial supremacy of period 3 is a staple of the modern criticism of *Marbury.* But in context *Marbury* merely repeated the period 2 claim of the equality of the branches in rejection of the legislative supremacy of period 1. The concluding paragraph made the same point: "Thus, the particular phraseology of the constitution of the United States confirms and strengthens the principle, supposed to be essential to all written constitutions, that a law repugnant to the constitution is void; and that *courts, as well as other departments,* are bound by that instrument."[15]

Marbury contained nothing as direct as Hamilton's claim that the judiciary could "ascertain [the] meaning [of the Constitution],"[16] and Hamilton's relative boldness was, most likely, the product of innocent intentions. Otherwise, Marshall followed Hamilton's lead in stressing the positive law components of existing doctrine, in avoiding overly detailed explication of the reasoning behind it, and in eliminating its overt links to natural rights.

10. Ibid., 178.

11. Compare ibid., 179, and 1 Va. Cases 20, 79–81 (1793).

12. *Lectures on the Law,* in *Works of Wilson,* ed. McCloskey, 329 and 330. Quoted above, chap. 3 at n. 71.

13. Compare *Marbury* v. *Madison,* 5 U.S. (1 Cr.) 137, 177 (1803), with *VanHorne's Lessee* v. *Dorrance,* 2 U.S. (2 Dall.) 304, 309 (1795). Quoted above, chap. 3 at n. 24.

14. *Marbury* v. *Madison,* 5 U.S. (1 Cr.) 137, 179–80 (1803). Emphasis in original.

15. Ibid., 180. Emphasis deleted and added.

16. *Federalist No. 78,* 506.

Marbury departed from the period 2 defense of judicial power over unconstitutional legislation in only two ways, neither of them recognizable at the time. The first was the hidden suggestion that the province and duty of the judicial department included saying what the law of the Constitution is, and the second was its liberal references to the written constitution. There were almost as many references to the written constitution in *Marbury* as in all the period 2 discussions combined.[17] The references to the written constitution in *Marbury* were bland. They carried neither the period 2 meaning of explicit fundamental law nor the period 3 meaning of supreme ordinary law. They served more than anything to associate the judicial refusal to execute an unconstitutional act with the written constitution, and to prepare the ground for judicial exposition of the constitutional text that was to begin at some opportune time in the future.

Natural Law and Positive Law in Marshall's Judicial Review

Marshall followed Hamilton's rather than Wilson's version of Iredell's argument, emphasizing its positive law elements and ignoring for the most part its natural law elements. *Marbury* contained no references to the reality or explicitness of American fundamental law, to its status as a social contract, or to judicial enforcement of it as a substitute for revolution. The only acknowledgment of natural rights in *Marbury* was indirect and came at the beginning of that opinion's defense of judicial review. After referring to "certain principles, supposed to have been long and well established," Marshall acknowledged the right to revolution without quite endorsing it: "That the people have an original right to establish, for their future government, such principles as, in their opinion, shall most conduce to their own happiness, is the basis, on which the whole American fabric has been

17. The word *written* is used nine times in *Marbury*. I have found it ten times in period 2 discussions: twice in Iredell to Spaight, *Correspondence of Iredell*, ed. McRee, 2:173, 174; twice in Tucker's *Kamper* opinion, 1 Va. Cases 20, 77, 78 (1793); once in Nelson's *Kamper* opinion, ibid., 23; and five times in Paterson's *VanHorne's Lessee* opinion, 2 U.S. (2 Dall.) 304, 308, 314 (1795).

erected."[18] In the next sentence he expressed reservations about the actual resort to revolution without, however, condemning it: "The exercise of this original right is a very great exertion; nor can it, nor ought it to be frequently repeated." He concluded the paragraph by touching on the problem of constitutional maintenance: "The principles, therefore, so established, are deemed fundamental. And as the authority, from which they proceed, is supreme, and can seldom act, they are designed to be permanent."[19]

Without rejecting the principle of consent or the right of revolution, Marshall was here pointing to the tension between these principles and the demands of political order and stability. In so doing he expressed concerns similar to those that had led Blackstone to parliamentary omnipotence and Madison to political checks and balances and the extended republic as ways of providing order, stability, and constitutional integrity. Examination of the similarities and differences among Blackstone's, Marshall's, and Madison's positions illuminates Marshall's unique strategy for constitutional maintenance, one pursued by restructuring period 2 judicial review.

Blackstone, Madison, and Marshall all accepted the prevailing natural law doctrine under which the rights to life, liberty, and property were understood to antedate the formation of civil government. Legitimate government was one based on consent and aimed at securing these rights; deprivation of these rights was legitimate ground for withdrawal of consent and revolutionary action. All three were aware, however, that although natural law provided the standard of justice for civil society and the basis for revolutionary action against it, it could not provide for the security of rights so identified. Security lay in civil society and good positive law, not in the state of nature, natural law, and revolution. Revolution not only could not secure private rights but might be a source of danger to them. It destroyed the existing order but could not guarantee a better one. Furthermore, frequent revolutions, even those rightly made in the name of natural rights, generated an instability that was incompatible with peace,

18. *Marbury v. Madison*, 5 U.S. (1 Cr.) 137, 176 (1803).
19. Ibid.

security, and private rights. Resort to revolution was a last desperate public recourse, not a welcome part of ongoing political life.

Blackstone manifested his acknowledgment of both the legitimacy and insufficiency of revolution in his failure in the *Commentaries* to assign a clear priority to either natural or positive law.[20] This failure did not reflect a confusion over priorities, as has sometimes been suggested, but rather the recognition that natural and positive law complemented rather than controlled each other directly. Natural law provided the standards for positive law but depended on positive law to achieve the ends to which it pointed. To the extent that positive law was the actual instrument through which these ends were achieved it was superior to natural law. But positive law remained, at the same time, dependent on natural law for its self-understanding and, in its broadest outlines, for its content. In that sense positive law was subordinate to natural law.

Despite allusions to the superiority of natural law, Blackstone ultimately supported positive law more strongly in his unequivocal defense of parliamentary omnipotence and in his refusal to recognize any right, including a judicial one, to challenge its authority. Blackstone also explicitly rejected any public recognition of a right to revolution. After quoting a passage from Locke expressing the people's inherent power to "remove or alter the legislative," he granted that Locke's conclusions were just "in theory." But he denied that "we [could] adopt it, [or] argue from it, under any dispensation of government at present actually existing." The right to revolution justly asserted by Locke

> includes in it a dissolution of the whole form of government [and] repeals all positive laws. . . . No human laws will therefore suppose a case, which at once must destroy all law, and compel men to build afresh upon a new foundation; nor will they make provision for so desperate an event, as must render all legal provisions ineffectual. So long therefore as the English constitu-

20. This reading of Blackstone follows that of Herbert J. Storing, "William Blackstone," in Leo Strauss and Joseph Cropsey, eds., *History of Political Philosophy* (Chicago: Rand, McNally, 1972), 594–606.

tion lasts, we may venture to affirm, that the power of parliament is absolute and without control.[21]

Blackstone was equally emphatic in refusing to acknowledge any legal right to challenge abuse of power:

> For, as to such public oppressions as tend to dissolve the constitution, and subvert the fundamentals of government, they are cases which the law will not, out of decency, suppose; being incapable of distrusting those, whom it has invested with any part of the supreme power; since such distrust would render the exercise of that power precarious and impracticable. For, wherever the law expresses its distrust of abuse of power, it always vests a superior coercive authority in some other hand to correct it; the very notion of which destroys the idea of sovereignty.[22]

To build afresh was a legitimate but desperate recourse that should not be dwelt upon publicly. At the same time, parliamentary omnipotence and the refusal to acknowledge a right to revolution would not remove this recourse from public life. Immediately after denying the availability of a legal remedy for public oppressions, Blackstone continued: "But, if ever they unfortunately happen, the prudence of the times must provide new remedies upon new emergencies." In the face of genuine oppression, he continued, "Mankind will not be reasoned out of the feelings of humanity; nor will sacrifice their liberty by a scrupulous adherence to those political maxims, which were originally established to preserve it."[23] The circumstances of such oppression will vary and cannot be predicted in advance. "Both law and history are silent" about the particular form that oppression may take, and "it becomes us to be silent too; leaving to future generations, whenever necessity and the safety of the whole shall require it, the exertion of those inherent (though latent) powers of society, which no climate, no time, no constitution, no contract, can ever destroy or diminish."[24]

21. *Commentaries*, 1:157.
22. Ibid., 237.
23. Ibid., 238.
24. Ibid.

Support for parliamentary authority over any invocation of first principles, including one made by the judiciary, was part of Blackstone's judgment that it was effective civil authority that needed bolstering, not revolutionary principles. Furthermore, the parliamentary omnipotence defended here related, as we have seen, to a parliament containing an effective system of checks and balances. Additional revolutionary action was not likely to improve on it. And having gone through a successful revolution, the English did not need instruction or encouragement on the subject. In any case, there was ultimately no reliable remedy against public oppression. Neither positive law nor natural law is capable of furnishing one. The revolutionary solution is an appeal beyond law to force, and the outcomes of such appeals remain in their nature beyond calculation.

Madison expressed comparable thoughts more directly than did Blackstone. They were the basis for his rejection of Jefferson's suggestion that popular conventions be used to enforce the Constitution and to resolve constitutional disputes among the branches. Madison raised and rejected Jefferson's suggestion in *Federalist 49*, which we examined briefly in the last chapter. Although Madison rejected Jefferson's proposal, he accepted its underlying premise that the people were the "only legitimate fountain of power" and the source of the "true meaning" of the Constitution.[25] Consequently, some provision for popular involvement in constitutional questions was necessary. But this should be reserved for "certain great and extraordinary occasions."[26] Madison opposed institutionalizing regular recurrence to the people on grounds similar to those that motivated Blackstone. For one thing, too frequent recurrence to the people on first principles threatened political stability. Stability required a certain degree of unthinking acceptance of the Constitution—a "veneration" and the support of the "prejudices of the community."[27] Too frequent popular discussion of constitutional questions "would carry an implication of some defect in the government, [and] frequent appeals would . . . deprive the government of that veneration which time bestows on

---

25. *Federalist No. 49*, 327, 328.
26. Ibid., 328.
27. Ibid., 328, 329.

every thing, and without which perhaps the wisest and freest government would not possess the requisite stability."[28]

Second, constitutional revision was an "experiment" of "too ticklish a nature to be unnecessarily multiplied."[29] Constitution making was intrinsically difficult and politically sensitive. Although Americans had so far been successful, there could never be any guarantee that they would be so again: "We are to recollect that all the existing constitutions were formed in the midst of a danger which repressed the passions most unfriendly to order and concord. . . . The future situations in which we must expect to be usually placed, do not present any equivalent security against the danger which is apprehended."[30]

Madison had no scruples about overthrowing the hopelessly inadequate Articles of Confederation, and indeed, he saw more risk in continuing under the articles than in trying something new.[31] But he clearly had no confidence that should the Constitution of 1787 fail, something at least as good would replace it. The task, then, was to maintain this Constitution, which included downplaying the fact that the people were the only legitimate fountain of power and the ultimate authority on the true meaning of the Constitution. As we saw in the last chapter, for Madison constitutional maintenance was to be achieved not by popular conventions but by properly designed institutional arrangements, by checks and balances and the extended republic. As indicated in *Federalist 51*, this solution was "commensurate with the danger of attack" and operated automatically, without the risks attendant on perpetual public discussion of first principle.

Marshall's consideration of these same issues was exceedingly brief and characteristically cryptic. It consisted first of his guarded acknowledgment of a right to revolution and his reference to the need for constitutional permanence, which we have already examined.

28. Ibid., 328–29.
29. Ibid., 329.
30. Ibid., 329–30.
31. See Madison to Edmund Pendleton, February 24, 1787, in *Writings of Madison*, ed. Hunt, 2:317–20, and "Vices of the Political System of the United States," April 1787, ibid., 361–69.

Next, Marshall added a legal check to the political ones already in place. This was not, however, the one he inherited from period 2—the judicial authority to refuse to execute a concededly unconstitutional act. With the passing of the revolutionary era and the establishment of the new Constitution, this restraint was for one thing already largely irrelevant. In addition, it depended too directly on invocation of first principles and relied too closely on the original right to revolution to be used safely.

Period 2 judicial review, furthermore, was unsuitable for Marshall's ambitious project of generating a new kind of check against official and popular abuse of power, one that neither challenged political authority directly nor involved repeated public recourse to first principles. This was to be the now familiar positive law restraint of the written constitution. This restraint is so familiar today that it is hard to believe that in 1803 it did not yet exist and that it was to take about half a century to construct. It was brought into being by making the restraint of the Constitution one of constitutional text rather than first principle. This was achieved in practice by establishing the meaning of the contract clause—the centerpiece of period 3 judicial review—by textual exposition rather than by invocation of the preexisting principle of vested rights. Next, under Marshall's leadership, judicially enforceable constitutional restraints were no longer reserved for the extraordinary, quasi-revolutionary situation but were applied to governmental acts whose conformity to the Constitution could be plausibly defended. These innovations blurred the distinction between the constitutionality and the wisdom or expediency of legislation while making implementation of first principles, for the first time, a judicial rather than a popular responsibility. Simultaneously, constitutionality became an external, continuously operating legal restraint on legislative and majority will analogous to the restraint of ordinary law on individuals. So too the Constitution's binding force lost the moral-political, quasi-revolutionary quality of fundamental law and took on the routine legal one of ordinary law.

This was the process that made the Constitution "so much law" and established "the peculiarly effective nature of American constitutional restrictions on legislative power."[32] This legal restraint was unprovided for in the Constitution and unanticipated in period 2 judicial review. At the same time, by making exposition of fundamental law a judicial rather than a popular responsibility, Marshall also introduced the judicial supremacy of period 3 and the unresolved tension between judicial review and democracy.

I shall show in the rest of this chapter precisely how Marshall legalized the Constitution, blurring the original distinction between fundamental law and ordinary law without challenging it openly. It should not be surprising to learn, in the meantime, that Marshall understood fully the force of the original distinction, particularly the judiciary's inability to enforce fundamental law against its genuine violation. Marshall alluded to this central difficulty in *Marbury* in the process of undermining its importance. In repeating the standard period 2 claim that the Constitution ended legislative omnipotence by establishing literally binding limits on legislative power, he said:

> The constitution is either a superior, paramount law, unchangeable by ordinary means, or it is on a level with ordinary legislative acts, and like other acts, is alterable when the legislature shall please to alter it.
>
> If the former part of the alternative be true, then a legislative act contrary to the constitution is not law: if the latter part be true, then written constitutions are absurd attempts, on the part of the people, to limit a power, in its own nature illimitable.[33]

There are many ways this thought could have been expressed. Marshall chose one that spoke of the illimitable nature of legislative power. His formulation reflected full appreciation of Madison's analysis of the political forces that threaten republican governments. It acknowledged the absurdity of thinking that there was any force strong enough to counter a majority bent on pursuing its will and ready to violate principles it had once agreed to follow. Marshall's

32. See Thayer, "Doctrine of Constitutional Law," 138, quoted above, chap. 2 at n. 34, and Wood, *Creation of American Republic*, 291, quoted above, chap. 1 at n. 10.

33. 5 U.S. (1 Cr.) 137, 177 (1803).

often noted caution in the use of judicial power is additional testimony to his recognition of the limited judicial capacity to maintain its exposition of the law of the Constitution over that of the majority.

Yet after conceding the absurdity of trying to control sovereign majority will by a written constitution, Marshall did make the law of the Constitution into a meaningful restraint. Though Marshall's judicial review has been too weak to enforce the Constitution against genuine violation and will likely remain so, it imparted to the restraint of political principle a force hitherto unknown—that is, some of the routine, internalized, binding quality that attaches to ordinary law. This is not the same thing as enforcing the law of the Constitution against its violation. It is more properly understood as reinforcement and internalization of the legitimacy of the restraint of principle.[34] It is a novel legal-political restraint unknown to the framers and still not properly understood. Marshall used this restraint exclusively to reinforce popular and legislative commitment to vested rights, the principle the framers thought most in jeopardy in a republican regime. In the ensuing public and professional receptivity to Marshall's innovations, constitutionality, judicially applied and expounded, has come to be accepted as a legal restraint against which all exercises of majority and official power could legitimately be judged.

The Rules for Statutory Interpretation

Marshall established modern judicial review by introducing two related innovations, neither of which he acknowledged openly and whose existence was barely recognized by others. First, he established the meaning of the Constitution, for the purpose of judicial review, through a process of textual exposition following the rules for statutory interpretation. In case after case Marshall painstakingly defined constitutional words and then examined their context. Only then did he consider the intent or spirit of the Constitution and in doing so insisted on the primacy of constitutional words.

34. The function of period 3 and modern judicial review will be discussed more fully below (chap. 7).

As we have already seen, period 2 judges did not use textual exposition to determine the meaning of fundamental law for the purpose of establishing the unconstitutionality of legislation but invoked instead natural law principle and common law precedent. The period 3 cases will show that Marshall's Supreme Court colleagues followed the period 2 practice. They also relied heavily on original intent or contemporaneous construction of the U.S. Constitution. In so doing, however, they reversed Marshall's procedure. Instead of determining constitutional intent through exposition of its words, they used those words to support an otherwise determined intent.

The significance and even the existence of this difference in approach were obscured by the fact that outside the federalism cases Marshall's constitutional law was limited to the contract clause. For Marshall's colleagues these cases were governed by the principle of vested rights and the common law of contracts. For the most part the results reached by Marshall's exposition of the contract clause text was the same as that reached by his colleagues' reliance on vested rights.

Marshall's second innovation was relaxation of the doubtful case rule. In keeping with the unacknowledged character of his innovations he never challenged the rule directly but actually reaffirmed it in the course of upholding legislation. But he never discussed the doubtful case rule in the course of overturning legislation whose unconstitutionality could plausibly be questioned. In these cases he was able, often enough to change the course of American constitutional law, to hold the Court together to invalidate acts that would likely have been upheld during period 2.

Marshall's ability to weaken the doubtful case rule without openly challenging it was made possible by the strength of contemporary commitment to the principle of vested rights.[35] This allowed him to bring the Court with him in overturning legislation in circumstances touching the outer limits of that rule. Marshall benefited also from the

35. For a discussion of the reliance of the Marshall Court's contract clause adjudication on a consensus on the meaning of vested rights see White, *Marshall Court and Cultural Change,* chap. 9.

degree to which the period 2 argument had overcome resistance to a judicial check on legislation. Even though period 2 judges adhered to a strict version of the doubtful case rule and overturned few pieces of legislation, their repeated and largely uncontradicted assertion that courts could legitimately refuse to enforce an unconstitutional act detracted from the boldness of Marshall's action.

The evidence that Marshall single-handedly transformed judicial review from enforcement of explicit fundamental law against conceded violation into the open-ended exposition of supreme written law lies in a comparison of his opinions with those of his colleagues. There are, unfortunately, few such opinions. This is not, however, an accident of history but the first piece of evidence. It was under Marshall's leadership that the Court abandoned the practice of seriatim opinion writing and united behind a single opinion.[36] Justice William Johnson has testified that it was only in response to his insistence that concurring and dissenting opinions were accepted.[37] In thus discouraging alternate opinions Marshall created the conditions for molding the relatively new and still pliable practice of judicial review. He eliminated effectively most expressions of alternate conceptions of its proper practice, while his own masterful style diverted attention from the few other opinions that do exist. When these are read carefully, however, they display a consistently different approach, one that continued period 2 understanding and practice.

The recently published history of the Marshall Court by G. Edward White provides an important insight into how Supreme Court justices understood judicial review, and this needs to be considered before turning to specific cases. White pointed out that a distinction existed on the Court between cases coming for review from lower federal courts, such as diversity suits, and those that came on appeal from state courts under section 25 of the Judiciary Act of 1789. For the former, it was agreed that the Court could overturn legislation on the ground that a statute violated general principle, as for example that of

36. See Donald G. Morgan, *Justice William Johnson: The First Dissenter* (Columbia: University of South Carolina Press, 1954), 45–47 and 168–89.

37. Johnson to Thomas Jefferson, quoted in ibid., 181–82.

vested rights. For cases coming from the state courts, by contrast, the Judiciary Act limited the Supreme Court's appellate jurisdiction to a determination of whether legislation violated the U.S. Constitution. This in turn was understood to mean violation of a specific provision and to exclude direct consideration of general principle.[38]

White did not focus on the difficulties of judicial review and assumed that Marshall Court justices read *Marbury* as it is read today.[39] But his identification of these two classes of cases is an important contribution to the understanding of period 3 practice, and it helps us to see the precise nature of Marshall's innovations. First, in revealing the extent to which period 3 judges accepted general principles as sufficient ground for declaring legislation void, even with the exception for section 25 cases, White's distinction indicates the continued

38. There is little overt acknowledgment of this distinction in the cases themselves. White's account documents that it was nevertheless widely accepted and that it played a significant role in the strategy of litigants. See *Marshall Court and Cultural Change*, 175–76, 606, 608, 611, 614–15, and 657–60. The clearest Court acknowledgment of the distinction was made by Justice Washington in a section 25 case, *Satterlee* v. *Matthewson*, 27 U.S. (2 Pet.) 380, 413–14 (1829). After sustaining a state statute against a claim that it violated the contract clause, Washington refused to consider whether that statute divested vested rights. In so doing, he restated Marshall's suggestion in *Fletcher* v. *Peck*, that legislative powers were limited by the principle of vested rights, and then said: "It is nowhere intimated in that opinion that a state statute, which divests a vested right, is repugnant to the Constitution of the United States, and the case in which that opinion was pronounced was removed into this Court by a writ of error, not from the Supreme Court of a state, but from a Circuit Court." Washington's opinion concluded: "We intend to decide no more than that the statute objected to in this case is not repugnant to the Constitution of the United States, and that unless it be so, this Court has no authority, under the twenty-fifth section of the judiciary act, to re-examine and to reverse the judgment of the Supreme Court of Pennsylvania." Justice Story made a similar allusion to the inapplicability of general principle as a ground for overturning legislation in section 25 cases in *Dartmouth College* v. *Woodward*, 17 U.S. (4 Wheat.) 518, 708 (1819). Story's comment is quoted and discussed below, chap. 5 at n. 77.

39. According to White, *Marbury* established "the proposition that the judiciary was to give constitutional language its operative meaning" (*Marshall Court and Cultural Change*, 670).

strength of the period 2 understanding and Chase's version of it. Next, White also pointed out that in cases on appeal from the federal courts, the Marshall Court during the 1810s adopted the position of declaring acts void on the alternate grounds that they violated general principles and the Constitution. Examination of these cases will show a consistent difference, following the lines indicated here, between Marshall and other justices in the way they treated each of these alternate grounds. Last, for section 25 cases, in which the only question was whether the legislation violated the Constitution, only Marshall established the meaning of the Constitution by application of the rules for statutory interpretation. For his colleagues the meaning of constitutional text was sought in some extratextual consensus combining the principle of vested rights and the common law of contracts.

In focusing on the novelty of applying the rules for statutory interpretation to the Constitution, I am not suggesting that no construction of the Constitution's words had ever taken place before Marshall. On the contrary, it had been done by members of all branches of government in circumstances where the Constitution's words were not self-executing and its precise intent was nonexistent. Had this not been the case, Marshall's actions would have been too great a departure from existing practice to be sustainable. It had never, however, been part of the determination of the unconstitutionality of legislation for the purpose of refusing to execute an unconstitutional act. In this setting, apart from the concurrent review of *Kamper,* there had never been Court reliance on its own exposition of the constitutional text over a plausible legislative exposition to the contrary, and thus no imputation that the judiciary was the authoritative expositor of the Constitution as it was for ordinary law.[40]

40. *Hylton* v. *United States,* 3 U.S. (3 Dall.) 171 (1796), and *Calder* v. *Bull,* 3 U.S. (3 Dall.) 386 (1798), provide examples of judicial construction of constitutional text. In each the Supreme Court upheld the legislation. In *Hylton* Chase specifically indicated that under the doubtful case rule he was obliged to defer to legislative construction of the Constitution: "The deliberate decision of the national legislature . . . would determine me, if the case was *doubtful,* to receive the construction of the legislature" (ibid., 173; emphasis in original).

The Contract Clause Cases

Fletcher v. *Peck*, the first contract clause case,[41] was a diversity suit in which Marshall held that the challenged legislation violated first principles of government as well as the contract clause. The idea that legislation could be void on these alternate grounds did not originate with Marshall. Alexander Hamilton had made a similar argument in 1796 in connection with the same issues litigated in *Fletcher* v. *Peck*, and his opinion had been put into pamphlet form and widely circulated.[42] Nevertheless, Marshall's *Fletcher* opinion remains unique in important ways. It was the only time Marshall rested a determination of unconstitutionality on natural law in an opinion for the Court, for either a diversity or section 25 case.[43] Excluding the concurrent review of *Marbury*, it was the opinion in which he first introduced the method of statutory interpretation into determinations of constitutionality. The opinion thus stands as a microcosm of Marshall Court contract clause adjudication, with its overlap of textual exposition and defense of the principle of vested rights. In addition, Marshall used his *Fletcher* opinion to acknowledge the peculiar qualities of constitutional limits and the political difficulties surrounding attempts to restrain sovereign power. His subsequent opinions, consisting exclusively of lawyer-like analysis of constitutional text, gave no hint of the problematic character of this kind of restraint.

Fletcher v. *Peck* grew out of what has become known as the Yazoo land fraud. In 1795 the Georgia legislature sold great amounts of state land in a transaction that was soon revealed to have involved large-scale bribery of the legislature. A subsequently elected legislature

41. 10 U.S. (6 Cr.) 87 (1810).

42. Hamilton's argument is quoted and discussed below, chap. 5, at n. 55. For an account of its circulation and influence see *Law Practice of Hamilton*, ed. Julius Goebel, Jr., and Joseph H. Smith (1980), 4:383–86 and 429–31. See also White, *Marshall Court and Cultural Change*, 603.

43. Marshall drew on natural law principles in his dissent in *Ogden* v. *Saunders*, 25 U.S. (12 Wheat.) 213, 344–47 (1827). Had he here been writing for the Court he likely would have maintained the exclusive reliance on textual exposition visible in all his other opinions.

rescinded the original grant but not until third parties had purchased some of the land. The rescinding act put these titles in question, and suit was brought to resolve the issue.

Fletcher held unanimously that the rescinding act was void and that the title of the third-party purchasers was valid. Marshall's Court opinion concluded:

> It is, then, the unanimous opinion of the court, that, in this case, the estate having passed into the hands of a purchaser for a valuable consideration, without notice, the state of Georgia was restrained, either by general principles which are common to our free institutions, or by the particular provisions of the constitution of the United States, from passing a law whereby the estate of the plaintiff in the premises so purchased could be constitutionally and legally impaired and rendered null and void.[44]

Marshall reached this conclusion after devoting almost equal attention to natural law principles and construction of the contract clause text. His discussion of first principles and vested rights, however, had a noticeably hesitant character. He observed:

> It may well be doubted whether the nature of society and of government does not prescribe some limits to the legislative power; and, if any be prescribed, where are they to be found, if the property of an individual, fairly and honestly acquired, may be seized without compensation.
>
> To the legislature all legislative power is granted; but the question, whether the act of transferring the property of an individual to the public, be in the nature of the legislative power, is well worthy of serious reflection.[45]

This statement avoided direct sanction of natural law as judicially enforceable law and lacked the forcefulness so obvious in every other contemporary judicial defense of first principle.[46]

44. 10 U.S. (6 Cr.) 87, 139 (1810).
45. Ibid., 135–36.
46. Contrast Paterson's formulation in *VanHorne's Lessee* v. *Dorrance*

Marshall ended this discussion with an even more equivocal expression: "It is the peculiar province of the legislature to prescribe the rules for the government of society; the application of those rules to individuals in society would seem to be the duty of other departments. How far the power of giving the law may involve every other power, in cases where the constitution is silent, never has been, and perhaps never can be, definitely stated."[47]

This oblique comment was the counterpart of Blackstone's qualified allusion to the supremacy of natural law in the *Commentaries*. The latter recognized that there were indeed limits to parliamentary omnipotence, and Marshall was here making a case for legislative omnipotence. The "power of giving the law" was the power to deal with societal needs. Judicial restraint on this power—understood either as the reassertion of natural law or the application and interpretation of the positive law of the Constitution—could, under some circumstances, hamper society's capacity to meet its needs. Different histories, social structures, and institutional arrangements led Blackstone and Marshall to different ways of balancing these considerations. Marshall, having decided that the tendency to legislative willfulness in the United States was serious enough to warrant institutionalization of a judicial check on legislation, not only anchored that check in a new kind of positive law but then took this one occasion to warn against its overly simplistic application.

When Marshall turned to the positive law grounds for reviewing the rescinding law, his equivocation disappeared. Georgia, he pointed out, was part of a union whose Constitution "imposes limits to the legislatures of the several States," among them that "no State shall pass any law impairing the obligation of contracts."[48] He then argued that the legislative grant was a contract within the meaning of the Constitution and that the rescinding act came within the prohibition encompassed in the words of the contract clause.

The textual exposition through which Marshall came to this last

---

quoted above, chap. 3 at n. 57, and Johnson's in *Fletcher* v. *Peck* quoted below, chap. 5 at n. 50. See also Story's Court opinion in *Terrett* v. *Taylor* quoted below, chap. 5 at n. 61.

47. 10 U.S. (6 Cr.) 87, 136 (1810).

48. Ibid.

conclusion is so commonplace by today's standards that it is not in itself worth examining. It concentrates in typical fashion on the meaning of constitutional words and the relationship of words to intent. Its significance lies in its difference from other justices' procedures for determining the unconstitutionality of legislation. To facilitate the comparison in this and subsequent cases it is helpful to reproduce part of Marshall's argument:

> Does the case now under consideration come within [the prohibition] of the constitution?
>
> In considering this very interesting question we immediately ask ourselves what is a contract? Is a grant a contract?
>
> A contract is a compact between two or more parties, and is either executory or executed. . . .
>
> . . . [A] grant is a contract executed, the obligation of which still continues, and since the constitution uses the general term contract, without distinguishing between those which are executory and those which are executed, it must be construed to comprehend the latter as well as the former. . . .
>
> If, under a fair construction of the constitution, grants are comprehended under the term contracts, is a grant from the State excluded from the operation of the provision? . . .
>
> The words themselves contain no such distinction. They are general and are applicable to contracts of every description. If contracts made with the State are to be exempted from their operation, the exception must arise from the character of the contracting party, not from the words which are employed.

Marshall explored this last point by examining constitutional intent. He referred to the framers' fears of legislative invasion of personal and property rights and their inclusion of limits on legislative powers to protect these rights. Returning to his emphasis on constitutional words, he concluded that he could find no motive "for implying, in words which import a general prohibition to impair the obligation of contracts, an exception in favor of the right to impair the obligation of those contracts into which the State may enter."[49]

49. Ibid., 136–38.

Fletcher v. *Peck,* although unanimous, contained a separate concurring opinion by Justice Johnson in which the invalidity of the rescinding act was established solely by its violation of the principle of vested rights. He expressed this in language that was perhaps the strongest expression of the natural rights foundation of limited government to be found in this literature and was strikingly different from Marshall's guarded formulation:

> I do not hesitate to declare that a state does not possess the power of revoking its own grants. But I do it on a general principle, on the reason and nature of things: a principle which will impose laws even on the deity.

Johnson continued: "When the legislature have once conveyed their interest or property in any subject to the individual, they have lost all control over it; [this interest] is vested in the individual; becomes intimately blended with his existence, as essentially so as the blood that circulates through his system."[50]

Johnson also explicitly disassociated himself from Marshall's construction of the contract clause. Although he had no "solid objection"[51] to including a grant within the term contract, he would not commit himself to Marshall's reading of the "obligation" of contracts. There was much scope for legitimate state regulation of contracts, and an overly strict definition of obligation, he argued, could deny states salutary authority. In thus upholding the principle of vested rights over legislation to the contrary without pointing to recognition of that principle in some explicit provision of the constitutional text, Johnson continued that strand of period 2 judicial review exemplified by Chase.

Last, *Fletcher* v. *Peck* demonstrated Marshall's calculated use of the doubtful case rule. At the beginning of his *Fletcher* opinion, Marshall pointedly affirmed acceptance of that rule. Among the issues raised in this suit was that the original legislation of 1795, as well as the

50. Ibid., 143.
51. Ibid., 144.

rescinding act, was unconstitutional. Before dismissing this challenge, Marshall declared:

> The question, whether a law be void for its repugnancy to the constitution, is, at all time, a question of much delicacy, which ought seldom, if ever, to be decided in the affirmative, in a doubtful case. The court, when impelled by duty to render such a judgment, would be unworthy of its station, could it be unmindful of the solemn obligations which that station imposes. But it is not on slight implication and vague conjecture that the legislature is to be pronounced to have transcended its powers, and its acts to be considered as void. The opposition between the constitution and the law should be such that the judge feels a clear and strong conviction of their incompatibility with each other.[52]

This is, first of all, a comparatively weak statement of the doubtful case rule, even though it is within existing conceptions. The judge need feel only a "clear and strong conviction" of the incompatibility between the legislation and the Constitution.[53] Marshall also repeated Iredell's comment that the invalidation of legislation was a "delicate" question but omitted Iredell's reference to its "awful" quality. More important, this statement was made in connection with legislation whose validity was never seriously questioned and which Marshall upheld without serious scrutiny: "In this case the court can perceive no such opposition. In the constitution of Georgia, adopted in the year 1789, the court can perceive no restriction on the legislative power, which inhibits the passage of the act of 1795. They cannot say that, in passing that act, the legislature has transcended its powers, and violated the constitution."[54]

52. 10 U.S. (6 Cr.) 87, 128 (1810).
53. Compare this formulation of the doubtful case rule with those made by Justice Chase in *Hylton* v. *United States*, 3 U.S. (3 Dall.) 171, 175 (1796); Justices Chase and Iredell in *Calder* v. *Bull*, 3 U.S. (3 Dall.) 386, 395, 399 (1798); and Justices Washington, Chase, and Paterson in *Cooper* v. *Telfair*, 4 U.S. (4 Dall.) 14, 18, 19 (1800). These period 2 statements are quoted above, chap. 3 at nn. 39–41, 43–45.
54. 10 U.S. (6 Cr.) 87, 128–29 (1810).

The validity of the rescinding act, however, which he did deny, was subjected to much greater analysis, and in this context he made no mention of the doubtful case rule. Its invalidation followed several rather dense pages of discussion including a construction of the contract clause that would be hard to defend as surviving challenge under the doubtful case rule. Johnson's disavowal of the applicability of the contract clause was enough to insulate the legislation from any textual challenge. By existing standards, as applied through the 1790s, the susceptibility of the Constitution to serious conflicting constructions was enough to sustain challenged legislation. Marshall's disassociation of judicial control over legislation from the defense of established principle and its link to an arguable judicial exposition of the constitutional text were begun here in *Fletcher* v. *Peck*, where his action was shielded by the strength of the vested rights challenge to the legislation and was accompanied by a declaration of support for the doubtful case rule as originally understood.

Although *Fletcher* contains no opinion that contrasts with Marshall's use of the rules for statutory interpretation to invalidate legislation on the ground that the law violated the Constitution, such a contrast is provided in Hamilton's pamphlet on the Georgia rescinding act:

> Without pretending to judge of the original merits or demerits of the purchasers, it may be safely said to be a contravention of the first principles of natural justice and social policy, without any judicial decision of facts, by a positive act of the legislature, to revoke a grant of property regularly made for valuable consideration, under legislative authority, to the prejudice even of third persons on every supposition innocent of the alleged fraud or corruption. . . .

> In addition to these general considerations, placing the revocation in a very unfavorable light, the constitution of the United States, article first, section tenth, declares that no state shall pass a law impairing the obligation of contracts. This must be equivalent to saying no state shall pass a law revoking, invalidating, or altering a contract. Every grant from one to another, whether the

grantor be a state or an individual, is virtually a contract that the grantee shall hold and enjoy the thing granted against the grantor, and his representatives. It, therefore, appears to me that taking the terms of the constitution in their large sense, and giving them effect according to the general spirit and policy of the provisions, the revocation of the grant by the act of the legislature of Georgia, may justly be considered as contrary to the constitution of the United States, and, therefore, null. And that the courts of the United States, in cases within their jurisdiction will be likely to pronounce it so.[55]

The similarities between this statement and Marshall's *Fletcher* opinion are as strong as those between Hamilton's and Marshall's defenses of judicial review in *Federalist 78* and *Marbury*. But in both instances apparently minor differences between their respective formulations were of critical importance in the construction of period 3 judicial review. The most important difference in their discussions of the rescinding act was the way Hamilton and Marshall determined that state grants were included within the prohibition of the contract clause. Hamilton fixed the meaning of the Constitution by "taking the terms of the Constitution in their large sense" and by appealing to the "general spirit and policy of the provisions." Marshall concentrated on constitutional words in the same "small" sense used in statutory interpretation and turned to intent to reinforce the meaning derived from the words. Hamilton's statement was not part of a court opinion, and no firm conclusion can be drawn from this single contrast. But an identical and more sharply drawn difference of method is visible between Marshall and his fellow justices in subsequent cases when they fixed the meaning of the Constitution in the course of invalidating legislation.

The next contract clause case was *New Jersey* v. *Wilson*.[56] In 1758

---

55. *Law Practice of Hamilton*, 4:431. Hamilton's original statement, in a letter to William Constable, contained an additional sentence: "But the question being in all its relations entirely new any opinion which can be given must be taken as problematical" (ibid., 430).

56. 11 U.S. (7 Cr.) 164 (1812).

New Jersey had entered into an agreement with some Indian tribes under which the state purchased land for the tribes in exchange for the relinquishment of all other claims. As part of the settlement, the land was exempted from taxation. The Indians eventually left the state after petitioning the legislature to sell their land. Arrangements were made in 1801 through legislation that made no mention of the tax exemption. In 1803 the land was sold and in the following year the tax exemption repealed. Upon assessment of taxes, the purchaser filed suit claiming the land could not be taxed.

New Jersey v. *Wilson* was a section 25 case. Marshall wrote for a unanimous Court and here, as for all his future opinions, there was no reliance on natural law and none of the elliptical language of *Fletcher*. After stating the facts, Marshall quoted the contract clause and cited *Fletcher* as having established that Article I, section 10, extended to contracts to which a state was a party. The question before the Court, consequently, was "narrowed to the inquiry whether in the case stated, a contract existed and whether that contract is violated by the act of 1804."[57] Marshall then reviewed the initial transaction between the Indians and New Jersey and concluded that it contained all the requisites of a contract. In return for the land, with the privilege of exemption, the Indians ceded all other land claims. Although it was not stated explicitly in the original transaction, Marshall held that the tax exemption annexed to the land and not to the persons of the Indians. He continued by indicating that the state could have insisted on a surrender of the exemption as a condition of sale. Having failed to do so, the purchaser succeeded with the assent of the state to all the rights of the Indians and could claim the benefit of their contract. "This contract," Marshall concluded, "is certainly impaired by a law which would annul this essential part of it."[58]

In the absence of concurring or dissenting opinions, *New Jersey* v. *Wilson* does not demonstrate Marshall's innovativeness. This is not the case for the next two contract clause cases, *Terrett* v. *Taylor* and *Dartmouth College* v. *Woodward*. *Terrett* was appealed from the

57. Ibid., 166.
58. Ibid.

District of Columbia Circuit Court and *Dartmouth* was a section 25 case.

Terrett, decided in 1815, invalidated a Virginia statute that had laid claim to property owned by the Episcopal church.[59] Writing for the Court, Justice Joseph Story held that the statute violated both the principles of natural justice and the letter of the Constitution.

Before independence the established church in Virginia owned considerable property. At independence the church was disestablished but its corporate existence and title to existing property were confirmed. In subsequent years the Virginia legislature passed a variety of measures regulating this property. In 1798 and 1801 it repealed the postrevolutionary legislation and asserted a claim to some of the church property.

Justice Story rejected the state's claim in an opinion whose most noteworthy aspects, for our purposes, were its disproportionate reliance on vested rights and natural law, and the fact that it was not written by Marshall. Story argued that regardless of the change in relationship between church and state accompanying the Revolution, the state had no power to divest the church of its property. The statute of 1776 explicitly confirmed the church's title and it acted, Story argued, as a "new grant" vesting "an indefeasible and irrevocable title."[60]

Story agreed that, under some circumstances provided for in common law, government could resume control over the property of private corporations, but he denied that "the legislature can repeal statutes creating private corporations, or confirming to them property already acquired under the faith of previous laws, and by such repeal can vest the property of such corporations exclusively in the state, or dispose of the same to such purposes as they may please, without the consent or default of the corporators." In the key passage of *Terrett* v. *Taylor,* Story continued: "And we think ourselves standing upon the principles of natural justice, upon the fundamental laws of every free government, upon the spirit and the letter of the constitution of the

59. 13 U.S. (9 Cr.) 43 (1815).
60. Ibid., 50.

United States, and upon the decisions of most respectable judicial tribunals, in resisting such a doctrine."[61]

Both *Fletcher* v. *Peck* and *Terrett* v. *Taylor* overturned legislation on the alternate ground of violation of general principle and the U.S. Constitution. Yet the contrast between Marshall's and Story's treatments of principle and of the Constitution could not be more striking. Story's reliance on natural justice is straightforward without any of Marshall's hesitancy. Taken together with all other judicial defenses of first principle, Story's underscores the uniqueness of Marshall's treatment of this point in *Fletcher*. And not only is there nothing in *Terrett* comparable to Marshall's determination of the meaning of the Constitution through exposition of its text, there is not even identification of which letter of the Constitution the Virginia statute violated. It is generally assumed to be the contract clause.[62]

Dartmouth College v. *Woodward*, decided four years after *Terrett*, was a section 25 case.[63] It included concurring opinions by Justices Washington and Story, in addition to Marshall's Court opinion, and provides another instructive contrast between Marshall's practice of judicial review and that of his colleagues.

Dartmouth College was incorporated by the king of England in 1769 after a group of benefactors had raised funds for its operation. After the Revolution New Hampshire assumed the responsibilities previously held by the king, and in 1816 the legislature changed the terms of the corporate charter in an attempt to bring the college under public control. The issue argued in Court was whether the U.S. Constitution imposed a bar to this assumption of state control, and an almost unanimous Court agreed that the contract clause constituted such a bar.[64]

Each of the *Dartmouth* opinions agreed that disposition of the case depended on the answer to two questions: whether the college charter

61. Ibid., 52.

62. *Terrett* v. *Taylor* is cited as a contract clause case in *Piqua Branch Bank* v. *Knoop*, 57 U.S. (16 How.) 369, 389 (1853). See also White, *Marshall Court and Cultural Change*, 609–10.

63. 17 U.S. (4 Wheat.) 518 (1819).

64. Justice Duvall dissented without an opinion.

was a contract within the meaning of the Constitution and, if so, whether the New Hampshire acts impaired the obligations of that charter.[65] Applicability of the contract clause to the charter was challenged on a variety of grounds. One important argument was that the Constitution covered only conventional contracts between individuals and not those establishing public corporations. The Dartmouth College charter, it was claimed, had created such a corporation, one similar to a municipality and like it open to legislative modification. It was also argued that the charter did not have the requisite attributes of a contract. Among the points raised was that there were no parties with vested interests cognizable in court and that no valuable consideration had passed to the king as part of the college's incorporation.

Marshall answered the first point by denying that Dartmouth College was a public corporation. The college, he concluded after examination of its origin and operation, was a private charitable institution devoted to the purposes designated by the founders. These were "the propagation of the christian religion . . . and the dissemination of useful knowledge among the youth of the country." Although New Hampshire benefited from the education of its citizens, "nothing particular or exclusive was intended for her."[66] In answer to the contention that there were no parties with legally cognizable vested interests, Marshall held that the corporation itself had such interests and that these could be asserted by the trustees. He discussed the point about valuable consideration in connection with the attributes of charitable corporations: "The objects for which a corporation is created are . . . universally such as the government wishes to promote. They are deemed beneficial to the country; and this benefit constitutes the consideration, and, in most cases, the sole consideration of the grant."[67]

Marshall's analysis of these and related points covered eighteen

65. See 17 U.S. (4 Wheat.) 518, 627, 656, and 666–67 (1819), for Marshall's, Washington's, and Story's respective formulations of these two questions.

66. 17 U.S. (4 Wheat.) 518, 640 (1819).

67. Ibid., 637.

pages in the *U.S. Reports*. The burden of his argument was that the corporation stood as would a private party in a valid contract. This argument was heavily dependent on the common law of private corporations and of contracts. Marshall acknowledged this dependence with two citations to Blackstone, the only citations in his entire opinion. The first was to Blackstone's discussion of a founder of a private corporation; the second to Blackstone's discussion of an "eleemosynary" corporation. These citations gave the relevant pages in the *Commentaries* but did not quote from Blackstone or summarize his argument.[68]

The implication of this part of Marshall's opinion was that the charter, by its conformity to common law requirements, was the kind of contract included within the constitutional prohibition against laws that impair the obligation of contracts. But Marshall did not make an explicit statement to this effect. On the contrary, in the scantiness of its legal citations the opinion reads as though the issues were being thought through for the first time. More to the point, when Marshall explicitly discussed applicability of the Constitution to the Dartmouth contract, he did so through the same kind of literal analysis of the contract clause text used in *Fletcher* v. *Peck*. As was the case there, it is necessary to reproduce Marshall's discussion to facilitate comparison with the constitutional arguments of other justices:

> This is plainly a contract to which the donors, the trustees, and the crown . . . were the original parties. It is a contract made on a valuable consideration. It is a contract for the security and disposition of property. It is a contract, on the faith of which, real and personal estate has been conveyed to the corporation. It is then a contract within the letter of the constitution, and within its spirit also, unless the fact, that the property is invested by the donors in trustees for the promotion of religion and education, for the benefit of persons who are perpetually changing, though the objects remain the same, shall create a particular exception, taking this case out of the prohibition contained in the constitution.
>
> It is more than possible, that the preservation of rights of this

68. Ibid., 633, 634.

description was not particularly in the view of the framers of the constitution, when the clause under consideration was introduced into that instrument. It is probable, that interferences of more frequent recurrence, to which the temptation was stronger, and of which the mischief was more extensive, constituted the great motive for imposing this restriction on the State legislatures. But although a particular and a rare case may not, in itself, be of sufficient magnitude to induce a rule, yet it must be governed by the rule, when established, unless some plain and strong reason for excluding it can be given. It is not enough to say, that this particular case was not in the mind of the Convention, when the article was framed, nor of the American people, when it was adopted. It is necessary to go farther, and to say that, had this particular case been suggested, the language would have been so varied, as to exclude it, or it would have been made a special exception. The case being within the words of the rule, must be within its operation likewise, unless there be something in the literal construction so obviously absurd, or mischievous, or repugnant to the general spirit of the instrument, as to justify those who expound the constitution in making it an exception.

On what safe and intelligible ground can this exception stand. There is no expression in the constitution, no sentiment delivered by its contemporaneous expounders, which would justify us in making it. In the absence of all authority of this kind, is there, in the nature and reason of the case itself, that which would sustain a construction of the constitution, not warranted by its words?[69]

In 1819 this kind of analysis was visible only in Marshall's opinions. The meaning of the Constitution, for the purposes of judicial review, was still generally thought to be established by its spirit, by the intent of its framers and of the people who adopted it, and by the sentiments of its contemporaneous expounders. Marshall acknowledged the importance of these sources in the very act of insisting on the primacy not only of the words but of their construction in court. Marshall's procedure takes on more significance when the Court opinion is contrasted with the concurring opinions of Justices Story

69. Ibid., 643–45.

and Washington. There were no substantive differences in the three *Dartmouth College* opinions, only one of approach.[70] There was nothing comparable in Story's and Washington's opinions to Marshall's emphasis on the words of the Constitution and their literal construction. For Story and Washington the nature of the Dartmouth College charter and the substantive law of the Constitution were established from sources outside the Constitution: from common law precedent and the doctrine of vested rights.

Story began his opinion with a discussion of the status of the original charter. Determination of its status depended on the substance of English common law: "It will be necessary . . . before we proceed to discuss [the constitutional] questions, to institute an inquiry into the nature, rights, and duties of aggregate corporations at common law; that we may apply the principles, drawn from this source, to the exposition of this charter, which was granted emphatically with reference to that law."[71]

This inquiry covered eleven pages and involved discussion and citation of more than a dozen English precedents. It also included full quotation of Blackstone's definition of a founder of an eleemosynary corporation. The most important case law on the nature of aggregate corporations was *Phillips* v. *Bury*, which established, as Story pointed out, that a corporation founded by private benefactors "is, in point of law, a private corporation, although dedicated by its charter to general charity."[72] Story then devoted five pages to the details of the Dartmouth charter and concluded that it was "a private eleemosynary corporation, endowed with the usual privileges and franchises of such corporations . . . among others, with a legal perpetuity."[73]

After thus establishing the nature of the charter, Story turned to the

70. The one substantive difference between Story's and Marshall's opinions affected future cases and issues, not the disposition of *Dartmouth*. Story emphasized that legislatures could regulate rights legally vested in a corporation if they reserved such power in the original act of incorporation (ibid., 708).

71. Ibid., 667.

72. Ibid., 669–70.

73. Ibid., 681–82.

constitutional issue: whether the charter was a contract contemplated by the contract clause. He cited *Fletcher* v. *Peck* to the effect that a grant of a state was a contract within the meaning of the contract clause. He then examined the various grounds on which the clause's applicability to the "charter or grant" in the present case was challenged. Before replying to the first objection, that the charter was not within the terms of the Constitution "because no valuable consideration passed to the King as an equivalent for the grant," Story said: "The constitution certainly did not mean to create any new obligations. . . . [O]n the other hand . . . the constitution did intend to preserve all the obligatory force of contracts, which they have by the general principles of law."[74] These general principles of law were those in the existing law of contracts. Over the next twenty-five pages Story answered the objection stemming from the alleged absence of valuable consideration as well as the related ones. He covered the same ground covered by Marshall and reached the same conclusions. Unlike Marshall, however, he canvassed and cited relevant English precedents at every point. To have established the substance of the law of contracts was to have brought the charter within constitutional protection. Story's opinion contained no other reference to the contract clause and included no counterpart to Marshall's textual exposition.

After establishing that the contract clause did apply to the Dartmouth College charter, Story inquired in the last five pages whether the New Hampshire legislation had impaired the charter's obligations. He found that it had. This was similar to Marshall's opinion, which devoted the last five pages of a thirty-page opinion to this last inquiry.

It is interesting to note that in his discussion of *Dartmouth* Professor White described Story's opinion as having "devoted forty-two of its forty-seven pages to the vested rights argument" and "his last five pages to an analysis of the Contract Clause argument."[75] This misconstrues Story's opinion and the period 2 understanding of con-

74. Ibid., 683.
75. White, *Marshall Court and Cultural Change*, 619.

stitutionality on which it was based. By today's standards, however, it is easy to miss Story's constitutional argument.

The references to vested rights that White notes and that do exist in Story's opinion were, first, part of the fusion of vested rights principles and contract clause application that lay at the heart of period 3 judicial review. What is anomalous in period 3 judicial review is Marshall's avoidance and minimization of vested rights, not its general prominence. And despite Story's references to vested rights his first forty-two pages *was* contract clause argument. This section of his opinion established the meaning of that provision in the context of the Dartmouth College charter. Whereas Marshall made the identical determination by exposition of the contract clause text, Story did it by establishing the substance of an extratextual referent, specifically the common law of contracts.

White was also misled by some of Story's remarks relative to the jurisdictional issue in Dartmouth, and by the politics connected with the case. *Dartmouth* reached the Supreme Court as a section 25 case after efforts to develop a diversity suit failed to materialize. In such a suit, as White has indicated, direct reliance on vested rights would have been possible. White also suggested that Story had likely drafted an opinion in anticipation of a diversity suit and then used that opinion as a concurrence in the section 25 case.[76] In addition, after invoking vested rights principles at the beginning of his inquiry into whether the challenged legislation did impair the obligations of the charter, Story said: "These principles are so consonant with justice, sound policy, and legal reasoning, that it is difficult to resist the impression of their perfect correctness. The application of them, however, does not, from our limited authority, properly belong to the appellate jurisdiction of this Court in this case."[77] This seems to be an allusion to the Court's limited jurisdiction in section 25 cases. Story then concluded his opinion by answering in the affirmative the case's second question, whether the New Hampshire legislation impaired the college's charter.

76. Ibid., 174–78, 618–19.
77. 17 U.S. (4 Wheat.) 518, 708 (1819).

It is these last five pages that White calls contract clause argument in contrast to the forty-two pages of vested rights argument. But all of Story's opinion, like Marshall's, was contract clause or constitutional analysis. Each devoted the same relative attention to the same two issues: applicability of the contract clause to the charter and determination of whether the New Hampshire legislation impaired the charter's obligations. Each gave the same answers to these questions. Each even structured his argument in the same general way. But Marshall downplayed extratextual references and lavished great attention on constitutional words. Story established the meaning of the Constitution by documenting the substance of extratextual "general principles of law."

Washington's opinion, though not as extensive as Story's, was similar to it in the absence of textual exposition and its dependence on common law. For Washington as for Story, *Phillips* v. *Bury* was the key precedent:

> It has been insisted in the argument at the bar, that Dartmouth College was a mere civil corporation, created for a public purpose, the public being deeply interested in the education of its youth; and that, consequently, the charter was as much under the control of the government of New Hampshire, as if the corporation had concerned the government of a town or city. But it has been shown, that the authorities are all the other way. There is not a case to be found which contradicts the doctrine laid down in the case of Phillips v. Bury, viz. that a college founded by an individual, or individuals, is a private charity, subject to the government and visitation of the founder, and not to the unlimited control of the government.[78]

Washington also gave considerable attention to *Terrett* v. *Taylor* and in the process focused on the vested rights component of *Dartmouth* more sharply even than had Story:

> The case of Terrett v. Taylor fully supports the distinction above stated, between civil and private corporations, and is entirely in

78. Ibid., 665.

point . . . [I]t is denied, that [the legislature] has power to repeal statutes creating private corporations, or confirming to them property already acquired under the faith of previous laws; and that it can, by such repeal, vest the property of such corporations in the State, or dispose of the same to such purposes as it may please, without the consent or default of the corporators. Such a law, it is declared, would be repugnant both to the spirit and the letter of the constitution of the United States.[79]

Story too, it should be noted, cited *Terrett* v. *Taylor* as well as *Fletcher* v. *Peck*. Marshall ignored not only English precedents but American ones as well. He summarized his own argument establishing the applicability of the contract clause to the Dartmouth College charter with the remark: "This opinion appears to us to be equally supported by reason, and by the former decisions of this court."[80]

Two insolvency law cases, *Sturges* v. *Crowninshield* and *Ogden* v.

79. Ibid., 663–64.
80. Ibid., 650. *Green* v. *Biddle*, 21 U.S. (8 Wheat.) 1 (1823), was another contract clause case in which the Court invalidated legislation, but the opinions in this case did not add anything not visible more clearly in other cases. On the separation of Kentucky from Virginia the two states entered into a compact which became part of the Kentucky constitution and which provided, among other things, that "all private rights, and interests of lands within [Kentucky] derived from the laws of Virginia prior to such separation, shall remain valid and secure under the laws of the proposed State, and shall be determined by the laws now existing in [Virginia]." Kentucky subsequently passed a series of measures providing compensation for individuals who occupied land to which they were later adjudged not to have had good title but who had improved the land during their occupancy. Compensation was to have come from the owner. In *Green* v. *Biddle* the U.S. Supreme Court invalidated this Kentucky occupying-claimant legislation. Marshall did not participate in this case. Story and Washington each wrote opinions for the Court in different stages of the litigation. Washington relied on Marshall's opinion in *Fletcher* v. *Peck* to establish that the compact was a contract included within the prohibition of the contract clause, while Story did not address this issue directly. Both concentrated on establishing that the Kentucky legislation violated the rights of the Virginia landowners as established in common law and protected by the compact. Neither engaged in examination of the contract clause text.

Saunders, provided the last major contrast among Marshall Court judges in the practice of judicial review outside the federalism context.[81] In *Sturges,* decided in 1819, the Court invalidated an insolvency law applied to a contract entered into before passage of the law. Marshall wrote for a unanimous Court, but this unanimity masked significant disagreement revealed nine years later by Justice Johnson in *Ogden v. Saunders.* In that case a similar law was applied to a contract entered into after passage of the law, and a Court majority upheld the law over Marshall's dissent. Justice Johnson commented in *Ogden* that "the Court was, in [*Sturges*], greatly divided in their views of the doctrine, and the judgment partakes as much of a compromise, as of a legal adjudication."[82]

Ogden contained four separate opinions written by the majority justices, in addition to Marshall's dissent, and here, in the face of sharp disagreement on the validity of the legislation, different approaches to the practice of judicial review came to the surface in a way not visible before. The contrast between Marshall's Court opinion in *Sturges* and the four majority opinions in *Ogden* constitutes some of the best available evidence of the changes Marshall introduced into prevailing conceptions of constitutional construction for the purposes of judicial review.

In *Sturges* Marshall sought the meaning of the Constitution through examination of the meaning of its words:

> We proceed to the great question on which the cause must depend. Does the law of New York, which is pleaded in this case, impair the obligation of contracts, within the meaning of the constitution of the United States? . . .
>
> In discussing the question whether a state is prohibited from passing such a law as this, our first inquiry is into the meaning of words in common use. What is the obligation of a contract? and what will impair it?[83]

81. *Sturges v. Crowninshield,* 17 U.S. (4 Wheat.) 122 (1819), and *Ogden v. Saunders,* 25 U.S. (12 Wheat.) 213 (1827).

82. 25 U.S. (12 Wheat.) 213, 272–73 (1827).

83. 17 U.S. (4 Wheat.) 122, 197 (1819).

He then defined the words *contract, obligation of contract,* and *impair.* His definitions led him to the conclusion that the law violated the Constitution: "The words of the constitution, then, are express, and incapable of being misunderstood. They admit of no variety of construction, and are acknowledged to apply to that species of contract, an engagement between man and man for the payment of money, which has been entered into by these parties."[84]

Despite this clarity in the meaning of the words, Marshall acknowledged that dispute existed over whether this law did indeed fall within the constitutional prohibition. He continued by recapitulating and refuting a variety of arguments made in support of the law. The first was that "as a contract can only bind a man to pay to the full extent of his property, it is an implied condition that he may be discharged on surrendering the whole of it."[85] Marshall rejected this argument with the observation that an individual's future acquisitions may be used to fulfill the obligation of a contract and that these are contemplated in the original obligation.

Next he turned to the argument from intent. The contract clause, it was argued, was intended to prohibit the widely condemned debtor legislation prevalent under the Articles of Confederation, such as paper money legislation, legislation allowing property payment of debts, and legislation extending the time schedule for the payment of debts. Bankruptcy laws, unlike these kinds of debtor legislation, antedated the Revolution and were widely regarded as necessary and beneficial. Because they were so widespread and so uncontroversial it was unimaginable that an intent to prohibit them would have gone unchallenged during the ratification process, or that such an intent would not have been manifested by a more specific constitutional prohibition.[86]

Marshall readily agreed that bankruptcy laws had a long history and pointed out that states could continue to have them under the Constitution as long as they did not impair the obligation of con-

84. Ibid., 198.
85. Ibid.
86. Ibid., 198–99.

tracts; for example, a law that discharged a bankrupt from imprisonment but did not dissolve the obligation would be permissible. He then turned to the proposition that bankruptcy laws must be constitutional if there was no specific prohibition against them, and in rejecting this argument Marshall came as close as he ever did to relying on constitutional principle and intent. He identified inviolability of contracts as the "principle [the framers] intended to establish" and "to hold sacred" and argued that the contract clause in its "plain, and simple declaration" covered all laws which breached this principle.[87] A more specific prohibition was not only unnecessary but would be too broad, as it would cover laws prohibiting imprisonment for debt.

That the inviolability of contract was the principle animating the contract clause was not subject to dispute. The question remained whether conventional bankruptcy laws did in fact breach the sanctity of contract. The argument in the negative "pressed most earnestly at the bar," Marshall continued, was that

> although all legislative acts which discharge the obligation of a contract without performance, are within the very words of the constitution, yet an insolvent act, containing this principle, is not within its spirit, because such acts have been passed by colonial and state legislatures from the first settlement of the country, and because we know from the history of the times, that the mind of the convention was directed to other laws which were fraudulent in their character, which enabled the debtor to escape from his obligation, and yet hold his property, not to this, which is beneficial in its operation.

Marshall prefaced his reply to this argument by observing:

> Before discussing this argument, it may not be improper to premise that, although the spirit of an instrument, especially of a constitution, is to be respected not less than its letter, yet the spirit is to be collected chiefly from its words.[88]

87. Ibid., 200.
88. Ibid., 202.

This statement, easily overlooked in the middle of a long opinion, is the heart of Marshall's innovation in constitutional interpretation. It is a statement of the applicability to the Constitution of the procedures used in statutory interpretation. For the most part Marshall simply followed these procedures without open discussion. At no time did he acknowledge that only he followed them in the process of determining the constitutionality of legislation. He addressed the issue of constitutional construction directly three times in the course of invalidating legislation. This statement in *Sturges* was the first and least extensive. Eight years later in dissent in *Ogden* v. *Saunders* he said:

> Much, too, has been said concerning the principles of construction which ought to be applied to the constitution of the United States.
>
> On this subject, also, the Court has taken such frequent occasion to declare its opinion, as to make it unnecessary, at least, to enter again into an elaborate discussion of it. To say that the intention of the instrument must prevail; that this intention must be collected from its words; that its words are to be understood in that sense in which they are generally used by those for whom the instrument was intended; that its provisions are neither to be restricted into insignificance, nor extended to objects not comprehended in them, nor contemplated by its framers;—is to repeat what has been already said more at large, and is all that can be necessary.[89]

In *Brown* v. *Maryland*, a federalism case, he made the most orthodox statement of the rules for statutory interpretation and their applicability to the Constitution: "In performing the delicate and important duty of construing clauses in the constitution of our country, which involve conflicting powers of the government of the Union, and of the respective states, it is proper to take a view of the literal meaning of the words to be expounded, of their connection with other words, and

89. 25 U.S. (12 Wheat.) 213, 332 (1827).

of the general objects to be accomplished by the prohibitory clause, or by the grant of power."[90]

After insisting in *Sturges* on the subordination of constitutional spirit to its words, Marshall proceeded to reject his opponents' arguments from intent with a masterful textual analysis. His discussion was similar to, but fuller than, that introduced in *Fletcher* and was comparable to that repeated later that session in *Dartmouth:*

> It would be dangerous in the extreme to infer from extrinsic circumstances, that a case for which the words of an instrument expressly provide, shall be exempted from its operation. Where words conflict with each other, where the different clauses of an instrument bear upon each other, and would be inconsistent unless the natural and common import of words be varied, construction becomes necessary, and a departure from the obvious meaning of the words is justifiable. But if, in any case, the plain meaning of a provision, not contradicted by any other provision in the same instrument, is to be disregarded, because we believe the framers of that instrument could not intend what they say, it must be one in which the absurdity and injustice of applying the provision to the case, would be so monstrous, that all mankind would, without hesitation, unite in rejecting the application.[91]

The rest of Marshall's *Sturges* opinion demonstrated why a literal application of the words would not be absurd and unjust. "Many . . . by far the greater number" of colonial and state insolvency laws were, he pointed out, limited to prohibitions on imprisonment for debt and so were not laws impairing the obligation of contract. Even if this were not the case, however, "it would not justify our varying the construction of the section."[92] The states, he continued, had passed paper money laws and had issued bills of credit, yet both were prohibited by the Constitution. Consequently, the mere existence of

---

90. 25 U.S. (12 Wheat.) 419, 437 (1827).
91. 17 U.S. (4 Wheat.) 122, 202–03 (1819).
92. Ibid., 203.

bankruptcy laws was not enough to establish their exemption from constitutional control.[93]

No "admissible rule of construction," he continued, could justify limiting the reach of the contract clause to the widely condemned postrevolutionary debtor legislation. Such a construction stands refuted by the rest of the words of Article I, section 10: "Let this argument be tried by the words of the section under consideration."[94] The contract clause could not be read to bar paper money because there was a specific bar against bills of credit in the Constitution. Similarly, it could not be read to bar the making of worthless property payment of debts because there was a specific provision barring anything but gold and silver as payment of debts. If the opposing construction were correct, the contract clause would have to refer to laws that changed the schedule for the payment of debts. But such a construction was highly unlikely. No such intent would have been expressed by the words of the contract clause: "No men would so express such an intention. No men would use terms embracing a whole class of laws, for the purpose of designating a single individual of that class. No court can be justified in restricting such comprehensive words to a particular mischief to which no allusion is made."[95]

After so testing the argument from intent by the words of the Constitution, Marshall concluded by linking the particular words of the contract clause to the principle of inviolability of contract:

> The fair, and, we think, the necessary construction of the sentence, requires, that we should give these words their full and obvious meaning. . . . It is probable that [debtor relief laws] produced the loudest complaints, were most immediately felt. The attention of the convention, therefore, was particularly directed to [them]. Had nothing more been intended, nothing more

93. Ibid., 203–04. In this context Marshall denied that the constitutional prohibition on bills of credit was "more express" than the prohibition on laws impairing the obligation of contract. Sanctity of contract, he asserted, was protected "in as appropriate terms as our language affords."

94. Ibid., 204.

95. Ibid., 205.

would have been expressed. But, in the opinion of the convention, much more remained to be done. The same mischief might be effected by other means. To restore public confidence completely, it was necessary not only to prohibit the use of particular means by which it might be effected, but to prohibit the use of any means by which the same mischief might be produced. The convention appears to have intended to establish a great principle, that contracts should be inviolable. The constitution, therefore, declares, that no state shall pass "any law impairing the obligation of contracts."

If, as we think, it must be admitted that this intention might actuate the convention; that it is not only consistent with, but is apparently manifested by, all that part of the section which respects this subject; that the words used are well adapted to the expression of it; that violence would be done to their plain meaning by understanding them in a more limited sense; those rules of construction, which have been consecrated by the wisdom of ages, compel us to say, that these words prohibit the passage of any law discharging a contract without performance.[96]

The rules of construction consecrated by the wisdom of the ages were those developed for and applicable to the enforcement of statutes. Although they were not totally inapplicable to the Constitution, they could claim no comparable longevity as part of the exercise of judicial review. The judicial authority to refuse to enforce an unconstitutional act had been established only during the 1790s, and it was necessary to make a special case for this authority precisely because the Constitution was so universally understood to be outside conventional judicial cognizance. Iredell had succeeded in making the Constitution cognizable in court as a paramount law; Marshall proceeded to treat that paramount law as ordinary law.

The four majority opinions in *Ogden* v. *Saunders* held that a comparable bankruptcy law operating on contracts entered into after passage of such a law did not come within the constitutional prohibition. None disavowed the holding of *Sturges*. As noted above, how-

96. Ibid., 205–06.

ever, Justice Johnson did state that *Sturges* had been a compromise.
The minority in that case, he reported, had concluded that a holding
limited to anterior contracts "could do no harm, but, in fact, imposed
a restriction conceived in the true spirit of the constitution."[97] That
spirit, the majority justices went on to indicate, was the prohibition of
retrospective legislation.

Johnson's comment on *Sturges* revealed much more than the judicial politics surrounding that particular case. It revealed at the same
time the underlying basis for the Marshall Court's entire contract
clause adjudication, and thereby for all period 3 judicial review. As
long as Marshall's exposition of the words of the contract clause and
his colleagues' conception of the true spirit of the Constitution coin-
cided, he could hold the Court together behind his opinions. While
they were enforcing a leading principle of fundamental law or upholding the spirit of the Constitution, he was applying and interpreting the text of the supreme law of the land. *Sturges*, it should be noted,
was a diversity suit but Marshall did not mention the availability of
alternate grounds for the invalidity of legislation or back up his
conclusions with an appeal to general principle condemning retrospective legislation. He was able to write such positive law opinions
long enough and skillfully enough eventually to redirect judicial review from the defense of first principle to the application and interpretation of the constitutional text.

Johnson's comment on *Sturges* also revealed how Marshall weak-
ened the doubtful case rule without attacking it directly. Striking

97. 25 U.S. (12 Wheat.) 213, 273 (1827). White reported that before
Sturges came to the Court it was known from a variety of sources, including
circuit court opinions, that the justices were divided on the constitutionality
of state bankruptcy laws. Division centered on two points: whether the
constitutional grant of power to the national government to establish a
uniform bankruptcy law had preempted state authority in the field, and
whether state bankruptcy acts were prohibited by the contract clause. The
precise compromise alluded to by Johnson in *Ogden*, White concluded, was
"Marshall's concession of a concurrent power in the bankruptcy area in
exchange for unanimous support for the proposition that the Contract Clause
invalidated at least those insolvency laws that affected contracts made prior
to them" (*Marshall Court and Cultural Change*, 634, 636).

down the retrospectively operating bankruptcy law was fulfillment of the "true spirit of the constitution." It could thus hardly be said to violate the doubtful case rule. Yet, without Marshall's insistence on its unconstitutionality there would have been no need for compromise and no invalidation of legislation.

Disagreement in *Ogden* centered on the meaning of the *obligation* of contracts protected by the Constitution. The majority held that the obligation of contract was created by civil law, which could regulate such things as the validity, the construction, the mode of discharge, and the evidence of agreement of contracts. Bankruptcy laws were a legitimate part of this kind of regulation, and as long as they operated prospectively they did not impair the obligation of contracts.[98] Marshall insisted that, although enforced by civil government, contracts had a preexisting intrinsic obligation conferred by the act of the parties. Governmental regulation of the validity and evidence of contracts did not impair the obligation of contracts, unlike laws, such as a bankruptcy act, that discharged the obligation without performance.[99]

For present purposes these differences over the meaning of the contract clause were less important than the contrast between the *Ogden* majority opinions and Marshall's *Sturges* opinion on how these meanings were established. Each of the majority justices in *Ogden* sought the meaning of the contract clause in intent, but none sought to collect that intent from its words. Reliance was placed overwhelmingly on contemporaneous construction, on common usage, and on identification of the leading principles of government sought to be protected by adoption of the specific limits on governmental power. In no case did the majority justices rely on an exposition of the words that was not clearly commanded by an otherwise established intent.

To defend the position that the obligation of contract came from

98. See Justice Washington, 25 U.S. (12 Wheat.) 213, 256–59; Justice Johnson, idem, 281–84; Justice Thompson, idem, 296–302; and Justice Trimble, idem, 318–22.

99. Ibid., 344–50.

municipal law, not natural law, Justice Bushrod Washington drew on the understanding and practice of "all the civilized nations of the world. . . . This law, which accompanies the contract as forming a part of it, is regarded and enforced every where, whether it affect the validity, construction, or discharge of the contract. It is upon this principle of universal law, that the discharge of the contract, or of one of the parties to it, by the bankrupt laws of the country where it was made, operates as a discharge every where."[100]

Justice Johnson's determination of constitutionality drew heavily on intent and contemporaneous construction. He started his *Ogden* opinion by considering and rejecting the contention, also raised in objection to the state bankruptcy law, that the constitutional grant of power to Congress to pass uniform bankruptcy laws was an exclusive grant which stripped the states of all power in this field. In rejecting this contention he argued:

> Let any one turn his eye back to the time when this grant was made, and say if the situation of the people admitted of an abandonment of a power so familiar to the jurisprudence of every State; so universally sustained in its reasonable exercise, by the opinion and practice of mankind, and so vitally important to a people overwhelmed in debt, and urged to enterprise by the activity of mind that is generated by revolutions and free government.
>
> I will with confidence affirm, that the constitution had never been adopted, had it then been imagined that this question would ever have been made. . . .
>
> With regard to the universal understanding of the American people on this subject, there cannot be two opinions. If ever contemporaneous exposition, and the clear understanding of the contracting parties . . . could be resorted to as the means of expounding an instrument, the continuing and unimpaired existence of this power in the States ought never to have been controverted. . . . In every State in the Union was the adoption of the constitution resisted by men of the keenest and most comprehensive minds; and if an argument, such as this, so calculated to

100. Ibid., 259–60.

fasten on the minds of a people, jealous of State rights, and deeply involved in debt, could have been imagined, it never would have escaped them.[101]

In establishing the meaning of the contract clause later in his *Ogden* opinion, Johnson continued his reliance on "the evidence of contemporaneous exposition deducible from well-known facts."

Every candid mind will admit that this is a very different thing from contending that the frequent repetition of wrong will create a right. It proceeds upon the presumption, that the contemporaries of the constitution have claims to our deference on the question of right, because they had the best opportunity of informing themselves of the understanding of the framers of the constitution, and of the sense put upon it by the people when it was adopted by them; and in this point of view it is obvious that . . . the whole history of the times . . . indicates a settled knowledge of the [constitutionality of prospectively operating bankruptcy laws].[102]

Johnson's opinion also contained the most direct criticism of Marshall's literal reading of the Constitution:

It appears to me, that a great part of the difficulties of the cause, arise from not giving sufficient weight to the general intent of this clause in the constitution, and subjecting it to a severe literal construction, which would be better adapted to special pleadings. . . .
If it be objected to the views which I have taken of this subject, that they imply a departure from the direct and literal meaning of terms, in order to substitute an artificial or complicated exposition; my reply is, that the error is on the other side.[103]

Justice Robert Trimble's determination of the "obligation of contract" shows the same reliance on an assessment of general intent and the same absence of textual exposition:

101. Ibid., 276, 277–78.
102. Ibid., 290.
103. Ibid., 286, 290.

The arguments, based on the notion of the obligation of universal law, if adopted, would deprive the States of all power of legislation upon the subject of contracts. . . . I cannot believe that such consequences were intended to be produced by the constitution.

I conclude that . . . it is the civil obligation of contracts; that obligation which is recognized by, and results from, the law of the State in which the contract is made, which is within the meaning of the constitution. . . . The whole frame and theory of the constitution seems to favor this construction.[104]

Although the *Ogden* majority rejected Marshall's literal reading of the contract clause they did not disavow all textual analysis. They used the text, however, to bolster a previously determined intent rather than as a guide to that intent. Great reliance was placed on the fact that the contract clause was placed together with the prohibitions on bills of attainder and ex post facto laws. These provisions, it was argued, were linked by their common subject of prohibiting retrospectively operating legislation. This provided additional evidence that prospectively operating bankruptcy laws were not within the constitutional prohibition.[105]

This prohibition on retrospective legislation contained in the Constitution was, moreover, the constitutional commitment to first principle, anchored in natural rights. The Constitution's explicit prohibition of retrospective legislation gave existing principles added protection; it did not create new legal rights that were to receive their application in particular cases through judicial exposition. As Justice Smith Thompson indicated, the prohibition of neither bills of attainder nor ex post facto laws

can strictly be considered as introducing any new principle, but only for greater security and safety to incorporate into this charter provisions admitted by all to be among the first principles of our government. No State Court would, I presume, sanction and

104. Ibid., 321–22.
105. See ibid., 265–67, 286, 303–05, and 329–31, for the discussions of Justices Washington, Johnson, Thompson, and Trimble, respectively.

enforce an *ex post facto* law; if no such prohibition was contained in the constitution of the United States; so, neither would retrospective laws, taking away vested rights, be enforced. Such laws are repugnant to those fundamental principles, upon which every just system of laws is founded.[106]

This position that the Constitution did not create any new principles but only provided greater security for existing ones was the same one taken by Judge Grimke in *Lindsay* v. *Commissioners* and Story in *Dartmouth College*. It reflected the merger of extratextual fundamental law and positive law that characterized period 2 judicial review and that remained into period 3.

In addition to their reliance on intent and contemporaneous construction of the Constitution, two of the majority justices invoked the doubtful case rule on behalf of the bankruptcy law's constitutionality. None, it should be noted, relied on it as the primary ground for upholding the legislation, because they were generally convinced of the legislation's constitutionality. Nevertheless the very existence of serious controversy brought the legislation within the operation of the rule. Justice Thompson opened his opinion by quoting Marshall's formulation of the doubtful case rule in *Fletcher* v. *Peck* and then added: "If such be the rule by which the examination of this case is to be governed and tried, (and that it is no one can doubt,) I am certainly not prepared to say, that it is not, at least, a doubtful case, or that I feel a clear conviction that the law in question is incompatible with the constitution of the United States."[107]

Justice Washington concluded his *Ogden* opinion with similar remarks:

I shall now conclude ... by repeating ... that the question which I have been examining is involved in difficulty and doubt. But if I could rest my opinion in favor of the constitutionality of the law ... on no other ground than this doubt so felt and acknowledged, that alone would, in my estimation, be a satisfac-

---

106. Ibid., 303–04.
107. Ibid., 294.

tory vindication of it. It is but a decent respect due to the wisdom, the integrity, and the patriotism of the legislative body, by which any law is passed, to presume in favor of its validity, until its violation of the constitution is proved beyond all reasonable doubt. This has always been the language of this Court, when that subject has called for its decision.[108]

Marshall, in contrast, did not mention the doubtful case rule here or in the unanimous *Sturges* opinion, where the difference later revealed by Johnson could have justified its use. On the contrary, Marshall's *Ogden* dissent described the judicial obligation in terms irreconcilable with the doubtful case rule as otherwise stated and used. After noting Court disagreement on the constitutionality of the bankruptcy law, he said:

> This court has so often expressed the sentiments of profound and respectful reverence with which it approaches questions of this character, as to make it unnecessary now to say more than that, if it be right that the power of preserving the constitution from legislative infraction, should reside any where, it cannot be wrong, it must right, that those [upon] whom the delicate and important duty is conferred should perform it according to their best judgment.[109]

It was only in *Fletcher*, in connection with legislation whose constitutionality was not at all doubted, and in *Dartmouth*, where there was no serious disagreement on the unconstitutionality of the challenged legislation, that Marshall made orthodox statements of the doubtful case rule.[110]

---

108. Ibid., 270. Washington continued: "And I know that it expresses the honest sentiments of each and every member of this bench. I am perfectly satisfied that it is entertained by those of them from whom it is the misfortune of the majority of the court to differ on the present occasion, and that they feel no reasonable doubt of the correctness of the conclusion to which their best judgment has conducted them."

109. Ibid., 332.

110. For the statement in *Fletcher* see above, chap. 5 at n. 52. For the statement in *Dartmouth* see 17 U.S. (4 Wheat.) 518, 625 (1819).

Although Marshall's *Ogden* dissent displayed many of the familiar features of his judicial review, it also departed from it in one significant way. He did begin by repeating the admonition of *Sturges* that constitutional "intention must be collected from its words."[111] He did not, however, follow this in *Ogden* with the same severe literal reading of the contract clause visible in his other opinions. After addressing a variety of contentions made in the defense of the legislation, he turned to natural law to help sustain the argument that the obligation of contract came from the act of the parties outside civil government.[112] This was the second and last time Marshall mentioned natural law, after having linked vested rights and the contract clause in *Fletcher*. Had he been able to hold a majority in this case, he undoubtedly would have relied exclusively on textual analysis without mention of natural law. At the end of his *Ogden* opinion he returned to the straightforward literal analysis of the text that characterized his Court opinions.

Craig v. *Missouri* was the last instructive exercise of judicial review by the Marshall Court outside the federalism litigation.[113] Although not one of the contract clause cases, it was similar to them in subject matter. In response to economic depression Missouri had issued certificates acceptable for the payment of taxes and used for the salaries of state employees. They were not introduced in general circulation and were backed by tangible resources, namely, the state's salt deposits.

The certificates were challenged as bills of credit prohibited by the Constitution, and Marshall, writing for a majority of four, invalidated them on this ground. Justices Johnson, Thompson, and McLean dissented, relying heavily on the doubtful case rule. Marshall and the dissenters agreed that if the certificates constituted a paper money emission they were void. The dissenters argued that the certificates could be understood either as paper money or as a state loan. In Johnson's phrase, they were "of a truly amphibious character," and

111. 25 U.S. (12 Wheat.) 213, 332 (1827).
112. Ibid., 344–47.
113. 29 U.S. (4 Pet.) 410 (1830).

the doubtful case rule demanded they be upheld.[114] McLean also explicitly invoked the doubtful case rule,[115] and Justice Thompson's dissent stated that he had "serious doubts" about the unconstitutionality of the certificates.[116]

Both the majority and minority opinions discussed the literal meaning of the term *bills of credit* and the intent of the framers, and both agreed that bills of credit were originally understood to refer to paper money emissions. Marshall, in his characteristic manner, stayed close to the constitutional text in arguing that these certificates came within the prohibition, which reached "the emission of any paper medium." Such a reading was necessary "if the prohibition means any thing, if the words are not empty sounds."[117] He also invoked other provisions of the Constitution, particularly the legal tender clause, to support his holding. If the Constitution prohibited only those emissions labeled legal tender, he argued, there would be no need for both the prohibition of bills of credit and the legal tender clause.[118]

The minority, in contrast, placed greater emphasis on original intent and contemporaneous construction. Johnson urged that the meaning of the clause be derived from "the great end and object of this restriction."[119] McLean concluded that the certificates did not violate "the letter and spirit of the constitution,"[120] and Thompson relied on the "state of things at the adoption of the Constitution."[121] Johnson's conclusion is typical of the minority opinions: "The whole history and legislation of the times prove that, by bills of credit, the framers of the Constitution meant paper money, with reference to that which had been used in the States from the commencement of the century, down to the time when it ceased to pass, before reduced to its innate worthlessness."[122] The dissents concluded that these certifi-

114. Ibid., 443.
115. Ibid., 458.
116. Ibid., 446.
117. Ibid., 432.
118. Ibid., 433.
119. Ibid., 442.
120. Ibid., 457.
121. Ibid., 448.
122. Ibid., 442.

cates were sufficiently different from the kind of paper money known to the founders to bring them within the doubtful case rule. That they might fit within the literal scope of the words was immaterial. Marshall, in *Craig,* ignored the doubtful case rule.

The Supremacy Clause Cases

Judicial invalidation of legislation raising issues of federalism stood on different grounds from that involving state authority under particular provisions of the Constitution. The supremacy clause made the Supreme Court arbiter of federal-state relations. As was the case in ordinary law, judges were society's appointed arbiters assigned to resolve designated conflict. Just as they could not resolve conflict over ordinary law without expounding that law, so they could not resolve conflicts over federalism without fixing the meaning of the Constitution. It should thus not be surprising to discover that there was never any mention of the doubtful case rule in federalism cases. The absence of preexisting agreement on the content of the constitutional division of power between the nation and the states also forced judges into more active determination of the meaning of the Constitution than otherwise had been the case.

Whether for these or other reasons the federalism cases generated less overt division on the Court than did the contract clause cases. There are only two opinions by judges other than Marshall in federalism cases overturning legislation—Johnson's concurrence in *Gibbons* v. *Ogden* and Thompson's dissent in *Brown* v. *Maryland.*[123] Both, however, reflected the same differences in approach to determination of constitutionality visible in the contract clause cases. Marshall focused first on the definition of words and the words in context, and moved from these to the objects or purposes of the Constitution. For his colleagues the objects or intent of the provision furnished the primary source of constitutional meaning.

Gibbons v. *Ogden* was the leading commerce clause case of the Marshall Court, and *Brown* v. *Maryland* involved construction of the

123. *Gibbons* v. *Ogden,* 22 U.S. (9 Wheat.) 1, 222 (1824); *Brown* v. *Maryland,* 25 U.S. (12 Wheat.) 419, 449 (1827).

constitutional prohibition on state taxation of imports, as well as of the commerce clause. *Gibbons* resolved a dispute stemming from a New York State monopoly on steamboat navigation within its waters, granted to Robert Fulton and his heirs. A state court had enjoined Gibbons, a nationally licensed ferryboat operator, from operating his ferry within New York, and Gibbons challenged this exclusion in the United States Supreme Court. *Brown* challenged the constitutionality of a state license fee imposed on wholesale importers.

Marshall wrote for the Court in both cases and in each held that the state action was unconstitutional. He started each opinion with a general statement on the proper method of constitutional analysis. In *Gibbons* Marshall said:

> As men, whose intentions require no concealment, generally employ words which most directly and aptly express the ideas they intend to convey, the enlightened patriots who framed our constitution, and the people who adopted it, must be understood to have employed words in their natural sense, and to have intended what they have said. If, from the imperfection of human language, there should be serious doubts respecting the extent of any given power, it is a well settled rule, that the objects for which it was given, especially, when those objects are expressed in the instrument itself, should have great influence in the construction. . . . We know of no rule for construing the extent of such powers, other than is given by the language of the instrument which confers them, taken in connection with the purposes for which they were conferred.[124]

In *Brown* he made his most complete statement of the applicability to the Constitution of the rules for statutory interpretation.[125]

Marshall started his discussion of the commerce clause in *Gibbons* by observing: "The words are, 'Congress shall have power to regulate commerce with foreign nations, and among the several states, and with the Indian tribes.' The subject to be regulated is commerce;

124. *Gibbons* v. *Ogden*, 22 U.S. (9 Wheat.) 1, 188–89 (1824).
125. *Brown* v. *Maryland*, 25 U.S. (12 Wheat.) 419, 437 (1827). Quoted above, chap. 5 at n. 90.

and . . . to ascertain the extent of the power, it becomes necessary to settle the meaning of the word."[126] He followed this with several pages devoted to the meaning of commerce and concluded that it could not be limited to traffic, or buying and selling. "Commerce . . . is intercourse" and included navigation.[127]

Having included Gibbons' activity under national authority, he turned to the central issue, the scope of that authority. There were at the time three contending interpretations of the reach of national power over commerce. One held that national power was dormant and barred all state regulation even in the absence of national regulation. The second held that it was a concurrent power whereby both state and nation could regulate the same subject. The third held that the commerce power was mutually exclusive, with both the states and the nation retaining the right to regulate some commercial activity. Marshall never resolved this issue. In *Gibbons* he rejected the concurrent power view and refused to commit himself on dormant power, arguing that there was no need to do so as Congress had acted in this case.[128]

Marshall's main discussion of the reach of the commerce clause was not couched in these terms but was made through analysis of the meaning of *among:*

> The subject to which the power is next applied, is to commerce, "among the several states." The word "among" means intermingled with. . . . Commerce among the states, cannot stop at the external boundary line of each state, but may be introduced into the interior.
>
> It is not intended to say, that these words comprehend that commerce, which is completely internal, which is carried on between man and man in a state, or between different parts of the same state, and which does not extend to or affect other states. Such a power would be inconvenient, and is certainly unnecessary.

126. 22 U.S. (9 Wheat.) 1, 189 (1824).
127. Ibid., 189–92.
128. Ibid., 197–200 (1824).

Comprehensive as the word "among" is, it may very properly be restricted to that commerce which concerns more states than one. . . . The genius and character of the whole government seem to be, that its action is to be applied to all the external concerns of the nation, and to those internal concerns which affect the states generally; but not to those which are completely within a particular state, which do not affect other states, and with which it is not necessary to interfere, for the purpose of executing some of the general powers of the government.[129]

It is clear from the entire historical record that Marshall supported a broad reading of national power and, probably, the dormant power view of the commerce clause. He was, however, also sensitive to the fact that this was not the dominant view in the country, and a decision to this effect would likely encounter strong opposition. His *Gibbons* opinion upheld national power in this case, rejected the narrowest reading of the commerce clause, and laid the basis for expanded national authority in the future.

He did this, moreover, through a lawyer-like discussion of the meaning of a word. Through the exposition of *among* Marshall mollified opponents of a strong national government by denying that national commerce power reached "completely internal" commerce. At the same time, he introduced national power into the "interior" of "each state" by attaching it to "that commerce which concerns more states than one" and which "affect[s] the states generally." In the reach of its implications Marshall's discussion of *among* is the high point of his textual exposition of the Constitution.

As usual the full significance of Marshall's opinion lies in its contrast to that of other justices. Johnson's concurrence defended the dormant power view of the commerce clause, and it did so with the same avoidance of textual exposition seen in the contract clause cases and the same reliance on intent. Johnson started by denying the need for extensive textual construction of the Constitution:

In attempts to construe the constitution, I have never found much benefit resulting from the inquiry, whether the whole, or

129. Ibid., 194–95.

any part of it, is to be construed strictly, or literally. The simple, classical, precise, yet comprehensive language in which it is couched, leaves, at most, but very little latitude for construction; and when its intent and meaning is discovered, nothing remains but to execute the will of those who made it, in the best manner to effect the purposes intended.[130]

From here he moved to a statement of constitutional purpose couched in exceedingly broad terms:

The great and paramount purpose, was to unite this mass of wealth and power, for the protection of the humblest individual; his rights, civil and political, his interests and prosperity, are the sole *end;* the rest are nothing but the *means*. But the principal of those means, one so essential as to approach nearer the characteristics of an end, was the independence and harmony of the states, that they may the better subserve the purposes of cherishing and protecting the respective families of this great republic.[131]

Johnson then turned to the history of the Confederation and the movement to replace the Articles of Confederation. Dissatisfaction with the conditions of commercial life, he argued, was the chief source of unhappiness under the articles, and by universal agreement the unsatisfactory conditions were to be remedied by giving the national government exclusive power over commerce:

The history of the times will, therefore, sustain the opinion, that the grant of power over commerce, if intended to be commensurate with the evils existing, and the purpose of remedying those evils, could be only commensurate with the power of the states over the subject. And this opinion is supported by a very remarkable evidence of the general understanding of the whole American people, when the grant was made.

There was not a state in the Union, in which there did not, at that time, exist a variety of commercial regulations; concerning which it is too much to suppose, that the whole ground covered

130. Ibid., 223.
131. Ibid. Emphasis in original.

by those regulations was immediately assumed by actual legislation, under the authority of the Union. But where was the existing statute on this subject, that a state attempted to execute? or by what state was it ever thought necessary to repeal those statutes? By common consent, those laws dropped lifeless from their statute books, for want of the sustaining power, that had been relinquished to congress.[132]

It was only after Johnson established the meaning of the commerce clause by drawing on the "history of the times," "the general understanding of the whole American people," and "common consent" that he turned to the constitutional text:

> And the plain and direct import of the words of the grant, is consistent with this general understanding.
>
> The words of the constitution are, "Congress shall have power to regulate commerce with foreign nations, and among the several states, and with the Indian tribes."
>
> It is not material, in my view of the subject, to inquire whether the article *a* or *the* should be prefixed to the word "power." Either, or neither, will produce the same result: if either, it is clear, that the article *the* would be the proper one, since the next preceding grant of power is certainly exclusive, to wit, "to borrow money on the credit of the United States." But mere verbal criticism I reject.
>
> My opinion is founded on the application of the words of the grant to the subject of it.[133]

Johnson not only reversed Marshall's order, subordinating constitutional words to intent or general understanding, but ridiculed what he obviously regarded as an inappropriate verbal quibbling.

The contrast between Marshall's and Thompson's opinions in *Brown* v. *Maryland* is not as striking as that between Johnson's and Marshall's in *Gibbons*, but it does reveal the same kind of differences. Marshall, writing for the Court, held that a Maryland license fee on

132. Ibid., 225–26.
133. Ibid., 226–27. Emphasis in original.

wholesale importers violated the prohibition on state taxation of imports and the commerce clause. He devoted most of his opinion to the clause prohibiting states from laying imposts and duties on imports. After repeating the applicability to the Constitution of the rules for statutory interpretation, Marshall asked, "What, then, is the meaning of the words, imposts, or duties on imports or exports?" He defined imposts and imports, appealing to "the lexicons" and to usage.[134] He continued by discussing the exception to the constitutional prohibition for "what may be absolutely necessary for executing [state] inspection laws."[135] The conclusions drawn from the existence of this exception reinforced the conclusions drawn from the initial definitions—the constitutional prohibition reached things imported and was applicable after goods had entered the country. The Maryland tax, operating on such imported goods in possession of the importer, was thus within the constitutional prohibition.[136] At the end of this discussion he defended application to the Constitution of the rule of interpretation governing exceptions to general words: "If it be a rule of interpretation to which all assent, that the exception of a particular thing from general words, proves that, in the opinion of the lawgiver, the thing excepted would be within the general clause had the exception not been made, we know no reason why this general rule should not be as applicable to the constitution as to other instruments."[137]

After so fixing the meaning of the Constitution, Marshall turned from "this narrow view of the subject" and "the literal interpretation of the words" to the "objects of the prohibition."[138] For a variety of reasons, including equality and harmony among the states, better commercial relations with foreign nations, and enhancement of national revenue, it was agreed by "the general opinion" that "the interest of all would be best promoted by placing [the] whole subject

---

134. *Brown v. Maryland*, 25 U.S. (12 Wheat.) 419, 437 (1827).
135. U.S. Constitution, Article I, section 10.
136. *Brown v. Maryland*, 25 U.S. (12 Wheat.) 419, 437–38 (1827).
137. Ibid., 438.
138. Ibid.

of [imports and exports] under the control of Congress.[139] Marshall's analysis of the objects of the prohibition led to the same conclusion drawn from the definition of the words. "It has already been shown," he concluded, "that a tax on the article in the hands of the importer, is within [the constitution's] words; and we think it too clear for controversy, that the same tax is within its mischief."[140]

Marshall's discussion of the commerce clause in *Brown* did not duplicate the textual analysis made in *Gibbons*, but it did draw on the propositions established in that case. It opened with a discussion of constitutional purpose rather than text and canvassed the depressed state of American commerce under the articles and the inability of the central government to remedy it. The grant of power over commerce was, he asserted, to be "as extensive as the mischief." In giving concrete expression to the extent of the grant he relied on *Gibbons*, which "declared [the commerce power] to be complete in itself, and to acknowledge no limitations other than are prescribed by the constitution. The power is coextensive with the subject on which it acts, and cannot be stopped at the external boundary of a state, but must enter its interior."[141] The power to enter the interior, in the context of *Brown*, included national authorization not only of the right to import goods into a state but also to sell them.[142]

Thompson's dissent began with the challenge to the Maryland act from the commerce clause. He pointed out first that national power was the surrender of power originally possessed by the states. The precise scope of national power was to be determined by a "fair and reasonable interpretation with reference to the object for which the surrender was made." This object, he continued, was "principally with a view to the revenue."[143] Citing *Gibbons*, Thompson then indicated that national power over commerce was confined to the external commerce of the United States. This, he argued, ended with the "importation of the foreign article." The Maryland license tax on

139. Ibid., 439.
140. Ibid., 440.
141. Ibid., 446.
142. Ibid., 446–47.
143. Ibid., 452.

wholesale domestic transactions touched internal commerce and was thus not covered by the commerce clause.[144]

Thompson then turned to the Constitution's prohibition on state taxation of imports and examined the contention that importing included the right of sale. He argued that the exemption of imported goods from all state taxes was an obviously untenable interpretation of the Constitution and that limitation of the exemption to the first sale, as argued in *Brown,* would not bear scrutiny. There was nothing in the letter of the Constitution to support such a conclusion, "nor does it fall within any reasonable intendment growing out of the nature of the subject-matter of the provision." That "intendment," again, was "to take from the states the power of imposing burdens upon foreign merchandise, that might tend to lessen or entirely prevent the importation, and thereby diminish the revenue of the United States."[145] Much of the rest of the opinion was devoted to showing that this object would not be served by limitation of the exemption to the first sale. In the course of his discussion he examined the meaning of the terms *impost* and *duty,* although this was not as extensive or prominent as Marshall's textual and definitional analysis.

"It Is a Constitution We Are Expounding"

Next to *Marbury* the most prominent of Marshall's opinions was *McCulloch* v. *Maryland.*[146] *McCulloch* was a federalism case in which the Court sustained the major piece of legislation under review. It thus involved neither of the most contentious aspects of American judicial review: the invalidation of legislation or this issue, outside the context of federalism. *McCulloch* was also a unanimous decision and so did not contain a specific contrast between Marshall's and other justices approaches to the Constitution. But it is one of Marshall's major opinions, moreover one that differed in important ways from his others.

144. Ibid., 452–53.
145. Ibid., 454, 455.
146. 17 U.S. (4 Wheat.) 316 (1819).

McCulloch reviewed the constitutionality of the national bank established by Congress and of a state tax on a bank branch. The central issue was whether Congress had authority under the necessary and proper clause to charter a bank. Marshall held that it did, but in reaching this conclusion he drew more on the objects or intent of the Constitution than on definitional and textual analysis. At the same time, opponents of the bank's constitutionality relied heavily on such analysis.

In *McCulloch,* Marshall also uncharacteristically called attention to the differences between a constitution and ordinary law. In one of the most quoted passages in American constitutional law he reminded his readers, "We must never forget that it is *a constitution* we are expounding."[147] By so arguing against treating the Constitution in terms devised for ordinary law and by relying in *McCulloch* on the objects or intent of the Constitution to establish the constitutionality of the bank, Marshall seemed to contradict the thrust of the analysis presented here.

McCulloch clearly did depart from Marshall's rule that the Constitution's intent is to be gathered from its words. Perhaps he followed this course because he thought that the necessary and proper clause text, by itself, could not sustain the substantive analysis he wanted to make. That his opponents relied heavily on a textual and definitional analysis may also have turned him away from it. Nevertheless, despite this departure from his usual approach, *McCulloch* did not undermine Marshall's larger effort.

For one thing, although Marshall's *McCulloch* opinion emphasized constitutional objects more than his other opinions usually did, it established these objects from the nature of the Constitution[148] and not, as had Johnson in *Gibbons,* from external sources such as the "history of the times" or "contemporaneous construction." Nor did Marshall abandon definitions or textual analysis altogether. He gave his own definition of *necessary,* showed why the contending one was wrong, and reinforced his reading by comparing use of the word

147. Ibid., 407. Emphasis in original.
148. Ibid., 405–18, 421–23.

necessary in the clause under consideration with that in the provision barring state taxes on imports "except what may be *absolutely* necessary for executing [state] inspection laws."[149]

Next, Marshall's insistence on expounding the Constitution differently from statutes, rather than contradicting his general approach to constitutional law, assumed the very point in contention between his own and period 2 judicial review, namely, judicial authority to expound the Constitution in the first place. It was precisely because a Constitution was not thought amenable to authoritative judicial exposition that period 2 judicial review sought its meaning in sources external to the text. To remind his readers that it is a constitution we are expounding was to assume judicial authority for such exposition and to reduce the differences between the Constitution and ordinary law to those of degree rather than kind. Such a difference in degree, as invoked by Marshall, remains to this day in the legalized modern judicial review with which we are familiar. The Constitution is universally acknowledged to be more general than statutes and to be open to adaptation to meet future unknowable needs. But it remains subject to authoritative *judicial* exposition, and that is the main difference between period 2 and 3 judicial review.

Because *McCulloch* is a supremacy clause case, neither Marshall's open assertion of judicial authority to expound the Constitution nor his opponents' textual analysis is as significant as it otherwise would be. As we have seen, the judiciary's assigned responsibility as arbiter of conflict over federalism made constitutional exposition unavoidable. It is testimony to the force of the original distinctions that even in this context Johnson, in *Gibbons*, relied on common consent and constitutional objects to establish the meaning of the Constitution.

Thayer's comment on *McCulloch* in "The Origin and Scope of the American Doctrine of Constitutional Law" is also of interest in this regard. Thayer's main aim was to revive the doubtful case rule for judicial invalidation of legislation. But in this article he also suggested that, in sustaining legislation, judges are to be understood not as declaring acts to be constitutional but rather as declaring them "not

149. Ibid., 413–15, 418–19. Emphasis added in original.

unconstitutional." He conceded that, in *McCulloch,* Marshall did not "in fact put the matter" this way, but Thayer maintained nevertheless that this was the proper course.[150]

Both the doubtful case rule for determinations of unconstitutionality and the "not unconstitutional" standard for sustaining legislation tapped ineradicable differences in kind that originally and clearly separated fundamental law from ordinary law. Thayer's position echoed the period 2 understanding without recognizing that it had already been decisively transformed. Thus, neither the doubtful case rule nor the "not unconstitutional" standard is coherent or internally consistent for modern judicial review. Thayer's call for a return to the doubtful case rule has proved to be unworkable and unpersuasive.[151] So, too, his observation that in *McCulloch* Marshall should have confined himself to a declaration that the law in question was "not unconstitutional" missed the key element in the construction of period 3 judicial review: the unacknowledged assumption by the judiciary of authority to expound fundamental law.

The Supreme Law of the Land

The differences between Marshall and his colleagues in determinations of constitutionality were not random ones, nor was modern judicial review the product of an undirected evolutionary process. Both followed from Marshall's deliberate design, one that transformed fundamental law into the supreme law of the land, subject on that ground to authoritative judicial rather than public or legislative exposition. This change, furthermore, was carried out with no public acknowledgment or discussion. The deliberateness of Marshall's design, as well as its public concealment, is visible, but only by hindsight, in *Marbury* v. *Madison,* in Marshall's portentous transformation of Tucker's argument made in *Kamper* v. *Hawkins.* What had been in *Kamper* a claim of judicial authority to "regard" the Constitution in order to make a just exposition of the ordinary law became, in

150. "Doctrine of Constitutional Law," 151.

151. This point will be more fully discussed below, chap. 6 at nn. 40–48.

Marbury, the suggestion of a judicial authority to say what the law of the Constitution is. This suggestion lay dormant and did not become the operative reading of *Marbury* until Marshall had applied and interpreted the Constitution and had gained public acceptance for such interpretation. Likewise, the period 3 willingness to invalidate legislation as contrary to general principles or the spirit of the Constitution and the absence of any textual exposition in opinions written by Marshall's colleagues indicate that, despite *Marbury*'s liberal references to the written constitution, the significance of that commitment to writing was not yet that attributed to it today. I shall show in the next chapter that the modern reading of *Marbury* did not emerge until some time near the end of the nineteenth century.

Marshall transformed fundamental law by taking existing raw materials and, with consummate skill, redirecting them to other purposes. By the time he came to the Court judicial refusal to enforce an unconstitutional act was well established and beyond controversy. Nor was judicial exposition of the constitutional text Marshall's invention, foisted on a compliant Court. Precedents for both existed, but what was unprecedented was the simultaneous exposition of the constitutional text and the invalidation of legislation supported by a plausible legislative construction to the contrary. In linking the two, Marshall asserted a judicial claim to be authoritative expounder of the Constitution in the same way the judiciary functions with respect to ordinary law.

Marshall applied not only the rules of statutory interpretation to the Constitution but, in the process, the logic of the lawyer and the form of the legal argument. In insisting on the primacy of the meaning of words, he established constitutional violations through a process of analytic reasoning. His colleagues, in contrast, still sought the substance of the Constitution directly through identification of its spirit, intent, or a few established principles outside the text. For them identification of a constitutional violation, even when made by the judiciary, was more a public or political act than an essentially judicial one.

Marshall's willingness and capacity to push constitutional law beyond the strict limits of the doubtful case rule comprised the last indispensable element in the legalization of fundamental law. Without this, judicial invalidation of legislation would not likely have proceeded at all. If it had, it would have been a fitful, sporadic activity reserved for the clearest invasions of vested rights. Invalidation of legislation that could be plausibly defended, as in *Dartmouth* and *Sturges*, stripped judicial enforcement of the Constitution of its extraordinary character and revolutionary potential and made it an ongoing phenomenon as routine and unexceptional as ordinary law enforcement. This last change was facilitated by the disappearance of period 1 fears of legislative willfulness and the general political stability accompanying period 3 judicial review.

Although Marshall's innovations were critical for the development of modern judicial review, it is unlikely that he could have succeeded without a favorable environment. The American commitment to limited government, as inherited from England, was the first component of this environment. The second was the agreement, evident from independence, on the end of legislative omnipotence and the invalidity of an unconstitutional act. The last was the period 2 debate that quieted opposition to judicial authority over unconstitutional acts. Marshall, over a thirty-year period, gave unconstitutionality a conventional legal identity. After engineering a near monopoly on opinion writing in long, detailed, masterful, and meticulous opinions, he treated the Constitution as though it were supreme ordinary law. Shielded by the overlap between the principle of vested rights and his own reading of the contract clause and by the judicial responsibility as arbiter of federalism, Marshall habituated the bench, the bar, and the public to the judicial application and interpretation of the constitutional text. The more Marshall framed his discussion in these terms, the more he invited litigants to do so and forced other judges to meet him on this ground. At the same time, the Constitution's success in ending preoccupation with concededly unconstitutional acts, and the seeming triviality of the difference between explicit social contracts or constitutions and supreme written law, obscured the nature and magnitude of Marshall's innovations from his own and future generations.

In Marshall's time, as now, the country was highly receptive to this judicial guardianship of the Constitution. But modern judicial review still could not have developed without the specific steps Marshall initiated. If seriatim opinion writing had prevailed and if the only precedents for the judicial refusal to enforce an unconstitutional act were those of *Bayard* v. *Singleton, VanHorne's Lessee* v. *Dorrance,* Johnson's opinion in *Fletcher* v. *Peck,* and Story's in *Terrett* v. *Taylor* and *Dartmouth College,* it is hard to see how modern judicial review could ever have come into being. The modern legalized practice depended on subordination of constitutional spirit and the general principles of free government to constitutional text, and that is nowhere to be found except in Marshall's opinions. Without this, even with *Marbury,* it is impossible to imagine how the Constitution could ever have come to be included within that kind of law for which it is the province and duty of the judicial department to say what the law is.

The Province and Duty
of the Judicial Department

THE MODERN READING of *Marbury* arose to accommodate the judicial review that evolved with acceptance of Marshall's innovations.[1] It was not the reading initially given to *Marbury* and I cannot say precisely when it emerged. By the 1830s it had not yet appeared, but by Thayer's time at the end of the century its key components were substantially in place.

The late emergence of the modern reading of *Marbury* is evident from its absence in three leading early nineteenth-century discussions of judicial review, those of Gibson,[2] de Tocqueville,[3] and Madison.[4] All three confirm that by the 1820s a form of modern judicial review was already entrenched and widely accepted. Their discussions also indicate that it was a transitional form, no longer that of period 2 but not yet the mature modern practice. Its most salient period 2 feature was its confinement to defense of the principle of vested rights.[5] Its

---

1. For statements of this modern reading see *Cooper* v. *Aaron*, 358 U.S. 1, 18 (1958), and *United States* v. *Nixon*, 418 U.S. 683, 703 (1974), quoted and discussed below, chap. 7 at nn. 1–2. In a reflection of the basic controversy over judicial review, these statements themselves are the subject of controversy. Nevertheless, they articulate the only basis for the power that courts exercise over legislation.

2. *Eakin* v. *Raub*, 12 Sergeant & Rawles (Pa.) 330, 344 (1825). Dissenting opinion.

3. Alexis de Tocqueville, *Democracy in America*, trans. George Lawrence (New York: Harper & Row, 1966; reprint ed., Garden City, N.Y.: Doubleday, 1969), 99–104.

4. Madison to ?, *Letters and Other Writings*, 4:349–50.

5. See Corwin, "Basic Doctrine," 258–76, for a discussion of judicial review in the state courts during the first half of the nineteenth century and its confinement to defense of the principle of vested rights.

most important departures from that practice were its disassociation from the concededly unconstitutional act and its association with authoritative judicial exposition of the Constitution. Judicial review at this time was also linked to a written constitution. But the meaning of that written constitution was neither the period 2 one of explicit fundamental law nor the modern conception of supreme ordinary law.

Gibson's opinion in *Eakin v. Raub* was the first and fullest of these assessments. Gibson's arguments are totally intelligible today, and some of his points have been incorporated in modern criticisms of *Marbury*. Yet there is also a certain indirectness in the presentation of his argument that is a reflection of the transitional status of mid-1820s judicial review and the fact that Gibson was not addressing directly either the pure period 2 or modern position. We have already examined important parts of Gibson's lengthy opinion. As we saw in his ridicule of *VanHorne's Lessee*, by 1825 the idea that judicial review was protection against acts such as denial of the franchise or of religious freedom was no longer intelligible.[6] Nor was it meaningful as a substitute for revolution, although Gibson did not deny that under the circumstances described by Paterson a judge could "as a citizen . . . throw himself into the breach" and defend the Constitution with "habeas corpus and mandamus."[7] By 1825 judicial review was operating as part of everyday checks and balances. The claim, as Gibson stated it in *Eakin v. Raub*, was that the judiciary was "*a peculiar organ*, under the constitution, to prevent legislative encroachment on the powers preserved by the people."[8] The burden of Gibson's reply was that such a claim was insupportable.

Gibson rejected routine judicial control over legislation as the illegitimate assumption of political power by the judiciary. He defined political power as that "by which one organ of the government is enabled to control another, or to exert an influence over its acts."[9]

6. See above, chap. 3 at nn. 68–69.
7. *Eakin v. Raub*, 12 Sergeant & Rawles (Pa.) 330, 356 (1825).
8. Ibid. Emphasis in original.
9. Ibid., 346.

Supervision of the division of power between nation and state was such a political power, but it was explicitly granted to the courts in the supremacy clause.[10] This power, like any political power exercised by the judiciary, was "*extraordinary* and *adventitious*," in contrast to the judiciary's civil power, "its *ordinary* and *appropriate* powers." The judiciary's civil power was defined in common law, as was the power of all the branches. It was "commensurate only with the judicial execution of the municipal law, or . . . the administration of distributive justice, without extending to anything of a political cast whatever."[11] It was, that is, confined to enforcement of ordinary law. Any modification of this power required specific positive authorization in the Constitution.

Gibson proceeded by raising and rejecting a variety of contentions used to support a judicial check on legislation. He stated the first point as follows:

> Nor can [support for judicial review be established] by saying, that in *England*, the constitution, resting in principles consecrated by time, and not in an actual written compact, and being subject to alteration by the very act of the legislature, there is consequently no separate and distinct criterion by which the question of constitutionality may be determined; for it does not follow, that because we have such a criterion, the application of it belongs to the judiciary. I take it, therefore, that the power in question does not necessarily arise from the judiciary being established by a written constitution, but that this organ can claim, on account of that circumstance, no powers that do not belong to it at the common law.[12]

In period 2 an "actual written compact" and a "separate and distinct criterion" of constitutionality marked the existence of explicit fundamental law, which countered the claim that the Constitution was a rule to the legislature only and supported a judicial right to "consider" or "regard" the Constitution as part of an equality of the

10. Ibid., 356–57.
11. Ibid., 346, 347. Emphasis in original.
12. Ibid., 347. Emphasis in original.

branches under explicit fundamental law. This right did not reach to application of the Constitution. Under the modern understanding an actual written compact came to mean supreme written law, which, like any other law, was routinely subject to judicial application or exposition.

Gibson, however, did not address himself directly to either the period 2 or the modern position. His remarks indicate that by 1825 the legislative supremacy of period 1 that had denied all judicial authority to regard or consider the Constitution had been so completely rejected that Gibson no longer had access to the importance of insisting on such authority. Iredell's successful argument and the continuing practice of judicial review had muted all challenge to the Constitution's cognizability in court. By the 1820s the issue had indeed become judicial application of the Constitution. But Gibson did not link this application to the modern idea that by virtue of its commitment to writing, the Constitution had taken on the status of supreme ordinary law. In 1825 the written constitution still retained important elements of explicit fundamental law. It was still a "separate and distinct criterion" of constitutionality. And Gibson rejected judicial application of the Constitution by simply denying that the existence of a separate criterion of constitutionality justified judicial application of fundamental law.

Gibson turned next to the assertion that the judiciary's political power could be established by implication: "The constitution is said to be a law of superior obligation."[13] This proposition was part of both period 2 and modern judicial review. In period 2, however, the law of superior obligation was also different in kind from ordinary law and subject to judicial enforcement only in the extraordinary case of undoubted violation. Subsequently the Constitution and ordinary law became the same kind of law, and the Constitution's superior obligation led to a relatively uncomplicated application of principles governing the conflict of laws. Again, Gibson's discussion indicates that in 1825 this transformation had not yet taken place. In answering the claim drawn from the Constitution's status as a law of superior

13. Ibid.

obligation, Gibson simply repeated the period 2 distinctions and reasserted the differences in kind between fundamental law and ordinary law under which the former remained of superior obligation without being subject to judicial exposition:

> What is a constitution? It is an act of extraordinary legislation, by which the people establish the structure and mechanism of their government; and in which they prescribe fundamental rules to regulate the motion of the several parts. What is a statute? It is an act of ordinary legislation, by the appropriate organ of the government; the provisions of which are to be executed by the executive or judiciary, or by officers subordinate to them. The constitution, then, contains no practical rules for the administration of *distributive justice*, with which alone the judiciary has to do . . . and it is generally true, that the provisions of a constitution are to be carried into effect immediately by the legislature, and only mediately, if at all, by the judiciary. . . .
>
> The constitution and the *right* of the legislature to pass an act, may be in collision; but is that a legitimate subject for judicial determination? . . . It is the business of the judiciary, to interpret the laws, not scan the authority of the lawgiver; and without the latter, it cannot take cognizance of a collision between a law and the constitution. So that, to affirm that the judiciary has a right to judge of the existence of such collision, is to take for granted the very thing to be proved.[14]

Gibson's canvass of the arguments in support of judicial review continued: "But it has been said to be emphatically the business of the judiciary, to ascertain and pronounce what the law is; and that this necessarily involves a consideration of the constitution."[15] This formulation is the most striking illustration of the maintenance of period 2 conceptions into the Marshall years. It retained the distinction between ascertaining and pronouncing what the (ordinary) law is and "considering" the Constitution. It is a paraphrase of the key para-

14. Ibid., 347–48. Emphasis in original.
15. Ibid., 349.

graph of *Marbury*, and suggests that as late as 1825 *Marbury* was still understood to have Tucker's meaning as stated in *Kamper v. Hawkins*. And once again Gibson's reply indicated that he had lost touch with the full thrust of the period 2 argument without being aware of any later one. "It does so; but how far? If the judiciary will inquire into anything beside the form of enactment, where shall it stop? There must be some point of limitation to such an inquiry; for no one will pretend, that a judge would be justifiable in calling for the election returns, or scrutinizing the qualifications of those who composed the legislature."[16] Gibson here accepted judicial consideration of the Constitution, but as the period 1 denial of judicial cognizability of the Constitution was no longer at issue the point had no real significance. At the same time, Gibson did not discuss the modern position that the business of the judiciary included ascertaining and pronouncing what the law of the Constitution is. He did not because this proposition had not yet been articulated.

Gibson went on to demand, as have subsequent critics of judicial review, judicial deference to the legislature's judgment of constitutionality as embodied in the statute under review. He insisted that this respect had to be granted.

> inasmuch as it is the foundation of [the opponents'] hypothesis; for all respect is demanded for the acts of the judiciary. For instance, let it be supposed that the power to declare a law unconstitutional has been exercised. What is to be done? The legislature must acquiesce, although it may think the construction of the judiciary wrong. But why must it acquiesce? Only because it is bound to pay that respect to every other organ of the government, which it has a right to exact from each of them in turn. This is the argument.[17]

This may have been the argument in 1825 but it has not been so for most of the last century. The obligation to accept the judicial interpretation of the Constitution comes, it is supposed, from the Consti-

16. Ibid.
17. Ibid.

tution's status as the kind of law properly subject to judicial application and interpretation. It comes from inclusion of the Constitution within that kind of law for which it is the province and duty of the judicial department to say what the law is.

Gibson neither alluded to nor discussed such a contention. He spoke instead of the difficulty in determining the meaning of the Constitution and of the absence of any presumption that one branch was better equipped than another to make such a determination. He insisted that judicial review, by withdrawing respect from legislative determinations, undermined the very respect for judicial determinations upon which their acceptance had to rest. The most likely consequence of the judicial claim to expound the Constitution, he argued, would be conflict among the branches.[18]

Having demonstrated to his own satisfaction that judicial authority over legislation could not be supported, Gibson conceded: "It might, perhaps, have been better to vest the power in the judiciary; as it might be expected, that its habits of deliberation, and the aid derived from the arguments of counsel, would more frequently lead to accurate conclusions."[19] He here anticipated a line of argument developed in the second half of the twentieth century. By this argument, approval for judicial review is connected with the institutional characteristics of judicial decision-making.[20] Actually, Gibson anticipated both sides of the twentieth-century debate, for he continued: "On the other hand, the judiciary is not infallible; and an error by it would admit of no remedy but a more distinct expression of the public will, through the extraordinary medium of a convention; whereas, an error by the legislature admits of a remedy by an exertion of the same will, in the ordinary exercise of the right of suffrage."[21]

We have not been able to resolve this dilemma either, and those unhappy with judicial review draw on Gibson's analysis to show that it is not a power inherent in a written constitution. The more interest-

---

18. Ibid., 349–50.
19. Ibid., 355.
20. See, e.g., Bickel, *Least Dangerous Branch*, 25–26.
21. *Eakin* v. *Raub*, 12 Sergeant & Rawles (Pa.) 330, 355 (1825).

ing observation to be drawn from Gibson, for our purposes, is that although in 1825 judicial review was linked to a written constitution, the intermediate position—that by commitment to writing, the Constitution became supreme ordinary law, amenable to judicial application and exposition—had not yet been established.

De Tocqueville's discussion of judicial review in *Democracy in America* did not provide such strong evidence of the transitional character of period 3 judicial review as did Gibson's, and I do not think it possible to draw firm conclusions from it. But it did lack key elements of the modern doctrine and on that score is worth examining.

Democracy in America confirms that by the 1820s the conception of judicial review as a substitute for revolution had disappeared. As de Tocqueville saw it, judicial invalidation of legislation was part of the regular judicial responsibility. He also noted that this authority brought with it political power otherwise unknown in law. His discussion of the legal-political components of American constitutional law is one of the more famous parts of *Democracy in America*. In America, de Tocqueville observed, judicial authority is "invoked in almost every political context,"[22] and "an American judge is . . . invested with immense political power."[23] The judiciary's political power stemmed from the fact that "Americans have given their judges the right to base their decisions on the *Constitution* rather than on the *laws*. In other words, they allow them not to apply laws which they consider unconstitutional."[24] Nevertheless, de Tocqueville continued, the American judiciary did not have any unusual political attributes but was composed of only the traditional ones associated with judicial power found elsewhere. The American judiciary was the societal "arbitrator" whose authority was invoked only to settle disputes. When courts acted they "pronounce[d] on particular cases and not on general principles," and they acted only when called upon.[25]

22. *Democracy in America*, 99.
23. Ibid., 100.
24. Ibid., 100–01. Emphasis in original.
25. Ibid., 99–100.

The political power de Tocqueville observed was the policy-making that accompanied weakening of the doubtful case rule and the judicial involvement in constitutional interpretation. As de Tocqueville expressed it, judges were allowed not to apply laws they *considered* unconstitutional. He did not have access to the period 2 formulation that the judicial authority over legislation was the refusal to enforce a (concededly) unconstitutional act. De Tocqueville's account of the political component of judicial review is thus the characteristically modern one; it is the political component of a legal act, not the earmark of a separate political responsibility.

When de Tocqueville turned from describing American judicial review to accounting for it, his arguments lost some of their modern character. He presented his justification through a comparison of American with English and French constitutionalism. The contrast with the English was clear and obvious. In England the constitution had no separate existence, and Parliament was acknowledged to be the body that "makes the laws" and "also shapes the constitution."[26] It thus made no sense to speak of a law as unconstitutional. The French, however, did have a separate constitution, which was, like the American, the "first of laws."[27] But the French did not have judicial review. De Tocqueville explained this difference by pointing out that the French constitution "is, or is supposed to be, immutable. No authority can change anything in it; that is the accepted theory." If French judges were to disobey an act of parliament, "the constitution-making power would really be in their hands . . . in that way they would take the nation's place and be the dominant power in society."[28]

This difficulty was obviated in America, where the Constitution was "the fount of all authority" and the "dominant power" in society, and subject to popular amendment as well:

In America the Constitution rules both legislators and simple citizens. It is therefore the primary law and cannot be modified

26. Ibid., 101.
27. Ibid., 102.
28. Ibid., 101. De Tocqueville continued: "So far as the inherent weakness of judicial power would allow them to play that part."

by a law. Hence it is right that the courts should obey the Constitution rather than all the laws. This touches the very essence of judicial power; it is in a way the natural right of a judge to choose among legal provisions that which binds him most strictly.

In France also the Constitution is the first of laws, and the judges there, too, have the right to take it as the basis of their decisions; but in exercising this right they would be bound to encroach on another right more sacred than their own, namely, the right of society in whose name they act. In this case ordinary reason must give way to reasons of state.

In America, where the nation always can, by changing the Constitution, reduce the judges to obedience, such a danger is not to be feared. So on this point politics and logic agree, and both the people and the judges can keep their proper privileges.[29]

Although it paraphrased fragments of *Marbury,* de Tocqueville's account of American judicial review was not quite the modern one. In particular it suggested that for him the "first of laws" and "the primary law" retained important period 2 attributes. This is visible first in de Tocqueville's failure to locate the American power of judicial review in the existence of a written constitution or even in the Constitution's legal identity. Ultimately it was the Constitution's amenability to popular amendment that supported the practice. De Tocqueville's statement that "it is in a way the natural right of a judge to choose among legal provisions that which binds him most strictly" was also a hesitant and awkward formulation that betrays the absence of key assumptions underlying the modern reading of *Marbury.* Today, the judge's authority in judicial review is a legal obligation, not a kind of natural right; and the judge does not "choose" which legal provisions bind him most strictly but expounds both ordinary law and the law of the Constitution and has no choice but to follow the latter in the event of conflict.

The last early nineteenth-century discussion to be examined is Madison's, made in a letter from which I have already briefly quoted.[30] Madison was commenting on the Court's position as "a constitutional

29. Ibid., 102.
30. *Letters and Other Writings,* 349–50. See above, chap. 4 at n. 20.

resort in deciding questions of jurisdiction between the United States and the individual States," and in it he repeated his commitment to concurrent review for resolving constitutional questions:

> As the Legislative, Executive, and Judicial departments of the United States are co-ordinate, and each equally bound to support the Constitution, it follows that each must, in the exercise of its functions, be guided by the text of the Constitution according to its own interpretation of it; and, consequently, that in the event of irreconcilable interpretations, the prevalence of the one or the other department must depend on the nature of the case, as receiving its final decision from the one or the other, and passing from that decision into effect, without involving the functions of any other.[31]

Difficulties stemming from the absence of an authoritative interpreter, he suggested, should be handled by practical accommodation among the branches. The proper model was the method of resolving differences between coordinate branches of the legislature.[32]

After stating this "abstract view of the co-ordinate and independent right of the three departments to expound the Constitution," Madison went on to acknowledge that "the Judicial department most familiarizes itself to the public attention as the expositor, by the *order* of its functions in relation to the other departments; and attracts most the public confidence by the composition of the tribunal."[33] By 1834 it could not be denied that

> it is the Judicial department in which questions of constitutionality, as well as of legality, generally find their ultimate discussion and operative decision: and the public deference to and confidence in the judgment of the body are peculiarly inspired by the qualities implied in its members; by the gravity and deliberation of their proceedings; and by the advantages their plurality

31. Ibid., 349.
32. Ibid.
33. Ibid. Emphasis in original.

gives them over the unity of the Executive department, and their fewness over the multitudinous composition of the Legislative department.

Without losing sight, therefore, of the co-ordinate relations of the three departments to each other, it may always be expected that the judicial bench, when happily filled, will, for the reasons suggested, most engage the respect and reliance of the public as the surest expositor of the constitution.[34]

Madison here acknowledged the development of period 3 judicial review with its judicial exposition of the Constitution and registered the public's and his own acceptance of it. His statement also revealed that this practice was evolving without theoretical or "abstract" justification. Madison still adhered to the period 2 rejection of judicial exposition of the Constitution as well as its distinction between questions of constitutionality and those of legality. This is the same position he took in *Federalist 49* and is not inconsistent with his support for judicial enforcement of the Bill of Rights as understood in period 2.[35] His acceptance of the emerging period 3 judicial review rested on practical considerations that included public receptivity to the practice and the quality of judicial exposition of the Constitution, as derived from the institutional characteristics of judicial decision-making.

Period 3 judicial review was not connected to any uniquely judicial relationship to the law of the Constitution for Gibson, de Tocqueville, or Madison. Each saw the practice in varying ways as a political enterprise, and each came to terms with it on political grounds. Madison emphasized the quality of judicial determinations and de Tocqueville the judiciary's ultimate responsibility to the people. Gibson, Thayer tells us, eventually shared in the widespread acceptance of period 3 judicial review. In 1845 he said: "I have changed that opinion [expressed in *Eakin* v. *Raub*], for two reasons. The late convention by their silence sanctioned the pretensions of the courts to

34. Ibid., 349–50.
35. See above, chap. 4 at nn. 1–20.

deal freely with the Acts of the legislature; and from experience of the necessity of the case."[36]

Madison, like Gibson, it is also worth noting, anticipated late twentieth-century discussions by identifying the character and quality of judicial reasoning as a key factor in support of judicial exposition of the Constitution. Those who make such a connection today have rejected the modern reading of *Marbury;* Madison's and Gibson's position on this point stemmed from the fact that the modern reading was not yet in existence.

By Thayer's time the modern doctrine of judicial review had caught up with its practice. The judiciary had now been expounding the Constitution outside the doubtful case rule for close to a century. Thayer accepted this practice with the statement of the modern *Marbury* doctrine referred to in chapter 2, in which he traced judicial review to the Constitution's status as "so much law." In addition, Thayer read this modern understanding back into all the period 2 discussions, from *Federalist 78* through *Bayard* v. *Singleton, Kamper* v. *Hawkins, VanHorne's Lessee* v. *Dorrance,* and Wilson's *Lectures on the Law.* In Thayer's words these defenses of judicial authority over legislation "began by resting it upon the very simple ground that the legislature had only a delegated and limited authority under the constitutions; that these restraints, in order to be operative, must be regarded as so much law; and, as being law, that they must be interpreted and applied by the court."[37]

This analysis still betrayed the period 2 emphasis on the limiting rather than the written constitution, but in its characterization of constitutional restraints as "so much law"—which, as law, must be "interpreted and applied by the court"—it reflected Marshall's total victory. The statement in *Marbury* that "those who apply the rule to particular cases, must of necessity expound and interpret that rule" had never before been thought to include the "rule" of the Constitution. By Thayer's time there was no other way to think about this rule.

Thayer's attribution of late nineteenth-century ideas to period 2

36. Quoted in Thayer, "Doctrine of Constitutional Law," 130, n. 1.
37. Ibid., 138.

sources also registers the silent, unacknowledged transformation of fundamental law into supreme ordinary law and his loss of access to period 2 assumptions. This is revealed too in Thayer's slight but significant misstatement of Wilson's argument in *Lectures on the Law*. After the passage just quoted, Thayer sketched the antecedents of *Marbury* as he understood them by quoting or paraphrasing key passages from leading period 2 sources. Wilson, according to Thayer, "said that the constitution was a supreme law, and it was for the judges to declare and apply it; what was subordinate must give way; because one branch of the government infringed the constitution, it was no reason why another should abet it."[38] Wilson said all these things except that it was for the judges to "declare and apply" the Constitution. Wilson's phrase was that the judges could "declare and enforce" the Constitution. Again, what earlier only Marshall had ambiguously suggested was now such entrenched common ground that Thayer could not contemplate enforcement of the Constitution that did not include its application and interpretation.

Although Thayer accepted the Constitution as "so much law," he also insisted that it could not be interpreted and applied as was other law. If it were, the judiciary would encroach on the power of the legislature, which also had an obligation to apply and interpret the Constitution. Theirs, Thayer argued, was actually the primary one, as demonstrated by the fact that the judiciary could pass on the constitutionality of legislation only in a lawsuit. For laws that never gave rise to lawsuits there could be no judicial assessment of constitutionality. Thayer concluded that the framers contemplated that legislative determinations of constitutionality would be final in most cases.[39] The primacy of legislative interpretation was reinforced by the obvious political content of constitutional interpretation, of the sort noted by de Tocqueville.

Thayer then embarked on the characteristically modern enterprise of seeking a way for judges to apply and interpret the Constitution that would not conflict with popular and legislative responsibility. He

38. Ibid., 139. For Wilson's full statement see above, chap. 3 at n. 71.
39. Ibid., 135–38.

sought this end by reviving period 2's doubtful case rule. As he understood it, under this rule judges were obliged to defer to legislative interpretation of the Constitution as embodied in the statute under review. Use of the rule constituted acknowledgment of the Constitution's amenability to a variety of legitimate interpretations and the primacy of the legislative one. According to Thayer, courts could overturn legislation only

> when those who have the right to make laws have not merely made a mistake, but have made a very clear one,—so clear that it is not open to rational question. . . . This rule recognizes that, having regard to the great, complex, ever-unfolding exigencies of government, much which will seem unconstitutional to one man, or body of men, may reasonably not seem so to another; that the constitution often admits of different interpretations; that there is often a range of choice and judgment; that in such cases the constitution does not impose upon the legislature any one specific opinion, but leaves open this range of choice; and that whatever choice is rational is constitutional.[40]

Thayer's attempt to revive the doubtful case rule gained impressive support on and off the Court, but it has not provided an enduring working standard for modern judicial review. It has never been consistently followed, even by its supporters. With the demise of Frankfurter's self-restraint during the 1960s it has, for now, been largely abandoned.

Thayer's solution failed because the doubtful case rule is neither practical nor internally coherent when applied to modern judicial review. Originally it was a rule not for application and interpretation of the Constitution but only for its enforcement against concededly unconstitutional acts. Indeed, it was devised precisely because there was no judicial authority whatever to apply or interpret the Constitution. Such authority developed only by disregard of the rule. Constitutional violations, moreover, were originally clearly and correctly understood as legislative willfulness, the products of an aggressive legislative supremacy willing to disregard or to reinterpret substan-

40. Ibid., 144.

tially previously accepted principle. In this form and under these circumstances the doubtful case rule marked a coherent boundary of judicial action with significant practical applicability. Thayer's attempt to use the rule as a standard for constitutional application and interpretation as practiced since period 3 is, in itself, a contradiction in terms. Moreover, under conditions of political stability and general legislative commitment to limited government, the rule can have no practical applicability. If conscientiously followed it means the end of judicial review.

The inapplicability of the doubtful case rule to modern judicial review is also revealed in Thayer's characterization of constitutional violations. These were in his words legislative "mistakes," and judicial review should be limited to those "so clear that it is not open to rational question." Constitutional law was thus for him the correction of legal error. This conception, however, corresponds to neither the nature of true constitutional violation nor the actual history of judicial review. It captures neither the defense of first principle that was period 2 judicial review nor the ongoing application of principle which marks that of period 3 and beyond. The idea that judicial review is the correction of legal error is a product of the unrecognized assimilation of fundamental law into ordinary law and the inappropriate attribution of ordinary law conceptions to the Constitution.

An equally important aspect of period 2 judicial review, which Thayer did not understand, was that its supporters were in fact ready to abandon the practice if conditions warranted it. As an additional political responsibility outside the judiciary's assigned function, it could easily be abandoned. By Thayer's time, however, constitutional law was an established branch of law. Thayer no more contemplated the possibility of abandoning judicial authority over legislation than anyone would contemplate abandoning judicial authority in ordinary law. Although he would confine judicial power to "fixing the outside border of reasonable legislative action," Thayer also insisted that "the ultimate arbiter of what is rational and permissible is indeed always the courts."[41] The net result of this position—of commitment to both the doubtful case rule and ultimate judicial responsibility for the

41. Ibid., 148, 152.

rationality of legislation—was a judicial review that could be neither used nor abandoned.

The doubtful case rule, applied to modern judicial review, not only loses its practical applicability but its capacity to maintain the Constitution's internal coherence. As Thayer understood it, the reasonableness test was the same one used in a variety of circumstances in ordinary law. One of its virtues, in his mind, was its very familiarity to judges. The test, Thayer pointed out, "marks a familiar and important discrimination, of daily application in our courts, in situations where the rights, the actions, and the authority of different departments, different officials, and different individuals have to be harmonized."[42] Thayer then gave several examples of its use, which included determinations of self-defense and negligence and review of jury findings. In the first two contexts it is used "in answering the question what might an individual who has a right and perhaps a duty of acting under given circumstances, reasonably have supposed at that time to be true?"[43] In the latter it constituted a weaker standard than the one used when judges made the determination under review.

After discussing these uses of the reasonableness rule Thayer presented and rebutted an argument challenging its applicability to constitutional questions:

> If it be said that the case of declaring legislation invalid is different from the others because the ultimate question here is one of the construction of a writing; that this sort of question is always a court's question, and that it cannot well be admitted that there should be two legal constructions of the same instrument; that there is a right way and a wrong way of construing it, and only one right way; and that it is ultimately for the court to say what the right way is,—this suggestion appears, at first sight, to have much force.[44]

Having thus stated and acknowledged the force of this objection, however, Thayer immediately rejected it:

42. Ibid., 146–47.
43. Ibid., 147.
44. Ibid., 150.

But really it begs the question. Lord Blackburn's opinion in the libel case related to the construction of a writing. The doctrine which we are now considering is this, that in dealing with the legislative action of a co-ordinate department, a court cannot always, and for the purpose of all sorts of questions, say that there is but one right and permissible way of construing the constitution. When a court is interpreting a writing merely to ascertain or apply its true meaning, then, indeed, there is but one meaning allowable; namely, what the court adjudges to be its true meaning. But when the ultimate question is not that, but whether certain acts of another department, officer, or individual are legal or permissible, then this is not true. In the class of cases which we have been considering, *the ultimate question is not what is the true meaning of the constitution, but whether legislation is sustainable or not.*[45]

The objection, however, cannot be so easily dismissed. "The ultimate question" in constitutional controversies is indeed "whether legislation is sustainable or not." Before legalization of fundamental law the judiciary not only could but was obliged to answer that question without establishing the true meaning of the Constitution. But it did so in the context of public agreement on the Constitution's true meaning. More important, the Constitution was then a set of first principles: constitutional limits were the "maxims of free government"[46] and an "observation at sea, with a view to correct the dead reckoning."[47] With the legalization of fundamental law, however,

45. Ibid. Emphasis in original. The libel case to which Thayer alluded was an English one, *Cap. and Count. Bank* v. *Henty*, 7 App. Cas. 741. He had referred to it earlier in discussing the reasonableness rule and quoted from Lord Blackburn's opinion: "When the court come to decide whether a particular set of words . . . are or are not libellous, they have to decide a very different question from that which they have to decide when determining whether another tribunal . . . might not unreasonably hold such words to be libellous" (ibid., 147).

46. Madison in *Writings of Madison*, ed. Hunt, 5:273, quoted above, chap. 4 at n. 9.

47. Gibson in *Eakin* v. *Raub*, 12 Sergeant & Rawles (Pa.) 330, 354 (1825), quoted above, chap. 4 at n. 40.

these same maxims and first principles had indeed become so much law. As a consequence their meaning now depended substantially on judicial exposition. Judicial refusal to declare the true meaning of the Constitution meant the withdrawal of legal recourse from legal problems. It undermined the Constitution's newly acquired legal status without being able to restore its earlier political one.

Thayer's difficulty is reflected in the fact that the reasonableness test he sought to apply to the law of the Constitution, although a familiar part of legal practice, was not a test for judicial resolution of legal questions. It was used in reviewing factual determinations and for resolving such mixed law-fact questions as negligence. So too the writing construed in a libel case, to which Thayer appealed, was not law. Precisely because "it is emphatically the province and duty of the judicial department to say what the law is," once Thayer had so completely accepted the Constitution as so much law he could not keep the judiciary from its authoritative exposition without undermining that status.

This was the problem Gibson anticipated when he pointed out that as part of the fulfillment of a legal responsibility, the doubtful case rule constituted an evasion of that responsibility.[48] And this problem keeps Thayer's and Frankfurter's reasonableness rule from being a viable standard for modern judicial review.

48. See above, chap. 3, n. 51.

CHAPTER SEVEN

The Rediscovery
of Fundamental Law

THAYER'S WAS the first of many attempts to reconcile the legal and political elements of modern constitutional law. All share his assumption that the Constitution is and always was so much law. None has yet been persuasive enough to quiet debate, and controversy over constitutional law remains deeper and more basic than that in any other area of law.

To come to terms with modern judicial review it is necessary to recognize that legalization of fundamental law occurred only in the middle of the nineteenth century with acceptance of Marshall's treatment of the written constitution as supreme ordinary law. Modern judicial review is Marshall's judicial review as developed in the contract and supremacy clause cases and not that of Iredell, Hamilton, and Wilson or even *Marbury*. It developed slowly and did not reach its mature form until sometime after Marshall left the Court. This development was mirrored in the gradual evolution of the modern *Marbury* doctrine. Although key elements of it were visible in Thayer's work it was not until 1958, in *Cooper* v. *Aaron,* that the Court identified the Constitution as the supreme law of the land, linked its authoritative judicial exposition to this status, and drew on *Marbury* to support these contentions:

> Article VI of the Constitution makes the Constitution the "supreme Law of the Land." In 1803, Chief Justice Marshall, speaking for a unanimous Court, referring to the Constitution as "the fundamental and paramount law of the nation," declared in the notable case of *Marbury* v. *Madison,* . . . that "It is emphatically the province and duty of the judicial department to say what the law is." This decision declared the basic principle that

the federal judiciary is supreme in the exposition of the law of the Constitution, and that principle has ever since been respected by this Court and the Country as a permanent and indispensable feature of our constitutional system.[1]

Cooper marks the culmination of the Constitution's transformation from fundamental law into the supreme law of the land, which began when Marshall reworked Tucker's argument in *Kamper* v. *Hawkins*. Its account of judicial review owes whatever cogency it has to public acceptance of Marshall's innovations, not to the inner logic of a written constitution, of the supremacy clause, or of *Marbury*. *Cooper* in fact acknowledged that the *Marbury* text cannot support the full weight of the argument made on its behalf. *Cooper* does not repeat the *Marbury* doctrine's strongest version, namely, that by its commitment to writing, a constitution becomes part of that law routinely amenable to authoritative judicial exposition. *Cooper* claims only that since *Marbury* the judiciary has been accepted as authoritative expounder of the Constitution. It is also the case that the *Cooper* doctrine itself has been subject to the reservation, usually voiced off the Court, that judicial exposition of the law of the Constitution cannot be the exclusive or final one.

That *Marbury* cannot support authoritative judicial exposition of the Constitution is not surprising. *Marbury* was a defense of period 2 judicial review, of judicial authority to refuse to enforce a concededly unconstitutional act. That it had ever been thought capable of supporting the modern practice reveals the depth of our loss of access to original intent and the degree to which we have yet to understand that practice. Nevertheless, for all its acknowledged difficulties this modern *Marbury* doctrine constitutes the only explanation for the power over legislation now exercised by courts. Twenty years after *Cooper* the Court repeated its main contention in insisting on the authoritativeness of its exposition of executive privilege over that of the president:

In the performance of assigned constitutional duties each branch of the Government must initially interpret the Constitu-

1. 358 U.S. 1, 18 (1958).

tion, and the interpretation of its power by any branch is due great respect from the others. . . . Many decisions of this Court, however, have unequivocably reaffirmed the holding of *Marbury v. Madison* . . . that "[i]t is emphatically the province and duty of the judicial department to say what the law is."[2]

In between the Court referred to itself as the "ultimate interpreter of the Constitution."[3]

Marbury's and *Cooper's* internal difficulties manifest themselves in the controversy that has accompanied all significant exercises of judicial review and in the unresolved debate over its proper scope. Retrieval of the original understanding will not by itself end this debate or resolve the controversy. Nor will it produce radically new ideas that have not been suggested in the course of sensitive observation of judicial review's functioning. But it can deepen our understanding of the modern practice and permit sounder judgments on the merits of contending positions.

The Persistence of Fundamental Law

The first observation is not so much that the framers did not intend modern judicial review, although that is the case, but that Americans accepted authoritative judicial exposition of the Constitution with no public deliberation or conscious consideration of the implications or commitments inherent in this acceptance. Most important, we have never recognized that fundamental law remains different in kind from ordinary law and that its legalization is a relatively superficial phenomenon. Legalization was achieved by application of ordinary law technique to the Constitution and by public acceptance of judicial application and interpretation of the Constitution. But differences between restraints on sovereign power and those on individual behavior are too deep to have been removed by adoption of ordinary law technique. To deal successfully with the modern practice it is necessary to recognize the enduring vitality of these differences.

2. *United States* v. *Nixon*, 418 U.S. 683, 703 (1974).
3. *Baker* v. *Carr*, 369 U.S. 186, 211 (1962), and cited in *McCormack* v. *Powell*, 395 U.S. 486, 521 (1969).

The silent, unacknowledged assimilation of fundamental law into ordinary law has left standing only one difference in kind between the two. Ordinary law, it is agreed, cannot change fundamental law. Otherwise, we speak of constitutions as being more general than statutes; of their need to last longer and to retain their applicability in a wider range of circumstances; of their being more difficult to change formally and to enforce; and of the political elements in their exposition. Given this generation's receptivity to the policy implications of statutory exposition, even this last characteristic is not thought to establish a difference in kind between constitutions and statutes. In the loss of access to the original distinctions our conception of the nature, texture, function, use, and abuse of constitutional law is derived by extrapolation from ordinary law.

Originally the distinction between fundamental law and ordinary law cut deeper than this and was manifestly self-evident in a way we must now strain to recreate. Statutes, and ordinary law generally, regulate the conduct of individuals. In the enactment of ordinary law there is an expectation of violation and of an enforcement process which includes definitive determination of the meaning of that law in each case where it is officially invoked. This authoritative exposition of ordinary law is made in court by judges who are assigned responsibility to say what the law is.

The judicial finality over ordinary law is a necessary part of the rule of law in the most rudimentary sense, and every society has some mechanism for the authoritative exposition of its commands whether it has a separate or an independent judiciary. It is this connection between judicial finality and the peaceful, legal resolution of human conflict that makes acceptable the inevitable concomitants of that finality, namely, the toleration of judicial "error" and what is acknowledged today as judicial policy-making.

Not only is the judicial authority to fix the meaning of ordinary law an unexceptional part of law enforcement, but law enforcement itself is a wholly unproblematic undertaking. In ordinary law the judge acts as the agent for the entire community, enforcing the collective will against individual violators. As he speaks for the entire society he is able to enforce the law against even the strongest individual violator, including, for example, a modern corporation.

A constitution, in contrast, is directed at sovereign power, not individual behavior. It provides for the distribution and organization of political power and stipulates certain restraints on the exercise of that power. Unlike statutes, a constitution contemplates compliance, not violation. The genuine constitutional violation is, of necessity, rare. If a regime were to encounter the breadth of constitutional violation contemplated by statutes, it would be in either constant turmoil or repression. Furthermore, should a regime somehow be able to tolerate repeated violation of its constitutional provisions, the judiciary could not enforce them as routinely as it does statutes. Genuine constitutional violations in a republican regime are by definition either large-scale popular disaffection from the existing order or a minority coup strong enough to succeed. Attempted violations that do not have such force behind them are amenable to correction through majoritarian political processes and are not violations in need of enforcement in the same sense that we speak of statutory violations. Under circumstances of real constitutional violation where, for whatever reason, the dominant force within the community has withdrawn support from the basic principles of the political system, the judge, attempting to enforce those principles, is no longer an agent of society carrying out its law. He becomes instead the agent of a forsaken principle, standing alone or for a minority of the community, confronting the superior numbers and power that no longer abide by the original agreement. Moreover, should a court succeed in such circumstances, it does so not by bringing societal force to bear against a violator but by rallying and reasserting a moral-political self-restraint. Enlightened by this perception, period 2 judicial review—the enforcement of the Constitution against genuine violation—was understood to be a political act, a judicial substitute for revolution. So, too, Madison's and Gibson's relative disinterest in judicial "enforcement" stemmed from their clear understanding that courts could not in fact meet this responsibility. Their understanding was, unfortunately but predictably, confirmed by the courts' weakness against the few genuine constitutional violations in American history: the denial of basic rights and protections to black Americans for almost a century after Reconstruction and the relocation of Japanese-Americans during World War II.

Constitutions, or fundamental law, not only contemplate general compliance but anticipate ongoing, legitimate differences of opinion over interpretation. Resolution of these differences is a policy question, an aspect of the wisdom of legislation, not its constitutionality. Before the assimilation of fundamental law into ordinary law, this distinction was untroublesome and unambiguous and was central in period 2 to the restriction of judicial enforcement of the Constitution to the clear violation. The extension of judicial review beyond the doubtful case rule not only rendered this distinction unserviceable but obscured the fact that unresolved controversy over the meaning of the Constitution in particular cases does not impair its functioning, as unresolved dispute over the applicability of a statute does impair the functioning of ordinary law. Freedom of speech, the obligation of contracts, and the requirements of equal protection of the laws, for example, retain their vitality while deeply held and conflicting applications of these principles vie for acceptance. As there is no need for finality in constitutional interpretation comparable to that in ordinary law, there is no need to accept the judicial policy-making that accompanies authoritative exposition of any text. There is, consequently, no analogy between the judicial policy-making in ordinary law and in constitutional law. The former is an inescapable part of the judiciary's assigned arbiter function and is the price gladly paid for peaceful and principled resolution of conflict under the rule of law. The policy-making of constitutional law, which occurs only and necessarily outside the doubtful case rule, is not connected to any enforcement role and is not essential for maintaining the integrity of the law of the Constitution.

Nothing in modern judicial review has changed these basic relationships. It is not much of an exaggeration to state that the judiciary routinely enforces ordinary law but can never enforce constitutions. If it could, the universal problem of abuse of political power would have been solved long ago. Moreover, if the exercise of constitutional law were confined to genuine violation—to the occasional severe crisis that many regimes are able to tolerate—it would be an irregular, sporadic, and quasi-revolutionary activity incapable of the systematization characteristic of law, including the constitutional law we know. Judicial exposition of the Constitution, *as a form of law*, can exist only as Marshall built it, detached from a true enforcement function. It can be only what it has been, the judicial, rather than the legislative, reinterpretation and adaptation of constitutional principle in circumstances where it is possible to defend contending implementations of principle, and where there is no need for an authoritative choice. This separation of judicial exposition from a true enforcement function and from an assigned arbiter role created the novel legal-political institution that is modern constitutional law, which thus simultaneously acquired the legal attribute of regularity and an ineradicable, extralegal policy component.

A New Form of Law:
The Redefinition of Function

Because constitutional law is unable to fulfill a true enforcement function, it is necessary to consider just what function it does fulfill. To the extent that the Constitution remains unenforceable against genuine violation, it retains its fundamental law character as moral commitment and exhortation rather than enforceable law. However, legalization of fundamental law did work some change in the Constitution's restraining force. Subjection of first principle to ongoing judicial application and interpretation outside the doubtful case rule and on the same terms as other law imparted to the moral restraint of principle some of the unthinking, internalized, compelling force associated with ordinary law. This merger of moral and legal restraints manifests itself in the internalized acceptance of law, as applied and interpreted in court, as a legitimate restraint on majority power. It has transformed fundamental law from popularly implemented and somewhat abstract commitment to limited government into an external, concrete restraint. Constitutionality so understood has even come to rival majority will as the nation's highest principle.

Acceptance of constitutionality as a legitimate restraint is not the actual acceptance of restraint in specific circumstances. To appreciate Marshall's achievement and to pinpoint the function performed by modern constitutional law, it is helpful to return to Madison, who spoke openly and instructively about the difficulties of restraining all power, including popular power. Marshall avoided calling attention to this last difficulty.

For Madison, as for all his contemporaries, popular government was the first check against abuse of power. It sought this end by placing power in the hands of the many and requiring that laws affect all individuals in the same way. But lodging power in the hands of the majority left unresolved the problem of majority abuse of power. Separation of powers, built on wholly republican branches, and the extended republic were Madison's not inconsiderable contributions to the solution of this problem. Moreover, Madison saw these devices as the achievable limit in restraining abuse of power. As late as 1821, he saw no restraint on majority will besides exhortation—"sound arguments and conciliatory expostulations," as he phrased it.[4] The only other possibility was the clearly unacceptable retreat from republicanism, the "creat[ion of] a will in the community independent of the majority [or] of the society itself."[5] Such a creation not only negated the basic tenets of republicanism but was a likely source of more serious abuse of power.

For this system Marshall devised the additional restraint of constitutionality, which he directed against what he considered the most likely abuse of power by a popular regime—the invasion of property rights. From hindsight it is clear that property rights were never in serious danger. The worst majority abuse of power in American history was violation of the rights of blacks, as sanctioned by the Constitution under slavery and in violation of it afterward. The inability of constitutionality to restrain this abuse is testimony to the cogency of Madison's analysis and his observation that, after lodging political and physical power in the same hands, republican government had no effective way to guarantee agreed upon limits that the majority was not willing to respect. This intractability of all power,

4. Madison to Roane, in *Writings of Madison*, ed. Hunt, 9:59. Quoted above, chap. 4 at n. 32.

5. *Federalist* 51, 339.

including popular power, makes significant acceptance even of the idea that constitutionality is a legitimate restraint. It is an achievement apart from individual court decisions and perhaps enough to compensate for poor ones. This is small comfort to the victims of abuse, but on the scale of human efforts to domesticate political power it is no mean achievement. Furthermore, an operating system of constitutional law and popular acceptance of the idea that constitutionality is a legitimate restraint furnishes victims with an opening for gaining relief.

Modern constitutional law, moreover, is more than majority acceptance of the legitimacy of restraint on its own power. In its ongoing operation it functions simultaneously to augment or enhance the role of principle in political life. The legal process is always open and provides a forum for probing the justice of particular uses of power.[6] The substance of constitutional law at any given time will be confined within some broad societal consensus,[7] but within this consensus there remains significant latitude. This regularized and institutionalized consideration of principle through the forms of law has become a more pervasive phenomenon than Marshall likely contemplated. At its best it elevates the quality of public life, but it is also capable of reinforcing harmful principle. *Brown* v. *Board of Education* is the least controversial example of the former, *Dred Scott* of the latter.

Last, the transformation of first political principle into supreme ordinary law removed the revolutionary potential that had been part of period 2 judicial review and that inheres in any direct challenge of principle. In its legal form the check of constitutionality is one of comparatively low stakes, couched in legalisms and directed to particular exercises of power without challenging political authority. In defiance of Blackstone's expectation Marshall found a way for law to

6. See Ronald Dworkin, "The Forum of Principle," *New York University Law Review* 56 (May–June 1981): 469–518, esp. 517–18. The idea that judicial review enhances or refines principle is central to all discussions that stress its educative role. See Eugene V. Rostow, "The Democratic Character of Judicial Review," *Harvard Law Review* 66 (December 1952): 208–10.

7. See Dahl, "Supreme Court as Policy-Maker."

"express its distrust of abuse of power" without "destroy[ing] the idea of sovereignty."[8]

A New Form of Law:
Legal and Democratic Accountability

As modern judicial review has evolved, its most persistent problem has been the inability to comply with the legal requirement that judges not make law, that is, to refute the charge that restraint of the law of the Constitution is in essence the restraint of judges. This difficulty had been anticipated in period 2 by denial of all judicial authority to expound the Constitution and restriction of judicial review to the concededly unconstitutional act.

During period 2 there was no open acknowledgment that exposition of ordinary law necessarily included a policy component. The contemporary acknowledgment that all interpretation includes such a component is sometimes relied upon to deny the significance of policy-making in constitutional law. But as we have seen, the period 2 understanding of a difference in kind between ordinary law and the Constitution is still relevant. In the absence of any societal need for authoritative exposition of the latter, the policy component associated with its interpretation remains unique and in need of its own justification. This problem is exacerbated by the breadth of policy-making in constitutional law. Even if we grant everything that can be said about the indeterminacy of statutory texts, most of them provide more substantive direction to an interpreter than do even relatively specific constitutional provisions. And the broadest statute has a discrete historical context capable of providing a level of guidance unavailable for the Constitution. Judicial interpretation of common and statutory law is also amenable to legislative correction, whereas a comparable check on constitutional interpretation requires the difficult amendment process.

Modern criticism of judicial review, which started with Thayer, has expended much effort in trying to eliminate judicial review's policy

8. *Commentaries*, 1:237. See discussion above, chap. 5 at n. 22.

component or at least to bring it in line with that with which we are comfortable in ordinary law. As was clearly understood in period 2, no such effort can succeed because it is precluded by the nature of fundamental law. Continued experience with modern constitutional law has made this increasingly obvious, and there is today a growing recognition that there is no alternative to the open acknowledgment of constitutional law's unique policy component.[9] Effort is better spent in finding a way to justify than to eliminate it. The most promising justification is in terms of the ends pursued by modern constitutional law. Just as the policy-making of ordinary law is accepted as an unavoidable part of the peaceful and principled resolution of social conflict, so the more significant policy-making of constitutional law can be accepted as part of the internalization of popular and legislative self-restraint and the systematic consideration of principled limits on political power. If there are to be limits on constitutional law's policy-making, as I believe there must be, they have to be essentially political in nature. Limits devised for the judicial exposition of ordinary law cannot meet the needs of fundamental law.[10]

Modern constitutional law thus is unable to meet two of the leading attributes of law: it cannot be enforced against genuine violation and it cannot conform in the usual way to the requirement that judges not make law. Yet it clearly is as some form of law that it has gained and maintained its legitimacy. This is the meaning of the modern *Marbury* doctrine, which links authoritative judicial exposition of the Constitution to its status as supreme ordinary law. However problematic this reading of *Marbury*, it articulates a key element of judicial review's self-understanding and public acceptance. Any workable reso-

9. This acknowledgment began tentatively with Herbert Wechsler, "Toward Neutral Principles of Constitutional Law," *Harvard Law Review* 73 (November 1959): 15. It was made more openly by Bickel, *Least Dangerous Branch*, 24. Others have been still more open. See, e.g., Arthur S. Miller and Ronald F. Howell, "The Myth of Neutrality in Constitutional Adjudication," *University of Chicago Law Review* 27 (Summer 1960): 661–95, and Ronald Dworkin, *Taking Rights Seriously* (Cambridge: Harvard University Press, 1977), chap. 5.

10. I develop this point more fully below, chap. 7 at nn. 26–41.

lution of judicial review's problems must bring it into some credible conformity with the requirement that it be some form of law.

I believe that constitutional law achieved its legal identity by conformity to a third legal requirement—namely, law's commitment to reason as its highest authority.[11] The status of reason in law is the subject of extensive controversy, and this is not the place to pursue that debate. I take seriously much of the argument challenging the sufficiency of reason to account for judicial decisions and I do not argue that the law produces disinterested results. Much of the reasoning in constitutional law is a reflection of opposing ideological positions, and over the long run the reasoning of groups and interests dominant in society generally dominates in court. Even if all this is granted, the commitment of law—including constitutional law—to reasoned judgment is still meaningful. Although constitutional law operates within boundaries forged by external political forces, it retains the opportunity for significant choice and for reasoned judgment in shaping the precise contours of these choices. The Warren Court, for example, functioned within the political boundaries set by the New Deal coalition, a national majority of the poor and of ethnic, racial, and religious minorities. This political support allowed it to expand existing conceptions of equality and to implement increased control on official arbitrariness, particularly at the local level. Yet no specific action was dictated by these larger political forces, and implementation of these ends was open to definition and delineation by reasoned argument. Also, the Warren Court's central legal legacy—acceptance of heightened scrutiny for individual rights guarantees and rejection of Thayer's and Frankfurter's reasonableness rule for these cases—survived the dominance of the New Deal coalition. One large part of that survival is the inability to argue persuasively to the contrary.

The inability of reason simply to transcend the disposition of politi-

11. The point that constitutional law's commitment to reason can compensate for its incapacity to meet other legal and democratic requirements has been made by others in related contexts. See above, chap. 6 at nn. 19 and 34, for Gibson's and Madison's observations. See also Bickel, *Least Dangerous Branch*, 25–26.

cal power and the ideological defenses of power is not unique to the reasoning of constitutional law, and the legal system cannot overcome the limitations of human reason generally. But whatever the human capacity to guide action by reason, that capacity is enhanced by the legal system's institutional commitment to reasoned discourse. The system forces articulated defense of all its actions, and its own decisions are open to criticism on the same terms.[12]

To the extent that constitutional law can maintain a credible legal identity, it can also maintain democratic accountability. With reason as its ultimate authority constitutional law does not introduce an essentially undemocratic restraint; it does not introduce a "will . . . independent of the society itself." In addition, constitutional law shares another characteristic of the legal process that helps it maintain democratic accountability, that is, law's openness to the ideas and values of the community, which work their way into court in contending briefs.[13] Through this ultimate democratic accountability constitutional law simultaneously meets the legal requirement that judges confine themselves to execution of policy made elsewhere. For modern constitutional law, "elsewhere" is not legal text or intent but the broad confines of public opinion.

As constitutional law's inability to conform to all the requirements of law and democracy is underscored anew each generation, critics most troubled by this nonconformity—Thayer, Wechsler, Ely, for example—have sought to bring about that conformity, not to dismantle the institution. Their efforts are testimony both to constitutional law's integrity as a form of law and to the attractiveness of law as a restraint on majority power. So entrenched has this new restraint become that no one since Gibson has rejected all judicial control over legislation. To do so would be to declare publicly that there are no

12. For similar discussion of the relationship between reason and power in law see Edward H. Levi, *An Introduction to Legal Reasoning* (Chicago: University of Chicago Press, 1948), 1–8, and E. P. Thompson, *Whigs and Hunters* (New York: Pantheon Books, 1975), 258–69. I am indebted to my colleague Lonnie S. Turner for calling my attention to Thompson's discussion.

13. Levi, *Legal Reasoning*, 5.

legitimate limits on the exercise of majority will. Judicial review, moreover, is stronger than ever in the second half of the twentieth century amid ever widening recognition that unprincipled use of power is a permanent political problem and not just a feature of insufficiently popular regimes.

The Rediscovery of Fundamental Law:
Alexander Bickel's *The Least Dangerous Branch*

The more experience the country has with judicial review, the more the original and enduring elements of fundamental law force themselves to the surface. Alexander Bickel's *The Least Dangerous Branch* is the best expression of this phenomenon. Bickel's discussion of judicial review as the defense of fundamental values captures significant aspects of fundamental law as originally understood and in the process provides a compelling account of modern constitutional law. At the same time, as I shall show, Bickel's work demonstrates the hold that inappropriate ordinary law conceptions still have on our thinking and the need to go still further in retrieving the full difference between fundamental law and ordinary law.

The Least Dangerous Branch, published in 1962, was a response to emerging difficulties confronting both judicial self-restraint and judicial activism as understood during the 1940s and 1950s. Each of these positions was an attempt to come to terms with judicial review in the aftermath of the court crisis of the 1930s. That crisis laid bare the policy content of constitutional exposition with an intensity that could not be ignored. Self-restraint, as championed by Justice Frankfurter, adopted Thayer's reasonableness rule and advocated systematic judicial deference to legislative interpretations of the Constitution. Activism rejected the reasonableness rule for adjudication of the individual rights guarantees of the Bill of Rights and the Fourteenth Amendment. This position was first articulated in *United States* v. *Carolene Products,* which suggested that judicial implementation of the explicit Bill of Rights guarantees, unlike substantive due process of the previous era, was a neutral judicial enterprise faithful to constitutional design. This was particularly so if implementation was directed to maintaining open political procedures and the rights of "discrete and insular" minorities permanently locked out of the democratic system.[14]

By the 1960s problems with each position were becoming apparent. First, Frankfurter's willingness to retreat from authoritative judicial application and interpretation of the Constitution, and of individual rights guarantees in particular, failed to gain widespread acceptance.[15] At the same time, there was no refutation of his contention that active judicial defense of these guarantees necessitated the same kind of judicial value choices condemned in judicial defense of economic rights.[16] Several decades of implementation of the *Carolene Products* program had made apparent its policy component and undermined its suggestion of neutrality. Similarly unpersuasive was the claim of Justice Black, leader of the activist wing on the Court, that a literal, absolutist reading of the Bill of Rights and its incorporation into the Fourteenth Amendment was policy-free application of constitutional text and intent. Thus if judicial review was to continue, as it was clear it was to do, it was necessary to confront the issue of policy-making once again.

This need was brought to a head by *Brown* v. *Board of Education*. On the one hand, its condemnation of public racial segregation was widely hailed as a major moral, legal, and political achievement. Yet in the early 1960s *Brown* was still controversial. Opponents routinely denounced it as extralegal judicial policy-making, and this charge was echoed even among those who enthusiastically welcomed its results.[17] Moreover, by the 1960s, after decades of experience with the mature,

14. 304 U.S. 144, 153–54, n. 4 (1938).

15. That Frankfurter's position had been bypassed was not openly acknowledged until the 1970s. See, e.g., Chief Justice Burger's recognition of "a far more demanding scrutiny" than reasonableness for review of "fundamental constitutional rights": *Nixon* v. *Administrator of General Services*, 433 U.S. 425, 506–07 (1977). The weakness of Frankfurter's position was manifested during the 1960s in Justice Harlan's failure to follow the reasonableness rule when he assumed leadership of the self-restraint wing of the Court after Frankfurter's departure.

16. For a good statement of Frankfurter's argument see *West Virginia Board of Education* v. *Barnette*, 319 U.S. 624, 648–50 (1943).

17. See Wechsler, "Neutral Principles."

modern practice, *Brown*'s supporters made no attempt to defend it in traditionally legal terms as standard judicial application and interpretation of the equal protection clause text and intent. Indeed, whatever evidence on specific intent existed argued as much against as for the decision. The response of *Brown*'s supporters to the charge that the decision lacked the neutrality necessary for law was more an attack on the concept of neutrality than a defense of *Brown*'s conformity with it.[18] Although not so stated it was also clear that if *Brown* could not be supported in these terms, no meaningful constitutional law could be.

Bickel acknowledged these problems by opening *The Least Dangerous Branch* with an exhaustive critique of the modern *Marbury* doctrine and its suggestion that judicial control over legislation was a legal responsibility that followed from the Constitution's status as supreme written law.[19] Criticism of *Marbury* had been made before, but always as part of an attack on judicial review. For Bickel criticism of *Marbury* was part of a deep commitment to the institution and prelude to a reformulation of its foundations. Judicial review, he recognized, had gained strong support through popular approval of its operation. But in the defect of its original legal self-understanding it lacked principled support. *The Least Dangerous Branch* was the attempt to provide this support.

As Bickel understood it, the deficiencies of *Marbury* meant that judicial review could not be defended as fulfillment of a conventional legal function. A principled defense needed delineation and justification of an alternate function, one that could account satisfactorily for judicial review's operation and the depth of its support, and that could be reconciled with legal and democratic requirements. Bickel identified this function as the defense of long-term principle or fundamental values.[20] In so doing he drew implicitly but heavily on *Brown*. References to the case, Bickel's leading example of successful court defense of fundamental values, permeated *The Least Dangerous*

18. See, e.g., Miller and Howell, "Myth of Neutrality," and Addison Mueller and Murray L. Schwartz, "The Principle of Neutral Principles," *U.C.L.A. Law Review* 7 (July 1960): 571–88.

19. *Least Dangerous Branch,* 1–14.

20. Ibid., 23–25.

Branch. If *Brown* was not credible as conventional legal application of equal protection clause text and intent, it was totally intelligible as defense of the principle of racial equality. Bickel also acknowledged that fulfillment of this function necessarily involved a judicial policy-making beyond that acceptable in ordinary law, one significant enough to implicate judicial review as a "counter-democratic institution."[21] Bickel went on to defend this policy-making in terms of institutional competence—the judiciary's political insulation and commitment to reasoned discourse made it, he argued, peculiarly suited to defend society's fundamental values.[22]

Bickel drew his analysis from observation of constitutional law's functioning and not from any reinterpretation of the original understanding. Yet in his emphasis on the Constitution as a statement of fundamental values, or long-term principle, rather than law, he got in touch with the original and enduring fundamental law elements of the Constitution that have never lost their vitality despite assimilation of fundamental law into ordinary law. This accounts for the receptivity and strength of the fundamental values view, a strength visible in the work of all who followed.

The Least Dangerous Branch, in its recognition that neither *Marbury* nor any traditional legal argument could justify authoritative judicial exposition of the Constitution, in its retrieval of fundamental law's status as first principle, and in its acceptance of the extralegal policy component in judicial exposition of fundamental law, stands as a watershed in our understanding. For all his innovativeness, however, Bickel did not do full justice to the complex legal-political phenomenon that is American constitutional law. Without recognizing the depth of the differences between fundamental law and ordinary law, the unacknowledged legalization of the former, and the novelty of the mature practice, Bickel, too, drew more than is sustainable on ordinary law conceptions, particularly its enforcement model. This was reflected in difficulties in Bickel's position as it developed over the succeeding decade.

In the years following publication of *The Least Dangerous Branch*

21. Ibid., 16–23.
22. Ibid., 25–26.

Bickel found it increasingly more difficult to support specific exercises of judicial review as he had supported *Brown*.[23] His initial stress on *Brown,* coupled with his discomfort with subsequent adjudication, betrayed the extent to which his defense of fundamental values was restricted to the judicial enforcement of those values against their unambiguous violation. This, however, is as unsatisfactory an account of the modern practice as was period 2 judicial review.

In the enormity of American racial injustice it was easy to conceive of *Brown* as enforcement of Fourteenth Amendment principle against clear violation, the judicial implementation of unchallengeable moral requirements. No other constitutional principle has been so openly, willfully, and protractedly violated as has the commitment to racial equality. But if judicial review, as the defense of principle, is to be confined to violations of this magnitude, as it was in fact for Bickel, we confront again the untenability of an enforcement model. If the regime were to face with any frequency departures from constitutional principle comparable to the country's flouting of the requirement of racial equality, it could not continue in recognizable form; if the judiciary were to confine itself to such mammoth violations of principle, its actions would be too infrequent and too irregular to be recognizable as law. Constitutional law, as an ongoing enterprise committed to the defense of long-term principle, necessitates more ongoing judicial implementation of principle than Bickel contemplated or seemed ready to accept.

Some Contemporary Implications

Although Bickel did not resolve many of the issues raised in *The Least Dangerous Branch,* his analysis of judicial review at midcentury retains major significance. It presaged the imminent demise of the activist–self-restraint debate as known in the 1940s and 1950s, retrieved essential elements of fundamental law, and was instrumental in emergence of the fundamental rights controversy, the latest version of

23. See Bickel, *The Supreme Court and the Idea of Progress* (New York: Harper & Row, 1970).

constitutional law's perpetual battle to establish legal and democratic accountability.

One group of judges and scholars in this controversy accepted without reservation Bickel's redefinition of judicial review's function and expanded its thrust. They did not confine judicial defense of principle to its clear violation, as exemplified in *Brown* v. *Board of Education*'s defense of racial equality, or to defense of the Bill of Rights, as had the *Carolene Products* and Warren courts. Rather, through exposition of the Constitution's more general limits, judicial defense of fundamental values now included values neither identified in the Constitution nor specifically contemplated by the framers.[24] In the process there developed a new form of judicial activism centered on two-tier equal protection and a revived substantive due process. In its overt reliance on extratextual sources of law this position called attention to constitutional law's departure from conventional legal practice and opened the prospect for broad judicial value choice.

The revival of substantive due process soon triggered a reformulated doctrine of self-restraint, one that drew on Black's, not Frankfurter's, position and that has been variously labeled 'interpretivism' or 'textualism.'[25] As a product of the 1970s and heir to Black, interpretivism accepted significant aspects of Bickel's analysis. In rejecting Frankfurter's deference it joined Bickel in reaffirming the American commitment to judicial review and its authoritative judicial application and interpretation of the Constitution. In addition, interpretivism did not challenge directly characterization of the Constitution as a statement of first principles or fundamental values. But it did draw

24. See, e.g., Thomas C. Grey, "Do We Have an Unwritten Constitution?" *Stanford Law Review* 27 (February 1975): 703–18, and Dworkin, *Taking Rights Seriously*, chap. 5.

25. The term *interpretivism* was used by Grey in "Unwritten Constitution." He later concluded that *textualism* was preferable. See "The Constitution as Scripture," *Stanford Law Review* 37 (November 1984): 1. For statements of the interpretivist position see Robert H. Bork, "Neutral Principles and Some First Amendment Problems," *Indiana Law Journal* 47 (Fall 1971): 1–20; Hans A. Linde, "Judges, Critics and the Realist Tradition," *Yale Law Journal* 82 (December 1972): 253–56; and Linde, "Constitutional Theory and State Courts," 179–81 and 193–200.

more deeply on constitutional law's legal and ordinary law component rather than its political and fundamental law strand and insisted
that, if the provisions of the Constitution were first principles, they
were first principles expressed as legal commands. The Constitution
was consequently subject to treatment on the same terms as other law.
Thus, interpretivism's central insistence was that judges restrict themselves to the standard legal practice of interpreting text and intent and
that they defend only those values stated or implicit in that text or
demonstrably contemplated by the framers.

The historical analysis offered here cannot mediate conclusively
between these contending positions. But I believe it does have substantial implications for each and for constitutional law's operation.
Most important it calls attention to the degree to which constitutional law is a new branch or form of law. The following comments
on the issues as posed by the fundamental values controversy illus-
trate the way I understand constitutional law to function as a new
form of law.

This account of judicial review's origin supports the widely made
criticism of interpretivism that text and intent cannot function for
constitutional law as they do for ordinary law. Once the doubtful case
rule is abandoned, as must happen in any ongoing practice of judicial
review, that practice cannot be guided or meaningfully limited by
constitutional text and intent. These ordinary law tools were never
expected to function in such a capacity, and nothing in the history of
American constitutional law indicates they can so function. Even if
constitutional law were confined to interpretation of the Constitution's relatively explicit provisions, it would retain fundamental law's
demonstrated policy content, one outside anything known in ordinary law. This problem is highlighted by the fact that interpretivism
accepts Black's textual emphasis and his commitment to active defense of the Bill of Rights while, as this name implies, rejecting Black's
literalism, his claim that constitutional exposition consists in judicial
application of a self-executing text. Black's literalism was an attempt
to avoid the extralegal policy-making present in all exposition of
constitutional text. In abandoning Black's literalism, interpretivism
conceded its untenability. But this abandonment undermined any

suggestion that fidelity to text is capable of removing significant judicial value choices from constitutional law.

A more telling expression of the inability of constitutional text to function comparably to statutory text is that the textual reliance of the 1970s, as was Marshall's, is a selective one. This type of reliance, however, is not textual at all but depends on the values guiding selection. The textual reliance of the 1970s and 1980s was limited to the first eight articles of the Bill of Rights and to a review of racial distinctions under the equal protection clause. This text represents those aspects of Warren Court adjudication that have survived criticism to become part of a new consensus on the role of the courts. It is helpful, in this regard, to remember that whereas interpretivism regards *Brown* v. *Board of Education* as adequately supported by equal protection text and intent, *Brown*'s opponents did not share this view but denounced that opinion in precisely the same terms currently used against substantive due process. The legal character that presumably attaches to *Brown* today does not in fact derive from a meaningful fidelity to text and intent, as interpretivism suggests, but from an extratextual consensus that has now developed supporting the decision. By the same token a judicial review centering on interpretation of the Bill of Rights and racial distinctions under the Fourteenth Amendment avoids a judicial choice of values only to the extent that it relies on an existing consensus that these values should be judicially protected and on the general contours of that protection. This extratextual consensus is the twentieth-century counterpart to the one on vested rights that informed judicial review at its inception. It is, moreover, reinforced by the international human rights movement that came into being after World War II. Interpretivism is thus a passable defense of the status quo but is unable to account for its own existence or to guide future practice. More seriously, in its focus on text and intent rather than first principle, it distorts the essence of American constitutional law.

The conception that constitutional law is the defense of fundamental values broadly understood remains, I believe, the best account of modern constitutional law. It explains what judges do when they take regular responsibility to expound fundamental law, to say what the law of the Constitution is. Beyond this it does not provide much guidance for specific cases. I will only suggest that the judicial defense of fundamental values needs to be coupled with some form of restraint.

This need grows out of the inherent and enduring differences between first principles and ordinary law and out of the fact that courts in constitutional law do not fulfill a true enforcement function. In its nature ordinary law must be authoritatively expounded and enforced in each case where it is invoked. First principles, outside a true enforcement context, need not receive authoritative exposition in each case in order to retain their integrity. Public debate over the proper implementation of principle can and does antedate Court decisions and continues after they are made. Furthermore, attempts to enforce principle with the same regularity with which ordinary law is enforced could easily become intolerable. Bickel captured this difficulty when he first developed the idea of judicial review as the defense of principle in his observation that "no good society can be unprincipled; and no viable society can be principle-ridden."[26]

Restraint in the judicial implementation of fundamental values is also warranted by the paucity of substantive direction in the first principles that make up the law of the Constitution. In the absence of such direction, to defend fundamental values with the same latitude with which ordinary law is enforced invites a breadth of judicial value choice not only beyond anything known in ordinary law but one hard to reconcile with any sustainable conception of democracy or law. This potential has in fact always been kept in check by the political system that limits the values to be defended in court. I am arguing here only for recognition of the legitimacy of some such restraint. Last, the case for restraint is connected with the fact that the core legal identity of constitutional law is its commitment to reasoned judgment. In constitutional law's inability to maintain ordinary law's arbiter function, the fallibility of human reason counsels restraint.

As I have indicated before, a workable restraint for constitutional law cannot be that of Thayer and Frankfurter or of interpretivism. Unlike the former it needs to be inseparable from the use of judicial

26. *Least Dangerous Branch*, 64.

power; unlike the latter its substance must be more overtly political. The kind of restraint appropriate for this novel legal-political institution is the kind implicit in the original work of John Marshall and, later, of John Marshall Harlan. I shall discuss it in the course of commenting on Harlan's constitutional law and particularly his defense of substantive due process. I end with Harlan because I believe his constitutional law best captures the merger of fundamental law and ordinary law that is modern judicial review.

Harlan did not engage in any historical reevaluation of the origin of judicial review, yet his work reflected the fact that constitutional law is a new branch of law assimilable to ordinary law but also significantly different from it. Harlan did not dwell on the political components of judicial review. In a manner reminiscent of Marshall he approached cases as the straightforward fulfillment of a legal responsibility. He did not hesitate to reaffirm *Marbury*[27] and insisted that "it is the Constitution alone which warrants judicial interference in sovereign operations of the States."[28] In so doing he acknowledged the Constitution's achieved status as the supreme law of the land, binding sovereign power with the same kind of force with which ordinary law binds individuals. But he also insisted that the Constitution must be approached "not in a literalistic way, as if we had a tax statute before us, but as the basic charter of our society, setting out in spare but meaningful terms the principles of government."[29] Accordingly, constitutional limits have to be understood as expressions of limited government generally rather than as an exhaustive list of specific restraints. Harlan's discussion of constitutional limits and especially of substantive due process is a twentieth-century update of Marshall's admonition that "we must never forget that it is a *constitution* we are expounding," applied now to exposition of constitutional limits and a legalized Constitution, subject to judicial application and interpretation.

Identification of the Constitution as the "basic charter of our so-

27. *Oregon* v. *Mitchell*, 400 U.S. 112, 204–09 (1970), and *Mackey* v. *United States*, 401 U.S. 667, 677–81 (1971).
28. *Poe* v. *Ullman*, 367 U.S. 497, 539 (1961), dissenting opinion.
29. Ibid., 540.

ciety" was made in *Poe* v. *Ullman* in the course of Harlan's seminal defense of substantive due process. He maintained that due process could not be properly confined to procedural fairness or incorporation. As one of the more important "spare but meaningful . . . principles of government," it "includes a freedom from all substantial arbitrary impositions and purposeless restraints."[30] Harlan defended this reading of the due process clause as the only one capable of doing justice to the society's basic charter and accounting satisfactorily for the substance of American constitutional law.[31] The liberties it protects against arbitrary and unreasonable restriction certainly included those explicitly mentioned in the constitutional text, but neither are they so limited nor is the textual reference decisive. In a constitution specific limits are written because they are fundamental, not fundamental because they are written.[32]

American constitutional law is the legalization of limited government, the judicial refinement and reinforcement of principle short of its clear violation. Whether oriented around protections of religious freedom and of speech, limits on governmental regulation of the economy, or intrusions on personal privacy, it is an ongoing inquiry into "substantial arbitrary impositions and purposeless restraints." Substantive due process extends the core legal protection originally developed to protect individuals from arbitrariness in the criminal process. Concern about arbitrary use of power, the heart of limited government and thereby of American constitutional law, accounts for the persistence of substantive due process despite its very real difficulties.

30. Ibid., 543.
31. Ibid., 541–44.
32. Harlan continued by indicating that the constitutional base for the liberties connected with child rearing, protected by the Court in *Meyer* v. *Nebraska* and *Pierce* v. *Society of Sisters*, was properly understood as "the right of the individual . . . to establish a home and bring up children," as *Meyer* held, although today it "would probably" be identified as part of First Amendment freedoms of expression and conscience. "For it is the purposes of those guarantees and not their text, the reasons for their statement by the Framers and not the statement itself . . . which have led to their present status in the compendious notion of 'liberty' embraced in the Fourteenth Amendment" (ibid., 544).

Although fidelity to the law of the Constitution demands subordination of the primacy of its text, Harlan recognized that other legal requirements, as known in ordinary law, remained intact. The major one is the judicial commitment to reasoned judgment: "But precisely because it is the Constitution alone which warrants judicial interference in sovereign operations of the State, the basis of judgment as to the Constitutionality of state action must be a rational one."[33]

Harlan did not treat reason as a source of values to be judicially implemented, nor did the insistence on reasoned judgment presume creative judicial wisdom. Reasoned judgment is, rather, an indispensable condition for the legal character of all judicial determinations. It is the identifying characteristic of legal decision-making, through which the disinterestedness associated with law is sought and against which its success is continually measured.

Harlan joined this reliance on reason with insistence on the need for restraint. In delineating the components of this restraint he rejected text and intent as an "artificial and largely illusory" one, incapable of confining constitutional law in a meaningful way.[34] This criticism was directed at Black's literalism, but it is also applicable to the textual reliance of interpretivism. Nor did Harlan seek restraint through systematic deference to any reasonable legislative or executive interpretation of the Constitution. Rather, restraint was to be found in "insistence upon respect for the teachings of history,"[35] including "what history teaches are the traditions from which [the country] developed as well as the traditions from which it broke,"[36] and in "solid recognition of the basic values that underlie our society."[37] Harlan did not use the term *consensus* in this context, but I believe that it can so be used appropriately. To invoke, as Harlan did, traditions from which the country has broken, as well as those that remain, and basic values underlying society is to invoke a changing consensus on basic values.

Harlan did not argue that respect for history, tradition, and con-

33. Ibid., 539–40. See also ibid., 542.
34. *Griswold* v. *Connecticut*, 381 U.S. 479, 502 (1965).
35. Ibid., 501.
36. *Poe* v. *Ullman*, 367 U.S. 497, 542 (1961).
37. *Griswold* v. *Connecticut*, 381 U.S. 479, 501 (1965).

sensus would end contention over the substance of judicial review: "No formula could serve as a substitute . . . for judgment and restraint."[38] Instead, this respect would bring constitutional law as close as possible to the legal requirement that judges apply law made elsewhere. Evolving conceptions of first principle and of the meaning of fundamental law are the counterparts in constitutional law to statutory text and intent in ordinary law. Within the confines of any tradition and consensus, however, there remains inescapable latitude, including the opportunity for judicial leadership in fostering particular implementations of that consensus. This is the challenge and the danger of constitutional law.

Harlan, as his judicial performance indicated, imposed a conscientious self-restraint on that latitude that still allowed judicial review to rise to the challenge of a legal defense of principle. Harlan's most significant use of judicial power was his support for substantive due process, particularly his forceful argument defending it. Beyond this, he probably defended governmental action more than he opposed it. But it is important that this defense did not rest in routine deference to legislative interpretations of the Constitution or follow in a predetermined way from a set of ideological preconceptions. On the contrary Harlan took seriously the force of contending arguments in each case and defended his decisions with reasoned judgments.[39] In the process he provided a model for the legal defense of fundamental values and its accompanying value choices. In this connection it is worth noting that Harlan, not his fellow Justices Black or Frankfurter, came to be known as a "lawyer's judge."[40] The strength of Harlan's reasoning and his genuine openness to contending positions gave litigants a meaningful day in court and conveyed a legal quality to the law of the Constitution. These were more important than Black's claim of value

38. *Poe* v. *Ullman,* 367 U.S. 497, 542 (1961).

39. See, e.g., *Alberts* v. *California* and *Roth* v. *United States,* 354 U.S. 476, 496 (1957); *Duncan* v. *Louisiana,* 391 U.S. 145, 171 (1968); *Shapiro* v. *Thompson,* 394 U.S. 618, 655 (1969); *Williams* v. *Illinois,* 399 U.S. 235, 259 (1970); *Chambers* v. *Maroney,* 399 U.S. 42, 55 (1970); *Boddie* v. *Connecticut,* 401 U.S. 371 (1971); and *Cohen* v. *California,* 403 U.S. 15 (1971).

40. See the *New York Times,* September 24, 1971, 20.

neutrality through fidelity to text and intent or Frankfurter's avoidance of policy choice through systematic deference to the legislature.

In key respects Harlan's stance echoed that of Marshall. The latter's commitment to active use of judicial power needs no comment. But it should also be remembered that Marshall's defense of constitutional limits was confined to the principle of vested rights and the contract clause, and that he compromised regularly with competing conceptions of constitutional requirements.[41] Marshall's constitutional law is also the prototype for the combination of lawyerlike argument and defense of fundamental values visible in Harlan's opinions.

Like Marshall, Harlan combined an unapologetic commitment to the use of judicial power over legislation with the understanding that this authority cannot be pursued as systematically as are ordinary law restraints on individual behavior. Their readiness to exercise regular control over legislation acknowledged the need to use judicial power if constitutional law is to retain its legal identity. Underuse destroys judicial review's legal character as a routine legal restraint on popular will. At the same time, overuse brings the judiciary too far from the legal requirement that it not make law. Modern constitutional law accommodates and even demands both great boldness and serious restraint. The substance and occasion for each require political judgments unprovided for in the ordinary law tradition.

I am not arguing that such conclusions are the only possible ones that flow from this reinterpretation of the origins of judicial review. Ultimately the most significant conclusion is that the discontinuities between ordinary law and constitutional law have created a new branch of law and a new check on popular power. Judicial review was designed as an addition to the Constitution's system of checks and balances. It was, in the spirit of the original checks, one that started from the republicanism of the new American regime and attempted to deal with republicanism's potential problems without invoking nonpopular authority. To this end Marshall sought out law as a restraint on popular will, weaning that law away from natural law, which helped make it acceptable but which was incompatible with political

41. See White, "Marshall Court and Cultural Change," chaps. 8–10.

order and institutionalization. In its place he introduced the restraint of the positive law of the Constitution. On one level it is connected with the centuries-old common law tradition. On another and more important level the practice that grew out of Marshall's innovations is a new branch or form of law. As its nature indicates and its history confirms, this new branch is always in danger of being merely the restraint of judges rather than law. But it is not simply so. It is also the restraint of reasoned judgment and principle, open in an orderly way to challenge in these same terms. Although constitutional law has not been strong enough to restrain the worst abuses of popular power, it has made law and constitutionality an accepted legitimate restraint beyond anything imagined by those most sensitive to the problem of democratic abuse of power. As a result, sustained public consideration of the principled limits on power has become routine. Over the years constitutional law has also maintained the support of those most sensitive to judicial abuse of power. In the second half of the twentieth century, amid renewed evidence of the urgency of restraining all political power, the restraint of law remains an exciting possibility, too rich in achievement and promise to be discarded. It has shown itself capable of transplantation to other political systems and may yet become more widely and deeply institutionalized.

Hand, Learned, 102
Harlan, John Marshall, 217–21
Hayburn's Case, 59–60, 87–88
Henry, James, 85
Hylton v. United States, 61

Insolvency acts, 144–47, 149–56,
159. *See also* Debtor relief legislation
Intent, role of, 12, 214–15. *See also*
Fundamental rights controversy;
Judicial review, period 3
Interpretivism. *See* Fundamental
rights controversy
Iredell, James, 2, 53, 54, 55, 57, 59,
72, 73, 77, 86; and written constitution, 3, 26, 66; letter to Spaight,
26, 46, 47, 52–53, 58; and real
social contract, 27, 47; and concededly unconstitutional act, 34;
influence on Hamilton and
Wilson, 45–46, 77–78; defense of
judicial review, 46–53; contrast
with Marshall, 49–53; conflict of
laws analogy, 52–53; on "taking
notice of" constitution, 58; success of argument, 59, 179; and
doubtful case rule, 61; debate
with Chase, 70–72

Jefferson, Thomas, 91, 94–96, 98–
99, 117
Johnson, William: on seriatim opinion writing, 123; on vested rights,
130, 175; on *Sturges v.
Crowninshield,* 145, 152; and intent, 154–55, 160, 161, 164–66,
170, 171; criticism of Marshall,
155, 166; and constitutional text,
156, 166; and doubtful case rule,
159–60

Judicial activism. *See* Activism, judicial
Judicial review: and trial by jury,
20–22, 23, 36–37, 45, 50, 67–
68; and end of legislative omnipotence, 30–32, 34, 46–48, 73, 76,
80, 109; at Constitutional Convention, 38–44
—period 1: reliance on English
sources, 2, 17, 18–19, 20, 21–22,
23; and written constitution, 3–4,
24–26, 43–44; as response to
early republicanism, 7, 16, 35–36,
63; opposition to, 20, 22, 33, 34,
59; and explicit social contracts,
23–26; and real state of nature,
26–30. *See also* Concededly unconstitutional act; Fundamental
law; Natural law
—period 2: as substitute for revolution, 2, 3, 6, 50, 50n, 73–75, 91,
177, 183; and explicit social contracts, 2–3, 37, 52, 55, 66, 70–
71, 73; and equality of the
branches, 3, 49–51, 55, 57, 77,
112; two points of, 32–33, 37–
38, 48, 56–57, 78–80, 109–10;
as merger of principle and text,
37, 42–43, 50–51, 65–72, 85–
88; and obligation to ordinary
law, 49–50, 54–55, 56n, 111;
and conflict of laws analogy, 52–
53, 55n, 78, 111; and written
constitution, 53–54, 56, 65–66,
76–78, 81–82, 89; and "regard-
ing" the constitution, 55, 58–59,
111–12; atrophy of, 59, 63, 108–
09. *See also* Doubtful case rule;
Fundamental law; Natural law
—period 3: and written constitution, 106, 113, 179; overlap of
principle and text, 119, 122,